List of Figures and Tables

Figures

Tables

This book is to be returned on
or before the date stamped below

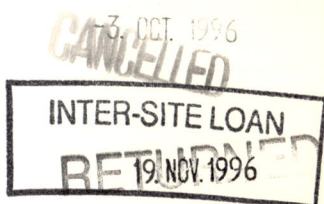

INTER-SITE LOAN
19. NOV. 1996

CANCELLED
26 MAR 2002

UNIVERSITY OF PLYMOUTH

ACADEMIC SERVICES
PLYMOUTH LIBRARY
Tel: (0752) 232323
This book is subject to recall if required by another reader
Books may be renewed by phone
CHARGES WILL BE MADE FOR OVERDUE BOOKS

MONETARY AND FISCAL POLICY, THE EXCHANGE RATE AND FOREIGN WEALTH

Monetary and Fiscal Policy, the Exchange Rate and Foreign Wealth

Patrizio Tirelli

Lecturer in Economics
Università Cattolica, Milan

St. Martin's Press

First published in Great Britain 1993 by
THE MACMILLAN PRESS LTD
Houndmills, Basingstoke, Hampshire RG21 2XS
and London
Companies and representatives
throughout the world

A catalogue record for this book is available
from the British Library.

ISBN 0–333–56579–7

Printed in Great Britain by
Antony Rowe Ltd
Chippenham, Wiltshire

First published in the United States of America 1993 by
Scholarly and Reference Division,
ST. MARTIN'S PRESS, INC.,
175 Fifth Avenue,
New York, N.Y. 10010

ISBN 0–312–08529–X

Library of Congress Cataloging-in-Publication Data
Tirelli, Patrizio, 1958–
Monetary and fiscal policy, the exchange rate and foreign wealth /
Patrizio Tirelli.
p. cm.
Originated from author's Ph. D. dissertation.
Includes bibliographical references and index.
ISBN 0–312–08529–X
1. Monetary policy—Mathematical models.   2. Fiscal policy–
–Mathematical models.   3. Foreign exchange rates—Mathematical
models.   4. Macroeconomics—Mathematical models.   I. Title.
HG221.T57 1993
332.4'06—dc20   92–12874
                                                          CIP

Contents

Preface

Macroeconomics is currently in a difficult position: no one theory of macroeconomic policy seems to meet general consensus. Both Keynesianism and, more recently, monetarism, have been welcomed and then fallen from favour. This book contributes to the search for a new framework for macroeconomic policy. Great emphasis is placed on two key ideas. The first is that both monetary and fiscal policies should be used in a well-designed policy package consisting of 'simple' rules, on the grounds that simple rules, which are easier to understand and monitor by private sector, would enhance the credibility of a government's precommitment to stick to the announced policy and help to stabilise expectations.

The second idea is that foreign wealth accumulation, operating through cumulating current account imbalances, plays a key role in the determination of open economy macroeconomic equilibrium (and its stability). Therefore open economy models should include wealth effects and the current account. Furthermore, policy evaluation should take into account, among other things, the implications of different rules for foreign wealth. We shall consider policy design both in a 'small' individual country and in the broader context of policy coordination.

This book originates from my PhD dissertation and has been written over a period of nearly four years. The Department of Political Economy of the University of Glasgow has offered fertile ground for conducting my research; I am particularly indebted to Professor D. Vines for (patiently) reading my work, for his many comments and for his constant encouragement. I am also very grateful to A. Muscatelli for his encouragement and for the time he has spent discussing my research with me.

For the last two years of my PhD I taught at the Department of Economics of the Catholic University of Milan. I wish to thank Professor L. Boggio for his constant support, and my colleague and dear friend M. Lossani, who was of great help in the revision of the final version of the book.

Finally, I wish to acknowledge financial contributions from Fondazione Einaudi, Torino, and Consiglio Nazionale delle Ricerche, Roma.

PATRIZIO TIRELLI

x

Part I

Simple Rules for the Open Economy

1 The Design of Simple Rules for the Open Economy

INTRODUCTION

It is often argued that macroeconomics is currently in a state of flux. Several schools of macroeconomists have competed in the intellectual arena to provide a suitable policy framework. But the alternative policy packages which have been advocated, either orthodox Keynesian, monetarist or new classical, seem to have been unable to tackle both the unprecedented levels of unemployment recently experienced and the trade imbalances which endangered the stability of the international monetary system.

More recently, new attempts have been made to design alternative macroeconomic policies aiming at improving the performance of the advanced economies. This book may be considered part of such efforts. The design of macroeconomic stabilisation policies requires the definition of objectives, instruments and of the methodology to be followed in the policy design. This chapter provides a preliminary discussion of the subject, establishing the necessary framework for the analysis of the alternative stabilisation policies which will be carried out in the following chapters.

1.1 MACROECONOMIC POLICY IN A HISTORICAL PERSPECTIVE

The philosophy of macroeconomic policymaking has undergone a thorough revision during the post-war era. Up until the collapse of the Bretton Woods regime, policy was guided by what has been labelled elsewhere[1] 'orthodox Keynesianism'. This policy framework had the following features. It was thought that in an 'uncontrolled' system prolonged periods of underemployment of resources would occur. It was also believed that nominal wage stability would prevail when productive resources were under-utilised. Therefore policy was mainly concerned with stabilising output at full employment by means of fiscal and monetary instruments. The existence for each country of an external objective was also recognised, as under an exchange rate regime of 'adjustable pegs' countries were in principle allowed to revise nominal parities when facing fundamental disequilibrium of the balance of payments.

After the end of the Bretton Woods era and the appearance of severe inflation problems in the major industrial countries during the 1970s, 'monetarism' took over from 'orthodox Keynesianism'. Monetarists held a rather optimistic view of the self-stabilising properties of a market economy. It was believed that wage and price flexibility would ensure a sufficiently high level of output and employment without need for any kind of Keynesian 'fine tuning'.[2] Furthermore, recognition of forward-looking behaviour in the private sector, combined with faith in market clearing, led to the famous 'policy ineffectiveness' proposition.[3] As a consequence, monetarists argued that macroeconomic policy should be reoriented. At the international level exchange rate flexibility would introduce a free market mechanism which would enable each country to obtain its own desired rate of inflation. On the domestic side, monetarists argued that policy should neglect output stabilisation, and focus instead on the domestic inflation rate by setting an intermediate money supply target. The emphasis on rules originated from a profound distrust of governments' capability to successfully manage the economy and from the belief that incumbent governments would exploit fine tuning for their own purposes at the expense of general welfare. Since the rational expectations revolution this argument has been replaced by a more sophisticated point, raised by Kydland and Prescott (1977), concerning the time inconsistency[4] of optimal policies. Over the last few years consensus on monetarism has too faded. Basically, dissatisfaction with the monetarist philosophy of policymaking is centred around four points: the self-stabilising properties of a market economy, the implications of forward-looking behaviour in the formation of expectations, the efficiency of monetary targets, and the insulating properties of a flexible exchange rate. I shall briefly state the reasons for dissatisfaction with these propositions, taking each in turn.

1.1.1 Wage-price flexibility

Monetarists held the optimistic view that anti-inflationary policies would not generate high unemployment to the extent that policies were known and fully understood.[5] Actual history has turned out to be quite different. A key feature of a modern market economy is the existence of a whole range of implicit and explicit contracts.[6] Hence the macroeconomic system exhibits a considerable degree of inertia and the adjustment of prices and quantities which is necessary in response to shocks can only occur gradually, leaving room for prolonged periods of disequilibrium. Furthermore, evidence of hysteresis has been found[7] in the labour market. This casts serious doubts on the supposed irrelevance of macroeconomic policies for the long-term position of the economy as 'full employment' equilibrium cannot be conceived as independent from the past evolution of the economic system nor from the history of the policy stance.

1.1.2 Rational expectations

It is now widely accepted that rational agents will form their expectations about future economic events by making use of all available information. But gathering information may be costly and access to the relevant information simply not be possible. As a matter of fact, forward markets have not spread to some key markets, such as investment goods.[8] This fact of life is probably another justification for the considerable degree of inertia that modern advanced economies exhibit. On the other hand, the so called 'efficient markets', where prices are flexible and information is quickly available, have witnessed high volatility and speculative 'bubbles': prices have often moved in sharp contrast with the predictions of economic theory.[9] Accepting the rational expectations hypothesis is a far cry from inferring continuous equilibrium in the real economy as postulated in the 'policy ineffectiveness' proposition! The simple recognition of the existence of contracts provides a rationale for the persistence of disequilibrium in the labour market even under the assumption of rational expectations.[10]

1.1.3 Money supply targets

At the beginning of the 1980s governments in a number of industrial economies adhered to the monetarist prescription of setting monetary targets. But the experience of targeting the money supply has been rather disappointing. This is so because, in contrast with former evidence, demand for money has been rather unstable. Furthermore, the task of monetary control has been complicated by the growing financial integration of open economies. Anti-inflationary policies which relied on attempts to control monetary aggregates often ended up in excessive interest rates hikes and exchange rate appreciation, imparting unduly contractionary stimuli to the real sector.

1.1.4 Flexible exchange rates

The widespread belief that exchange rate flexibility would insulate national economies has also been contradicted. Fifteen years of unmanaged float have witnessed wild fluctuations in exchange rates, persistent trade imbalances and the resurgence of protectionism. Recently, calls for increased international policy coordination and for a reform of the international monetary system have gained ground.[11]

1.2 THE SEARCH FOR A NEW POLICY FRAMEWORK

Given the difficulties monetarist policies have run into, it should not come as a surprise to learn that a great deal of research has recently been devoted to attempts at redesigning macroeconomic policies.

The search for alternative policy strategies has focused on the following aspects.

- Establishing the theoretical framework necessary for the advocacy of new policy rules.
- Defining an appropriate methodology for policy design. This should not be considered a merely technical aspect. The debate on the time inconsistency of optimal policies has clearly shown how the design of policy is crucially affected by the way the economy is conceived to work.
- Setting policy targets and instruments.

In this section we shall discuss these issues in turn.

1.2.1 The resurgence of more interventionist policies

Recent years have witnessed the resurgence of a more 'activist' philosophy of policymaking. The case for interventionist policy rules has been reformulated, allowing for forward-looking behaviour in the private sector. In a seminal article, Buiter (1981) contrasted fixed rules, of the type advocated by Friedman, with contingent rules, involving a higher degree of discretion. The terminological distinction between the two can be drawn as follows.

- *Open loop rules*, or fixed rules, require all present and future values of the policy instrument to be known when the planning period starts.
- *Closed loop rules*, or contingent rules, specify the value that policy variables will take in the future as a function of the information that will be available at the time when these values will actually have to be assigned.

A key difference between contingent and fixed rules is that the latter require the initial determination of instrument values regardless of future world conditions, whereas the former only require the functional form of the policy feedback to be defined in advance, the actual future values of the policy instruments depending on the occurring disturbance. Closed loop policies allow for a flexible response to unforeseen disturbances and in so doing exploit new information which would not be considered under open loop policy rules.

Buiter showed that the optimal closed loop rule always outperforms the optimal open loop rule. Particularly relevant for the purpose of this book is his criticism of the new classical proposition that only unanticipated policy shocks will affect the economy.[12] Buiter demonstrated that, as long as private and public opportunity sets differ, known contingent policy rules will affect real outcomes. It is well known that if multi-period wage contracts are non-contingent, that is make use of initial information only, a contingent monetary rule, which at any period is a known function of the information publicly available, may be effective and increase welfare.[13] The point is very simple but quite important: to the extent that shocks hit the economy and contracts delay the necessary wage-price adjustment, room is left for contingent policy rules which may reduce the welfare loss that would otherwise be generated. This conclusion applies despite the fact that the functional form of the rule is known in advance: the policy is effective as long as private contracts are not made contingent on future information.

This would seem to leave room for a resurgence of the use of optimal control techniques which seemed so promising at the beginning of the 1970s.[14]

1.2.2 Optimal policies and the time inconsistency critique

The definition of the optimal policy involves two conceptual tasks.

The first is the definition of an appropriate mathematical framework, where the three sets of endogenous (state), exogenous (forcing) and policy (control) variables are specified,[15] along with the stochastic properties of the economic system and the set of dynamic equations which link the above variables. The standard controlled system may be represented as follows:[16]

$$dx(t) = Ax(t) + Bw(t)$$

where $x(t)$ is the $n, 1$ vector of state variables, w is the $m, 1$ vector of control variables, d represents the time derivative. All variables are defined as deviations from equilibrium, so that the forcing variables do not explicitly appear. Matrices A and B are time-invariant. The second step in the optimal control exercise is the definition of a performance measure:

$$J = \int\limits_{0}^{\infty} exp(-rt)[x(t)Qx(t) + w(t)Rw(t)]dt$$

where r is a discount factor, Q is a symmetric positive semidefinite matrix of order n, n and r is a positive definite time-invariant matrix of order m, m. J shows that the controller penalises deviations of state and control variables from their long-term values.

The optimal control problem involves choosing the sequence of $w(i)$ which minimises J given the dynamic system, the initial state of the system and some appropriate terminal condition. The resulting outcome satisfies Bellman's principle of optimality, which states that at any point in time the optimal policy is merely the following up of the original plan computed at the beginning of the control exercise.[17] This initial plan is described as time consistent because no incentive exists for the controller to revise it. Such time consistency holds when the control technique is applied to a non-intelligent system, but not when the controlled variables themselves react to the initial optimal plan, as is the case in rational expectation models.

In this class of models at least some state variables are non-predetermined and instantaneously respond to shocks and to policy announcements. As a result, a difference can arise between the optimal policy sequence $w(t + 1), w(t + 2), \ldots w(t + i)$ computed at time t and the optimal policy sequence $w(t + 1), w(t + 2), \ldots w(t + i)$ computed at time $t + 1$. To understand why this happens, it must be borne in mind that at year one the controller takes into account the fact that policy actions planned for the years ahead affect the current state of the economy because some variables immediately respond to expectations about the future. But at year two bygones are bygones, and the current optimal policy will be based on the influence of present and future policy actions on the current state of the economy, ignoring their influence on year one. And it is precisely at this stage that an incentive exists for the controller to revise his policy.

Consider an example drawn from Miller (1985). Suppose that in an open economy the government announced at year one a future interest rate rise in order to fight inflation. Rational agents who believed such an announcement would discount this and increase demand for domestic currency. The resulting exchange rate appreciation would deflate the domestic economy before the monetary contraction actually took place. But in year two the optimal policy would not contemplate the same monetary contraction as that previously announced, since the past anticipation of an interest rate rise would have already deflated the economy. The initial policy plan is therefore time inconsistent because the government has an incentive to fool the private sector, announcing a future course of action and then revising it. But if rational agents anticipate this incentive their actions may be different from the ones implied in the optimal control exercise, and attempts to optimise might be counterproductive.

This point was forcefully raised by Kydland and Prescott (1977). They argued that rational agents would recognise the existence of an incentive for the government to 'renege' on announced policies and would therefore base their expectations on the anticipation of future reoptimisations. A possible equilibrium of the resulting game would be a policy accounting for the private sector expectation that the government will reoptimise, taking the behaviour of the private sector as given. The following example, drawn from Barro (1985), might further clarify the issue. First, assume that anticipated monetary policy only affects the price level. Second, monetary 'surprises' may alter real output. Third, the government welfare function positively values an output expansion above the 'natural' rate.[18] Fourth, inflation is a social evil. At any point in time an incentive exists for the policymaker to generate unexpected inflation and raise output. But forward-looking agents anticipate this incentive and expect an inflation rate which is higher than announced. Therefore the government must accommodate a higher inflation rate just to keep output at the natural rate. In this context, Barro and Gordon (1983) describe an equilibrium solution where, although inflation surprises may still occur, the policymaker lacks the incentive for inflating the economy because the inflation rate rises to just that level at which the marginal cost of a monetary surprise is equal to its marginal benefit in terms of higher output. As may seem obvious, the time consistent equilibrum is greatly inferior to the one which would prevail under the optimal time inconsistent policy. Kydland and Prescott argued that governments should constrain themselves to following a non-optimising, arbitrarily fixed rule:

> economic theory [should] be used to evaluate policy rules and that one with good operating characteristics be selected . . . it is preferable that selected rules be simple and easily understood, so that it is obvious when a policymaker deviates from the policy. There should be institutional arrangements which make it a difficult and time-consuming process to change the policy rules in all but emergency situations.[19]

Referring to the former example, a fixed rule would spare the economy the higher expected inflation rate which is necessary to render the marginal cost of an inflation surprise equal to the benefit accruing from the corresponding output expansion.

An important line of the literature following the work of Kydland and Prescott has stressed the importance of government precommitment to implement the plan implied by the initial optimisation and has suggested that the loss of reputation following a policy surprise might impair the success of future policies, deterring governments from reneging on announced policies.[20] In this context it might be superfluous that governments be forced by law to abide by the rules, provided that departures from the announced policy can be easily detected.

A further development, which is of key importance for the research to be carried out in this book, has been the search for simple contingent rules which are easily understood by the private sector, that is, they do not involve the degree of complexity typical of optimal policies. This issue is discussed in the next two subsections, in which the connections between the time inconsistency problem and the use of simple rules is also investigated.

1.2.3 The design of simple macropolicy rules

Typically, an optimal policy must be contingent on all state variables. It should be clear that this is the most efficient way of steering the controlled economy, as the fully optimal rule controls everything. But a rule which is exceedingly complex and difficult to understand and monitor might raise serious problems of credibility. For the policy to be credible in the eyes of the private sector, it is crucial that policy assessment may be carried out easily. Simple feedback rules may well serve this purpose. Furthermore, there must be considerable doubt as to whether complex optimal policies may be realistically implemented.[21] Rather than run the risk of considerable and casual simplification at the stage of implementation, the obvious alternative is to build in the requirement of simplicity from the outset.[22]

Robustness is another reason for advocating the choice of simple rules.[23] An obvious reason why optimal policies outperform simple rules is that the former exploit the details of the dynamic system to be controlled. But to the extent that these aspects are model-specific, highly uncertain and subject to frequent changes over time, the gains from full optimisation may prove illusory. Optimal policies may perform badly in the face of even minor alterations of the dynamic structure of the economy. By contrast well-designed simple rules may turn out to be more robust in the presence of such changes.[24]

A third source of skepticism with fully optimal policies concerns the way the loss function J is defined. Very often the range of variables included in the objective function is not related to plausible considerations about social welfare;[25] instead its choice is made with the aim of obtaining acceptable results.[26] Methods have been suggested for tuning the penalty matrices so that dynamic instability is prevented[27] or the optimal solution trajectories are kept reasonably close to the target path.[28] But under no circumstances could policies designed in accordance with such methods be regarded as the outcome of a genuine optimisation process. Ad-hocery is certainly an inherent feature to the design of simple rules when the functional form and the strength of control parameters are selected, but very often full optimisation removes it only to reintroduce arbitrariness in the design of the objective function.

It has been argued elsewhere that simple rules should be selected according to the following principles:[29]

- the dynamic structure of the rules should be simple.
- each instrument should respond to a limited set of variables.

Of preeminent interest for the present work is that class of simple rules (assignment rules) which assign each instrument to a specific set of target variables. Within this set of rules we shall be concerned with decoupled control rules[30] which entail the assignment of each instrument to a specific target variable.

The simple rules we shall be dealing with throughout the book will take the following general form:

$$dw = h_1 I dT + h_2 I T$$

where d is the time derivative, w and T respectively are the vectors of control and target variables, h_1 and h_2 are the vectors of control parameters and I is the identity matrix. We shall therefore consider decoupled rules involving proportional and integral control.[31]

1.2.4 Time inconsistency and simple rules

The problem of time inconsistency potentially applies to simple rules as well as to full optimal control. Consider again the Miller example of an interest rate rise to fight inflation through currency appreciation. Suppose that a simple proportional rule were operated which required merely an interest rate x per cent above the world interest rate for every 1 per cent that inflation was above target. An inflation shock would lead to an immediate raising of interest rates. It would also immediately lead to a currency appreciation determined by the knowledge that interest rates would remain high throughout the disinflation period. The expectation that, according to the rule, interest rates would be high in the future would therefore appreciate the currency and bring down inflation immediately. But when the future arrived there would be an incentive for the government to revise the rule so as to lower interest rates. In fact the partial relaxation of the high interest rate policy would be desirable because the past anticipation of the high interest rate policy has already deflated the economy.

This example shows that simple rules, as well as optimal policies, run into the time inconsistency problem when the private sector adopts forward-looking behaviour. This book does not tackle this problem – it is assumed that reneging would involve a loss of reputation whose cost, in terms of a lesser chance to implement policies requiring this reputation, would be sufficiently high to prevent the government from redesigning its policy. In this context the adoption of simple rules is intended to help the private sector to understand government behaviour and so more accurately build this into their expectations.[32]

Throughout the book we shall therefore assume that the government sticks to announced policies and that the private sector fully trusts the government.

1.2.5 Targets and instruments of macroeconomic policy

This section is concerned with the choice of the targets and instruments of macroeconomic policy, and with the ensuing implications for the modelling strategy to be adopted in the rest of the book.

1.2.5.1 Nominal income targets

I have already mentioned that the experience of setting monetary targets has been disappointing. Basically, this failure is to be ascribed to the frequent shifts in the velocity of circulation which have occurred over the last few years. The adoption of new policy targets obviously reflects the underlying philosophy of policymaking. Whatever the merits of a money supply target *per se*, monetarist policies relied on the presumption that governments should only be concerned with inflation control and should neglect output fluctuations. If policy were to retain this principle and the only required change was to allow for the apparent inefficiency of monetary targets as a result of velocity shifts, then the natural substitute would be a price level target, or an inflation rate target.[33] Barro (1985) has advocated the choice of a price level target, on the ground that it would enable the policymaker to offset shocks originating in the money market. As an alternative he considered the adoption of a nominal exchange rate rule. Obviously, such a rule would raise the issue of international leadership in the definition of the global inflation target.[34]

Others have suggested[35] that policy should aim at stabilising nominal GDP. In contrast with the former proposals, this rule prescribes a policy feedback on both the price level and real output. It relies on the presumption that wage-price stickiness leaves room for policy effects on output. Weale *et al.* (1989) put forward two reasons for adopting a nominal income target. The first is that it would discourage inflationary wage claims in the labour market. In fact trade unions would anticipate that an inflation rate above target would be matched by a loss of output and employment, even though such a loss would be smaller than if the policymaker adhered to a price level target. The second reason is that, should prices rise because of some unforeseen event, the money GDP target would set a ceiling on the corresponding output loss, whereas under a price rule the recession would need to be intensified as long as the price level were above target. A widespread criticism of this proposal is that it implies that the policymaker puts equal weight on output and price fluctuations. Fischer (1988a) argues that, if put explicitly, it is unlikely that such a trade-off would be accepted.

In principle, there is nothing that should prevent the policymaker from setting a target which exactly reflects his preferences in terms of output and inflation. A boundless range of targets would then be available, but to the extent that some cost is attached to output fluctuations such targets would still be in the spirit of a nominal income target, whose basic feature is the explicit recognition of the influence of policy on output fluctuations. In some recent attempts to evaluate the performance of simple rules nominal income targets have been adopted.[36] The same choice will be made in this book, in Chapters 4 and 6.

1.2.5.2 *Foreign wealth targets. Is there a rationale for current account control?*

Nominal income targeting might not be enough to avoid adverse results in the long term. Weale *et al.* (1989) argued that national wealth targets should be adopted along with money GDP targets. They suggested that policy should aim at controlling the distribution of national resources between investment and consumption. The first reason for doing so is obviously that an adequate investment level would help in achieving sustained productivity growth in the long term. The second reason is that a wealth target would prevent stabilisation policies that curb current inflation at the expense of lower growth in the future. An obvious example of how such an outcome might occur is a policy combining a lax fiscal stance with relatively high real interest rates. In this case domestic output and inflation would be kept on target but the policy mix would raise consumption relative to investment, with adverse results in the future.

In an open economy, such a policy would generate another undesirable consequence: higher interest rates would appreciate the exchange rate and penalise the trading sector. The wrong policy mix would cause a current account deficit. In the long term the inevitable exchange rate depreciation would require a contraction of domestic demand to offset the inflationary consequences of the devaluation, and to free resources for the improvement of the trade balance. Furthermore, the permanent accumulation of foreign debt would cause a permanent reduction in future national disposable income, which is necessary for servicing the foreign debt. Indeed, setting a national wealth target implies, for a given capital formation path, the adoption of a residual current account target.

Adopting a foreign wealth target is a fundamental departure from the monetarist orthodoxy. Followers of the monetary approach to the balance of payments argue that governments should focus on the internal objective, neglecting the evolution of the current account, whose balance is regarded as the result of saving–consumption decisions by the private sector. Typically, monetarists assert that, as long as the budget is balanced, governments should not be concerned with external disequilibria simply because the private sector will not run a permanent, unsustainable deficit. Over the last few years this approach has found increasing acceptance within the economic profession, and a new consensus seems to have emerged about the monetarist position.

According to the 'New View',[37] optimal saving–consumption decisions by the private sector may well imply a sequence of current account deficits which should not be the object of governmental concern. Muellbauer and Murphy (1990) cite several cases where optimal consumption decisions imply a current account deficit, such as greater productivity growth coupled with an initial capacity loss, permanently lower taxes and greater financial integration. Corden (1991) provides another illuminating example. Suppose domestic investment rose because productivity was seen to be above the interest rate paid on foreign funds and that the expected higher production led to an increase in domestic consumption. The current account would unambiguously worsen, but this should raise no government concern at all.

> There are numerous factors determining optimal savings and investment, and also divergences between actual levels of these and the optimal levels, and it is these that are relevant for policy consideration.[38]

No one would seriously dispute the above statement; however there may be situations when policy action would be appropriate. Consider the following examples, acknowledged by Corden himself.

- '*Unsound*' *domestic spending boom*. This might be the consequence of either myopic private behaviour or existing domestic distortions.[39] In the past there have been examples of cumulating external debt which compelled the government to take over private debts.[40] Less extreme and paradoxical outcomes imply that current overconsumption would impose the burden of servicing foreign debt on future generations.
- *Contamination effect*. The argument goes as follows. An increase in foreign loans will raise the share of national debt in international portfolios and increase the risk factor of domestic borrowers. To the extent that a change in the individual risk factor is not wholly internalised for the various agents, that is, to the extent that a 'country risk' factor is applied indiscriminately, a negative externality is imposed on future borrowers by the marginal borrower.
- *Trade distortions*. By and large, a spending boom will raise inflation and domestic interest rates. The resulting exchange rate appreciation will squeeze the relative profitability of the domestic tradable sector and generate 'structural' external imbalances because the supply of tradables has fallen.
- *Persistent external deficits lead to increased foreign ownership and control of the domestic economy*. The argument holds to the extent that domestic control of capital is preferable, but this issue does not enter into private borrowing decisions.

The above examples show that current account imbalances might signal a discrepancy between socially optimal and actual national net savings. Nevertheless, those who accept the 'new view' maintain that even when private saving and spending decisions are subject to microeconomic distortions, current account targeting is inappropriate. They argue that, instead of being concerned with the external imbalance itself, policy should aim at removing the distortions which generated it (Artis and Bayoumi, 1990). However, if correcting such distortions is not feasible, a second-best alternative may be for the government to target the current account (Evans, 1990). There is an obvious analogy with the advocacy of policies aiming to stabilise nominal income when labour market distortions limit nominal wage flexibility. The best policy would certainly involve the removal of distortions, but as long as this is not accomplished there is scope for macroeconomic stabilisation. Indeed macro and micro policies do not conflict with each other!

There are other reasons for advocating a foreign wealth target. First, ensuring intergenerational equity is the strongest justification for governments' concern with national savings, and the point holds even if the private sector is not subject to private myopia and there are no microeconomic distortions. It is well known that if consumers behave according to the life-cycle model and there is a lack of effective intergenerational linking of preferences, future generations are not represented in current decisions,[41] therefore individual optimising behaviour does not lead to socially optimal outcomes. This brings us back to the issue of current account targeting: as Boughton (1989) pointed out, arguing that governments should be concerned with intergenerational wealth transfers is equivalent to arguing that they should be concerned with the external current account balance.

Second, the danger of withdrawal on short notice might turn external debt into a serious threat to the independence of national policy (Dornbusch and Park, 1987). Third, a substantial net foreign assets position compels the policy to pay excessive attention to the capital gains or losses which might arise from swings in the exchange rate (Cooper and Sachs, 1985). Fourth, it is widely acknowledged that exchange rate expectations respond to current account 'news' and that balance of payments crises are often associated with large current account imbalances (Claessens, 1991).

Capital flights may be generated either by a sudden reversal of belief about the sustainability of the external deficit or by the uncertainty about government policies in response to it. Setting a foreign wealth target and a policy rule to achieve it would probably help to stabilise expectations in the financial markets.[42]

The debate on the external balance constraint has been centred around two fundamental questions:

- should we regard current account imbalances *per se* as 'bad'?
- under what circumstances should the policy aim at current account targeting?

From the above discussion the answer to the first question is unambiguously no. By contrast, no clear-cut answer can be given to the second. Followers of the 'new view' would probably incline to a 'benign neglect' attitude. Others do not share such an optimistic view.[43] There are several reasons why actual and socially optimal current account balances may diverge, and governments may legitimately seek to influence the level of net domestic savings. Indeed, a great deal of the recent debate on rules for policy stabilisation has focused on the importance of pursuing policies that are consistent with the external balance. The well-known target zones proposal is specifically designed with the aim of avoiding unsustainable trade imbalances.[44] In this book we shall evaluate policy proposals which include a wealth target. The scope of the research is restricted to the analysis of stabilisation policies in a context which does not explicitly account for capital accumulation, therefore we shall only consider a foreign wealth target, defined as net financial claims on foreign residents held by the domestic private sector.[45] We shall take such a foreign wealth target[46] as given and study the performance of some macroeconomic policy rules devised to attain it.[47] Throughout the book we shall be concerned with the current account implications of policy actions. This is one of the main innovative elements of the research.

1.2.5.3   Instrument selection

Traditionally, Keynesian policies relied on both monetary and fiscal instruments. The monetarist 'counterrevolution' stressed the role of the monetary instrument. Controlling monetary aggregates has proven extremely difficult, but manipulation of interest rates has been quite effective. The monetary feedback policies analysed in this book will therefore involve control of a short-term *real* interest rate. Rules of this kind have recently found growing acceptance.[48] It is well known, since Poole's (1970) seminal article, that pegging the interest rate insulates the economy from instability arising from the adverse effects of demand for money. The traditional monetarist objection to an interest rate peg is that such a policy would leave the economy without a nominal anchor. This argument does not apply here, as (a) an interest rate feedback rule is being considered and (b) this operates on the real rate. There is a danger that pegging the interest rate instead of monetary aggregates might cause instability because when inflation rises the real rate falls. But here we are operating a control rule on the real interest rate, so that a rise in inflation causes a rise of the nominal rate and this is part of a feedback policy designed so that real rates would be *raised* when inflation increased. Controlling a real interest rate obviously implies facing the difficulty of measuring the actual inflation rate but, as Edison, Miller and Williamson (1987) suggest, this is by no means more difficult than measuring and interpreting monetary aggregates.

The existence of a second target, besides the domestic objective, raises the issue of selecting an additional instrument if policy goals are to be met. Fiscal policy would seem the most obvious candidate. After a period of widespread acceptance of the monetarist prescription that governments should simply opt for a balanced budget, in recent years there has been a resurrection of policy 'packages' which involve active use of the fiscal instrument for the purpose of macroeconomic stabilisation.[49] New classical theorists[50] would point to the Ricardian equivalence theorem to assert that fiscal policy cannot affect the saving–consumption decisions of rational forward-looking agents. But the work of Blanchard (1985) has shown that such an ineffectiveness proposition only holds under the assumption of infinitely-lived agents. When this restrictive hypothesis is removed it is shown that even rational, forward-looking consumption decisions made in the context of a life-cycle hypothesis are affected by the current fiscal policy stance.

The fiscal instrument will be part of some of the policy proposals to be assessed in this book. Shifts of the fiscal stance can be operated on either side of the budget accounts, that is, by manipulating either expenditure or revenue. Vines *et al.* (1983) have argued in favour of tax rate rules, as such an instrument is likely to be more flexible and less costly to alter than public expenditure. In Chapter 4 the tax rate is adopted as the fiscal instrument, whereas Chapter 6 uses the more general concept of a fiscal stance index.[51]

1.2.5.4 Modelling the consumption function

The emphasis in this book on foreign wealth targets and on the importance of fiscal intervention obviously finds a logical counterpart in the modelling strategy for the aggregate consumption function. Over the last few years current account issues have been investigated using models which assume a forward-looking consumption function. Models assuming perfect foresight and infinitely lived agents are ill-suited for the purpose of this book, since they generate outcomes where Ricardian equivalence holds and no divergence may arise between actual and socially optimal savings. Models in the Blanchard–Yaari tradition, where finite horizons are assumed, leave room for the effectiveness of fiscal policy. However, as is often the case in forward-looking models, stability requires consumption to jump immediately in response to an increase in permanent income.[52] This may happen only if consumption is not restricted by liquidity constraints. Theoretical models embedding a forward-looking consumption function usually sweep this issue aside by assuming efficient financial markets. However, adverse selection and/or moral hazard problems may prevent people from borrowing the desired amount (Stiglitz and Weiss, 1981).

Several empirical studies have pointed out that liquidity constraints do affect a significant proportion of consumers.[53] Furthermore, very recent research has pointed to the 'excess sensitivity' of consumption to current income (Campbell and Mankiw, 1989 and 1991). These studies support the view that a substantial proportion of consumers follow a simple rule of thumb: consumption falls when current income falls and vice versa, and this generates a significant welfare loss.

The growing empirical evidence on liquidity constraints and the importance of current income has affected the way I have chosen to model the consumption function. The models set out in Chapters 3, 4 and 6 imply that consumption responds to *wealth*, the *real interest rate* and *current income*, while forward-looking behaviour is not accounted for. As pointed out in Weale *et al.* (1989), the long-term implications of this specification do not substantially differ from those that would obtain assuming forward-looking behaviour. By contrast, significant differences arise in short-term dynamics.

1.3 SUMMARY

This chapter has pointed out how new progress has been made in the search for a policy which framework provides an alternative to monetarist orthodoxy. This framework is built on the following basic hypotheses.

- Sluggish price adjustment leaves substantial room for disequilibrium and for macroeconomic stabilisation policies.
- Such policies are designed to provide a stable environment. Hence they are publicly announced and policymakers recognise that agents will behave according to their perceptions of government's policies. Therefore credibility and sustainability are essential prerequisites of policy packages. In this context simple feedback rules might turn out to be more appealing than full optimisation. Besides, I believe that, even if optimal policies were to be preferred, investigating simple rules is still helpful for the clarification of issues such as the danger of wealth instability and the policies needed to remove it, which would be shadowed by the inevitable complexities of optimal policies.

- Policy actions should be concerned with both inflation and output; I opt for nominal income targets. Furthermore, the adoption of national wealth targets might raise welfare by keeping actual and socially optimal savings as close as possible.

These points have inspired my work and will form the basis for the rest of this book.

1.4   OUTLINE OF THE REMAINDER OF THE BOOK

Chapter 2 is a review of existing models of floating exchange rates. It enables us to build up the key pieces of our model. It points to the importance of wealth effects for exchange rate determination, as has been emphasised by Branson (1979) and by Dornbusch and Fischer (1980). But it also shows that scant attention has been paid to the problem of exchange rate determination in models where goods prices are sticky, exchange rate expectations are forward-looking, and wealth effects occur.

Chapter 3 presents a more general model of this kind and highlights the danger of instability inherent to such models under a monetarist regime. Several criticisms of monetarist policies have been raised;[54] in this chapter another reason for dissatisfaction is stressed by showing that under such policies dynamic instability might occur. Furthermore, it will be shown that the danger of instability arises because the process of wealth accumulation, operating through the current account, is deliberately not controlled under a monetarist regime. Indeed the emphasis on the adoption of foreign wealth targets is a key issue throughout the following chapters.

Chapter 4 is a central part of this book, which Chapters 2 and 3 lead up to. The standard money supply rule is abandoned at this point and we move on to evaluate the relative performance of four alternative simple policy rules. This is done by means of both algebraic analysis and numerical simulations of a small theoretical model. The rules to be considered can be described as follows.

Assignment 1, a monetarist rule, assigns a real interest rate feedback to a nominal income target. Assignment 2, which originates from Weale *et al.* (1989), and from Boughton (1989), adds fiscal control of a foreign wealth target to the monetary control of the internal objective. Assignment 3, the Mundell assignment, sets fiscal control of domestic nominal income and monetary control of the foreign wealth target.

Finally, Assignment 4 applies in a small country context the kind of rules advocated in the target zones proposal by Williamson (1987): the government is supposed to dispense with monetary policy altogether and to assign fiscal policy to the domestic target. I shall obviously comment later on the results of the analysis. One general point I wish to stress from the outset is the importance of fiscal policy in a well-designed policy package, especially if it is assigned to a wealth target.

In part two, Chapters 5 and 6 apply my ideas to issues of policy coordination. Chapter 5 is a survey which mainly concentrates on those issues in the policy coordination debate that are relevant for an application of simple rules. Chapter 6 is the innovative section. In a two-country setting we consider a disinflation experiment and assess the relative performance of three alternative proposals, which assign the same instrument to the control of global, or average, inflation, but differ in their strategy to reduce intercountry inflation differentials and their strategy of foreign wealth control. The first rule is Williamson's well-known target zones proposal (1987). The second is a standard monetarist rule. The third is a two-country version of Assignment (2). The analysis crucially differs from the one carried out in Chapter 4 as it accounts for the international repercussions of individual policy actions. Furthermore, it gives a detailed account of the influence of global disinflation policy on intercountry inflation differentials, which occurs through the international transfer of wealth determined by the fluctuation of world interest rates.

2 Open Economy Models: The Macroeconomic Approach

INTRODUCTION

This chapter surveys some contributions to the theory of exchange rate determination which follow the so called macroeconomic approach[1] (MAC) in order to provide the theoretical background for the policy experiments to be presented in later chapters.

A huge amount of research has been devoted to the search for plausible explanations of the exchange rate volatility observed during the 1970s. A common feature of the models discussed here is the well-known overshooting of the exchange rate, a phenomenon which has found different theoretical explanations. The celebrated Dornbusch model emphasises the role of price stickiness. Further research, stressing the importance of wealth effects and imperfect capital mobility, has pointed to the connections between exchange rate and current account dynamics. The view that the exchange rate is 'the relative price of two national monies'[2] has been substantially amended. In the short term the exchange rate is still regarded as an asset price, although its level is set to clear financial markets where a wider bundle of assets than the two traditional money supplies matters. In the longer term the exchange rate depends on economic fundamentals, that is terms of trade and net domestic holdings of foreign assets. This implies that flexible exchange rate models must embed the constraint that the wealth accumulation/decumulation which arises from trade imbalances cannot be indefinitely sustained.

Possible alternatives to MAC are the equilibrium approach[3] (EA) or the new classical economics[4] (NCE). In contrast with the 'ad hoc' MAC models, both EA and NEC rely on explicit utility maximisation to derive behavioural equations from microeconomic foundations and emphasise intertemporal consumption and investment choices. However the two approaches present some unattractive features. For instance, the EA assumes that *all* markets clear and wages are flexible. Therefore, EA models are inconsistent with the philosophy of

23

policymaking outlined in Chapter 1. The NEC approach largely overlaps the EA, except for an occasional focus on situations where not all markets clear: for instance, some NEC models assume short-run price stickiness. However, the widespread assumption of perfect credit markets, combined with a forward-looking consumption function, generates the overoptimistic conclusion that external imbalances do not matter, as long as the government budget is balanced, and emphasises Ricardian equivalence effects which undo much of the potential role of fiscal policy. The approach is now being somewhat modified by imposing ad hoc credit constraints or introducing Blanchard-type non-neutrality. An authoritative scholar[5] has pointed out that when the task is completed and NEC models account for the critical 'rigidities' and imperfections of the economy, their predictions will not substantially differ from those obtained from MAC models. Since a great deal of this book investigates the foreign wealth implications of alternative fiscal rules, it is still preferable to stick to traditional MAC models which do not arbitrarily dismiss the relevance of the issue to be studied.

The rest of this chapter is organised as follows. First there is an analysis of the Dornbusch extension of the traditional Fleming–Mundell model,[6] which accounts for the sluggish adjustment of the price level to demand shocks. The second part focuses on the Dornbusch and Fischer model, relating wealth accumulation to domestic expenditure and the exchange rate. Finally, Branson's portfolio model is taken into account.

2.1 THE DORNBUSCH MODEL

Dornbusch shows that sluggish price adjustment leaves room for short-term disequilibrium in the money market and generates overshooting of nominal and real exchange rates. The model is composed of two building blocks, describing the financial and the goods sector respectively.

$$m - p = - ki \tag{2.1}$$

$$i - i^* = Ede \tag{2.2}$$

$$Ede = de \tag{2.3}$$

Equations 2.1, 2.2 and 2.3 describe[7] the equilibrium conditions in the financial sector of the economy, all variables being defined as deviations from equilibrium. Equation 2.1 is a standard demand for money function, where output does not appear because it is assumed to be constant at the natural rate. Equation 2.2 shows that, once perfect capital mobility is assumed, a divergence between domestic and foreign interest rates must be offset by expected exchange rate changes. Equation 2.3 entails the rational expectations hypothesis: the expected exchange rate variation is set equal to its actual rate of change.

$$dp = \epsilon D \tag{2.4}$$

$$D = \beta(e - p) - \sigma i - \delta s \tag{2.5}$$

Equation 2.4 links domestic inflation to excess aggregate demand, D. Aggregate demand, Equation 2.5, depends on terms of trade, $(e - p)$, the nominal interest rate, i, and an indicator of real taxation, s.[8] Substituting Equation 2.1, 2.3 and 2.5, in 2.2 and 2.4 we obtain the system in state–space form:

$$X_1 = AX_2 + BX_3$$

where $X_1' = (dp, de)$, $X_2' = (p, e)$, $X_3 = (s, m, i^*)$

$$A = \begin{bmatrix} -\epsilon(\beta + \sigma/k) & \epsilon\beta \\ 1/k & 0 \end{bmatrix}$$

$$B = \begin{bmatrix} \epsilon\delta & \epsilon\sigma & 0 \\ 0 & 1/k & -1 \end{bmatrix}$$

The equilibrium values of the dynamic endogenous variables, p and e, are:

$$p_\infty = ki^* + m$$

$$e_\infty = (k + \sigma/\beta)i^* + (\delta/\beta)s + m$$

In equilibrium purchasing power parity holds after a monetary shock: $dm = dp = de$, the money supply has no long term effect on real variables. Fiscal policy permanently alters aggregate demand and requires an offsetting variation of the terms of trade. A fiscal expansion, for example a reduction of the tax rate, causes an exchange rate appreciation to be matched by a revaluation of the terms of trade. The absence of any long-term link between p and s depends on the assumptions of perfect capital mobility and no wealth effects in demand for money.[9] A rise in the world interest rate lowers demand for money and causes a price increase. Hence the exchange rate must depreciate[10] in order to stabilise the terms of trade. Furthermore, the negative impact of i^* on demand must be offset by a real devaluation, which is achieved by a further exchange rate rise.

Let us turn now to the analysis of price and exchange rate dynamics. As is well known, rational expectations models can be stable and uniquely determined only if the number of unstable roots of the characteristic Equation of the dynamic matrix is matched by the number of non-predetermined variables, which are allowed to make discrete jumps in response to shocks.[11] Therefore the Dornbusch model can be stable if its characteristic equation

$$|A - \theta I| = 0$$

has two roots of different sign, a result which is ensured by the structure of the transition matrix, A. The two roots are:

$$\theta_s = -\epsilon(\beta + \sigma/k)/2 - (1/2)[\epsilon(\beta + \sigma/k)^2 + 4\epsilon\beta/k]^{1/2}$$

$$\theta_u = -\epsilon(\beta + \sigma/k)/2 + (1/2)[\epsilon(\beta + \sigma/k)^2 + 4\epsilon\beta/k]^{1/2}$$

Ruling out the possibility of unstable paths[12] exchange rate and price dynamics can then be described as follows:[13]

$$p_t = p_\infty + C\theta_s k \exp(\theta_s t)$$

$$e_t = e_\infty + C \exp(\theta_s t)$$

where C is a constant which can be defined as a function of $p_0 - p_\infty$.

$$C = (p_0 - p_\infty)/k\theta_s$$

Once C is determined, it is a simple matter to compute the initial overshooting/undershooting of the exchange rate:

$$e(0) - e_\infty = (p_0 - p_\infty)/k\theta_s$$

Consider a money supply increase. In this case $p_0 < p_\infty$ and $e(0) > e_\infty$, since $\theta_s < 0$. Hence the actual amplitude of the initial exchange rate jump depends on the size of the exogenous shock, of the stable root and of the interest rate semielasticity of demand for money. The dynamic path must be monotonic[14] because θ_s is real. At any point in time the gap between the current and the equilibrium exchange rate is negatively related to the gap between the current and the equilibrium price level.[15]

We can interpret the overshooting result as follows. In the aftermath of unanticipated shocks, that is an increase in the money supply, the exchange rate immediately jumps, but the sluggish price adjustment prevents e from settling at its new long term equilibrium value. In fact the monetary shock causes disequilibrium in the money market and a fall of the domestic interest rate. From Equation 2.9 it is clear that, due to international arbitrage, the expected exchange rate change must be negative. Hence the instantaneous exchange rate jump must overshoot the long term depreciation. The terms of trade devaluation and the interest rate fall gradually drive the price level upwards. This increases the demand for money and brings the interest rate back to its equilibrium level. In the meantime the exchange rate appreciates steadily. When purchasing power parity is restored the system returns to equilibrium. These concepts can be illustrated graphically (Figure 2.1). Just before the monetary shock occurs the system is in equilibrium at point a. When m shifts from m_0 to m_1 the new equilibrium position is set at point b, along the 45 degrees line, since in equilibrium:

$$\Delta e/\Delta m = \Delta p/\Delta m$$

The AA and BB loci represent the combinations of e and p that ensure equilibrium in the goods and money markets, for a given set of values of the exogenous variables. In this case the position of AA and BB depends on the new level of the money supply, $p_0 = p(m_0)$ is fixed, $e(0)$ jumps on to the saddlepath associated with the new equilibrium point. From there the combinations of e_t and p_t are described by the QQ line: the exchange rate initially overshoots its long term depreciation and then constantly appreciates; the price level gradually increases.

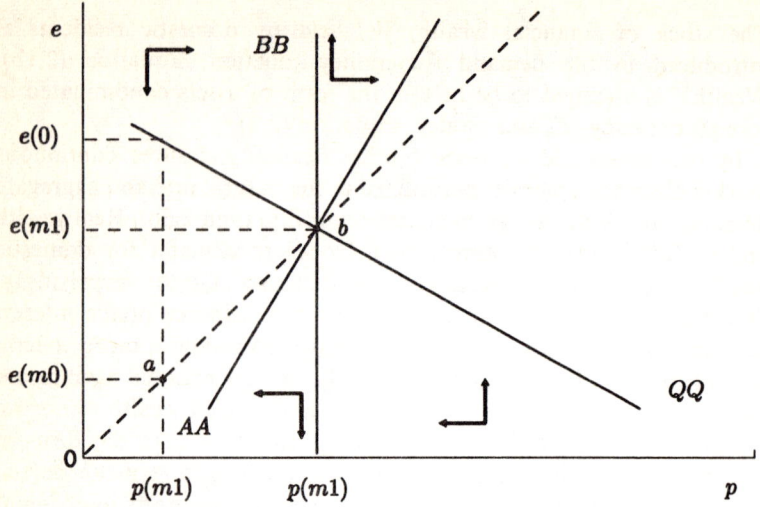

Figure 2.1   Overshooting in the Dornbusch model

2.2   WEALTH EFFECTS, EXCHANGE RATE OVERSHOOTING AND CURRENT ACCOUNT DYNAMICS IN THE DORNBUSCH AND FISCHER MODEL

In this section we shall investigate the connections between the current account, the international redistribution of wealth and the variation of relative prices. Presenting the results obtained by Dornbusch and Fischer requires some substantial modifications of the Dornbusch model. Basically, we need to assume perfect price flexibility and to introduce wealth effects.[16]

$$m - p = -ki + k_w(W - p) \tag{2.1b}$$

$$i - i^* = Ede \tag{2.2}$$

$$Ede = de \tag{2.3}$$

$$D = X^* + \beta(e - p) - \sigma i - \delta s + \tau(W - p) = 0 \tag{2.5b}$$

$$W = (1 - w_1)m + w_1(e + F) \tag{2.6}$$

$$dF = -\Omega(W - p) \tag{2.7}$$

The stock of financial wealth, W, held by domestic residents is introduced in the demand for money function, Equation (2.1b). Wealth[17] is assumed to be held in the form of assets denominated in foreign currency, F, and money, Equation (2.6).

In the goods sector, perfect price flexibility ensures continuous market clearing, hence output is fixed at the natural rate and aggregate demand cannot deviate from equilibrium (Equation 2.5b). Real wealth and a shift term, X^*, representing shocks to demand for domestic goods, are included in aggregate demand. Quite surprisingly, Dornbusch and Fischer do not consider the influence of the interest rate on domestic demand. We have chosen to follow a more general specification, as in Equation 2.5b. In this model national savings are assumed to be a negative function of real financial wealth. Since no capital accumulation occurs, net savings can only take the form of foreign assets accumulation. Equation (2.7) is a typical partial adjustment dynamic Equation, where agents are assumed to accumulate/reduced assets gradually over time, according to the gap between current and 'desired' levels of wealth.[18] Dornbusch and Fischer define Equation (2.7) as the current account. To derive a proper description of the current account, consumption according to the life-cycle theory should first be defined:

$$c = b_1 y^* + b_2(W - p)$$

Foreign wealth accumulation is then determined by the difference between ouput, y^*, and consumption and by the service of foreign investment.[19]

$$dF = S = y^* - c = (1 - b)y^* - \tau(w - p) + i^* F \qquad (2.7b)$$

Even assuming that output is fixed, the only way to reconcile 2.7b with 2.7 is to drop the terms describing the influence on savings of output and foreign interest payments. Dornbusch and Fischer apparently do this and we shall follow them here.[20] Obviously, a correct specification of the current account would lead to alternative conclusions concerning both comparative statics and the stability condition. Furthermore, the inclusion of foreign interest payments would highlight the potential instability inherent to this class of models.[21] In Chapter 3 we shall further discuss the issue using a more general model which accounts for wealth effects, imperfect capital mobility, flexible output and sticky prices.

In order to obtain the model in state–space form we shall proceed as follows. First by combining Equations 2.1b, 2.5b and 2.6 we define the endogenous non-dynamic variables, p and i, in terms of e, F, m, s, X^*.

$$\pi_1 p = \pi_2 e + \pi_3 F + \pi_4 m - \delta s + X^* \tag{2.8}$$

$$i = [-\pi_5 m + \pi_6 e + \pi_7 F + (1 - k_w)(X^* - \delta s)]/\pi_1 k \tag{2.9}$$

where

$$\pi_1 = (\beta + \tau + \sigma(1 - k_w)/k)$$

$$\pi_2 = (\beta + \tau - \sigma k_w w_1/k)$$

$$\pi_3 = (\tau - \sigma k_w w_1/k)$$

$$\pi_4 = [\tau + \sigma(1 - k_w)(1 - w_1)/k]$$

$$\pi_5 = [1 - (1 - w_1)k_w - (1 - k_3)\pi_4/\pi_1]$$
$$\quad = w_1 k_w + (1 - k_w)[\beta + \sigma(1 - k_w)w_1/k$$

$$\pi_6 = [k_w w_1 + (1 - k_w)\pi_2/\pi_1]$$

$$\pi_7 = [k_w w_1 + (1 - k_w)\pi_3/\pi_1]$$

π_1 describes the feedback effects of price variations in aggregate demand. A price rise appreciates the real exchange rate and lowers domestic demand because real wealth falls. But the reduction of wealth weakens the demand for money, so that the interest rate falls and domestic demand is stimulated. On the other hand, in the money market lower real money balances and wealth require a higher interest rate, which has a negative impact on demand. The term $\sigma(1 - k_w)/k$ accounts for this effect. Under the plausible assumption that $k_w < 1$ it is obviously negative. π_3 describes the influence of financial wealth changes. An increase in F stimulates domestic consumption but raises demand for money and the interest rate. π_2 differs from π_3 because the exchange rate affects both foreign demand and financial wealth.[22] Obviously the price change necessary to offset variations of e and F is less than proportional. π_4 shows that an expansion of the money supply raises wealth and lowers the interest rate: its effect on aggregate demand is unambiguously positive. $\pi_4/\pi_1 < 1$, because the price level has a broader effect on aggregate demand than the money supply. π_5, π_6 and π_7 describe the influence of money, the nominal exchange rate and foreign wealth on the domestic interest rate. These variables exert both a direct and indirect impact on i, the latter operating through the changes in the price level that are necessary to keep the goods market in equilibrium.

Let us now turn to the analysis of the system in state–space form. Substituting Equations 2.3, 2.8, 2.9 into 2.2 and 2.7 we get:

$$X_4 = C_1 X_5 + C_2 X_6$$

where

$$X_4' = (de, dF)$$

$$X_5' = (e, F)$$

$$X_6' = (m, X^*, s, i^*)$$

$$C_1 = \begin{bmatrix} \pi_6/k & \pi_7/k \\ -\Omega(w_1 - \pi_2/\pi_1) & -\Omega(w_1 - \pi_3/\pi_1) \end{bmatrix}$$

$$C_2 = \begin{bmatrix} -\pi_5/k & (1-k_w)/\pi_1 k & -(1-k_w)\delta/\pi_1 k & -1 \\ -\Omega(1-w_1-\pi_4/\pi_1) & \Omega/\pi_1 & -\Omega\delta/\pi_1 & 0 \end{bmatrix}$$

Variations of e, F and m positively affect financial wealth, exerting a negative pressure on desired wealth accumulation, which is proportional to their shares on W. For the goods market to clear the variation of nominal financial wealth must be offset by a movement of the price level in the opposite direction.

Note that

$$w_1 - \pi_2/\pi_1 = w_1\sigma k_w/k - (1-w_1)(\beta+\tau)/\pi_1$$

$$w_1 - \pi_3/\pi_1 = w_1\sigma k_w/k - (1-w_1)\tau/\pi_1$$

Unlike Dornbusch and Fischer we are not able to define unambiguously the effect of changes of e and F on W. This is so because we include the interest rate in aggregate demand. Nevertheless saddlepath

stability obtains anyway, as in Dornbusch and Fischer. The two roots
of the characteristic equation $|C - \theta I| = 0$ are:

$$\theta_u = 0.5[\pi_6/k - \tau(w_1 - \pi_3/\pi_1)] +$$
$$+ 0.5\{[\pi_6/k - \tau(w_1 - \pi_3/\pi_1)]^2 + 4(\tau\beta/k)J\}^{-1/2}$$

$$\theta_s = 0.5[\pi_6/k - \tau(w_1 - \pi_3/\pi_1)] -$$
$$- 0.5\{[\pi_6/k - \tau(w_1 - \pi_3/\pi_1)]^2 + 4(\tau\beta w_1/k\pi_1)\}^{-1/2}$$

At any point in time, the relation between current and equilibrium
values of the endogenous dynamic variables is defined as follows.

$$e_t = e_\infty + Nexp(\theta_s t)$$

$$F_t = F_\infty + Nu_s exp(\theta_s t)$$

where $[1, u_s]$ is the right eigenvector associated with the stable root.
$u_s = (\theta_s k - \pi_6)/\pi_7$ is negative. This means that $N = (F_0 - F_\infty)/u_s$ is
negatively related to $F_0 - F_\infty$.

Whenever a change in the exogenous variables occurs that requires a
long-term rise of foreign assets, the exchange rate must overshoot its
equilibrium value. θ_s is real, therefore after the initial jump in the
exchange rate the exchange rate path will be monotonic. When
unexpected shocks occur, current account surpluses will be associated
with appreciation of the exchange rate and vice versa. This is shown
more clearly with the aid of the familiar state–space diagram.

$$dF = 0 : \quad e = [-(w_1\pi_1 - \pi_3)/(w_1\pi_1 - \pi_2)]F$$

$$= \left\{ \frac{-[(w_1 - 1)\tau + w_1\beta + w_1\sigma/k]}{[(w_1 - 1)\tau + w_1\beta + w_1\sigma/k - \beta]} \right\} F \qquad (2.10)$$

$$de = 0 : \quad e = -(\pi_7/\pi_6)F$$

$$= -\left\{ \frac{[k_w w_1(\beta + \tau) + (1 - k_w)\tau]}{[k_w w_1(\beta + \tau) + (1 - k_w)(\beta + \tau)]} \right\} F \qquad (2.11)$$

Equation (2.11) represents locus *ee* in Figures 2.2, 2.3 and 2.4. It is
negatively sloped because e and F exert the same kind of influence on
demand for money,[23] hence if e rises F must fall. Points located above

the *ee* locus are associated with a devaluation because they imply that demand for money is above the current level of real money balances and an interest rate increase is then necessary to equilibrate the money market.

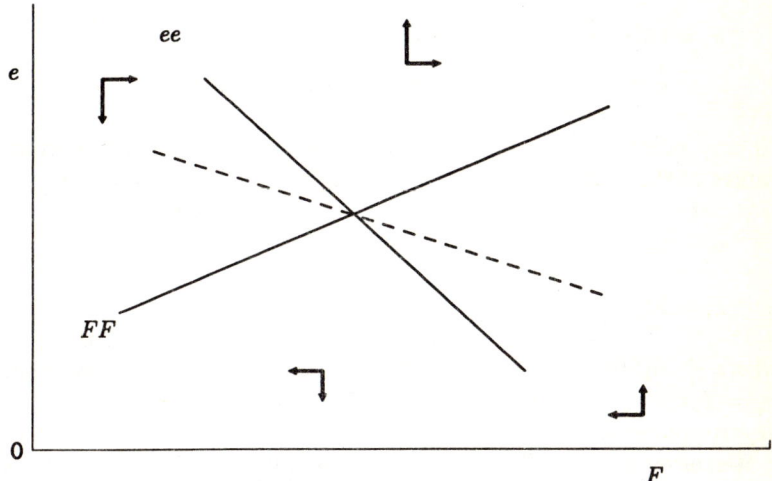

Figure 2.2   Dynamics when wealth imbalances are self-correcting and the *FF* is positively sloped

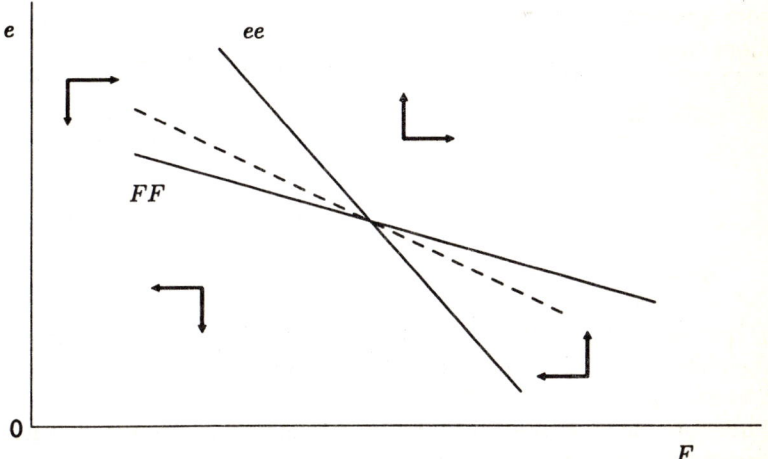

Figure 2-3   Dynamics when wealth is not self-correcting

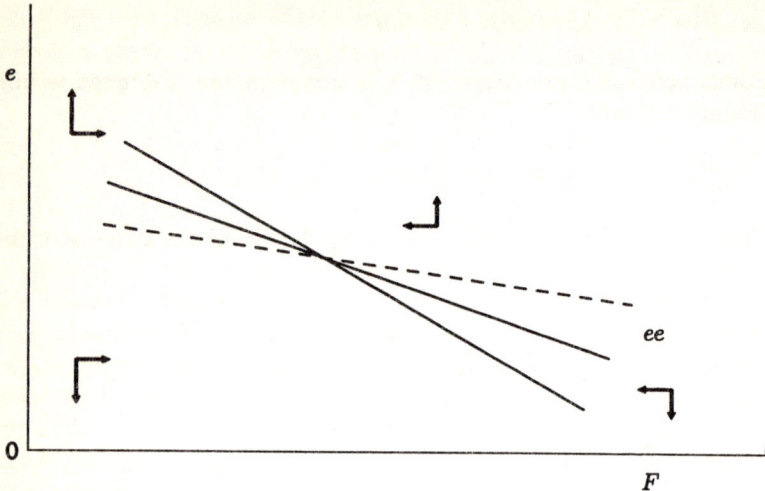

Figure 2.4   Dynamics when wealth is self-correcting and the FF is negatively
          sloped

The slope of the FF locus, described by Equation 2.10, depends on
the terms

$$[(w_1 - 1)\tau + w_1\beta + w_1\sigma/k]$$

$$[(w_1 - 1)\tau + w_1\beta + w_1\sigma/k - \beta]$$

If they have the same sign FF is negatively sloped. If

$$[(w_1 - 1)\tau + w_1\beta + w_1\sigma/k] > 0$$

and

$$[(w_1 - 1)\tau + w_1\beta + w_1\sigma/k - \beta] < 0$$

FF is positively sloped.[24] In this case, Figure 2.2, a low level of
financial assets, for a given exchange rate, triggers wealth accumulation
and vice versa.

On the other hand, assuming that FF is negatively sloped, points
below the FF locus are associated with a reduction in foreign wealth
(Figure 2.3) when:

$$[(w_1 - 1)\tau + w_1\beta + w_1\sigma/k] < 0$$

Points below FF are consistent with accumulation of foreign wealth (Figure 2.4) when

$$[(w_1 - 1)\tau + w_1\beta + w_1\sigma/k] > 0$$

Thus we are left with three alternatives, but from the analysis of the roots of the characteristic Equation we know that the system is saddlepath stable anyway. In each case an initial negative shock to F is associated with instantaneous depreciation of the exchange rate followed by gradual wealth accumulation and appreciation of the exchange rate towards equilibrium. For aggregate demand to be in equilibrium after a loss of foreign wealth the price level must fall. This, in turn, raises real money balances and lowers the interest rate. As in the Dornbusch model, a jump in the exchange rate is then necessary to generate the expectation of a future appreciation, which compensates for the low level of the interest rate.[25]

2.2.1 Comparative statics

$$e = m + (\delta s - X^*)/\beta + (k/\beta)[\sigma/k + (\beta + \tau)(1 - 1/w_1)]i^*$$

$$F = -(\delta s - X^*)/\beta - (k/\beta)[\sigma/k + (\beta + \tau)(1 - 1/w_1)]i^*$$

Changes in the money supply are fully offset by price variations, whereas the proportional exchange rate adjustment holds constant the terms of trade and real wealth. Domestic holdings of foreign assets are not affected at all.

A hike in the foreign interest rate raises the price level because equilibrium in the money market requires lower real money balances. The adjustment of foreign assets and of the exchange rate must keep wealth constant and balance aggregate demand. It is not possible to define the sign of changes of F and e. It can only be said that if the exchange rate appreciates the stock of foreign assets must increase. On the other hand, if the exchange rate is devalued foreign assets could either rise or fall. Foreign demand and fiscal policy shocks are offset by exchange rate variations. An increase in foreign demand causes an appreciation in the exchange rate whilst a fiscal contraction requires a devaluation. Variations of domestic holdings of financial assets keep real wealth stable. F increases in the former case and falls in the latter.

A comparison with the Dornbusch model immediately points out that no difference arises in the equilibrium variations in the price level nor in the exchange rate in response to changes in m, X^* and s, whilst the sign of the exchange rate change after an interest rate shock might be reversed. It will be shown that these results are substantially modified when (a) the assumption of perfect capital mobility is relaxed, and (b) a more satisfactory description of the current account is introduced. However, even under the overrestrictive assumptions made by Dornbusch and Fischer, the model shows that static equilibrium cannot be achieved unless wealth accumulation is absent. Furthermore, their model shows that wealth and exchange rate dynamics are closely related.

2.3 PORTFOLIO EQUILIBRIA AND EXCHANGE RATE AND CURRENT ACCOUNT DYNAMICS: THE BRANSON MODEL

This model focuses on the impact of portfolio allocation on the exchange rate and foreign wealth. Branson relaxes the assumption of perfect substitutability between assets denominated in different currencies. Perfect substitutability implies that agents are neutral towards the risk associated with investment in foreign currency,[26] but this can be considered just a special case in the theory of portfolio allocation. In general agents will perceive investment abroad as riskier than investment in domestic currency because of the default risk and because of uncertainty about the future level of the exchange rate level. Such perceived risk has to be compensated for by a differential between the rates of return on domestic and foreign assets. As a result, steady state equilibrium cannot be achieved unless the current account flow equals zero: a non-zero current account balance would require portfolio reallocation, and changes in the differential between the rates of return on domestic and foreign assets would be necessary to equalise demand and supply for each asset.

The financial sector of the model is defined as follows.

$$M = -\phi_1 i - \phi_2(i^* + Ede) + W \tag{2.12}$$

$$B = \phi_3 i - \phi_4(i^* + Ede) + W \tag{2.13}$$

$$e + F = -\phi_6 i + \phi_5(i^* + Ede) + W \tag{2.14}$$

$$W = w_1 B + w_2(e + F) + (1 - w_1 - w_2)M \tag{2.15}$$

Equations 2.12–15[27] describe the financial sector of the economy. Agents are supposed to hold three assets: money, M, domestic bonds, B, and assets denominated in foreign currency, F. Financial wealth, W, is a linear approximation of the sum of these three assets. At any point in time demand for each asset, defined on the right-hand side of Equation 2.12–15, must equal the corresponding outstanding stock. Demand for each asset is homogeneous to degree one in wealth. Obviously demand for money is negatively related to the rates of return on both foreign and domestic assets. Note that the former includes both the expected variation in the exchange rate and the foreign interest rate. Demand functions for B and F are positively related to their own rates of return and are negatively affected by the rate of return on the other interest-bearing asset.

For the sake of simplicity it is assumed that both output and the price level are constant. Therefore, to close the model we need only to define wealth dynamics, since the supplies of M and B are assumed to be exogenous.

$$dF = H^* + \beta_1(e - p) + i^* F \tag{2.16}$$

In this model the current account includes the trade balance, expressed as a function of terms of trade and a shift factor, H^*, as well as interest payments on foreign investment.

The familiar rational expectations hypothesis completes the model.

$$Ede = de \tag{2.17}$$

In order to reduce the model to state–space form we need a proper description of exchange rate dynamics which result from portfolio allocation. Given Walras' law we need to analyse Equation 2.12) and 2.15) only. By doing so we obtain i and Ede in terms of e, F, B, M, i^*.

From Equation 2.12) and 2.15) we get:

$$X_7 = (\phi_1 \phi_5 + \phi_2 \phi_6)^{-1} E_1 E_2 X_8$$

where

$$X_7' = (i, Ede)$$

$$X_8' = [(e + F), M, B, i^*]$$

$$E_1 = \begin{bmatrix} \phi_5 & \phi_2 \\ \phi_6 & -\phi_1 \end{bmatrix}$$

$$E_2 = \begin{bmatrix} -w_2 & (w_1 + w_2) & -w_1 & \phi_2 \\ 1 - w_2 & -(1 - w_1 - w_2) & -w_1 & -\phi_5 \end{bmatrix}$$

This system yields:

$$
\begin{aligned}
de = &\{[\phi_6 w_2 + (1 - w_2)\phi_1/(\phi_1\phi_5 + \phi_2\phi_6)\}(e + F) \\
&\{-[\phi6(w_1 + w_2) + (1 - w_1 - w_2)\phi_1/(\phi_1\phi_5 + \phi_2\phi_6)\}M \\
&[w_1(\phi_6 - \phi_1)/(\phi_1\phi_5 + \phi_2\phi_6)]B - i^*
\end{aligned}
\tag{2.18}
$$

$$
\begin{aligned}
i = &\{[\phi_5 w_2 - (1 - w_2)\phi_1]/(\phi_1\phi_5 + \phi_2\phi_6)\}(e + F) \\
&\{[-\phi_5(w_1 + w_2) + (1 - w_1 - w_2)\phi_2/(\phi_1\phi_5 + \phi_2\phi_6)\}M \\
&[w_1(\phi_5 + \phi_2)/(\phi_1\phi_5 + \phi_2\phi_6)]B
\end{aligned}
\tag{2.19}
$$

An increase in the supply of foreign assets affects de and i in two ways: (a) the wealth effect, which keeps the money market in equilibrium after a change in W.[28] It is proportional to the initial equilibrium share of $e + F$; (b) the substitution effect, defined as the variation of the differential between rates in return which is required for the portfolio to be in equilibrium after the change in the composition of wealth.

The increase in W raises demand for money. For a given stock of M, equilibrium in the money market requires both rates of return to be higher. But the new composition of wealth requires that the relative rate of return of $(e + F)$ should rise. As a result, an increase of foreign assets is positively related to de, whereas the impact on the domestic interest rate is ambiguous: the wealth effect will certainly push i up, but the substitution effect will make it fall. After an expansion in the money supply the adjustment of the two rates of return must increase demand for money and reduce demand for foreign assets, according to the change in the composition of wealth. As a result the rate of return on $e + F$ must fall, whereas the sign of the domestic interest rate change is undetermined. An expansion in the supply of domestic bonds raises wealth and demand for money, therefore equilibrium in the money market can obtain only if the rate of return on at least one interest-bearing asset increases. The substitution effect requires that the relative profitability of foreign assets falls. The overall effect of a change in B on the domestic interest rate is unambiguously positive, whilst the impact on de depends on the the patterns of substitutability. If $\phi_6 > \phi_1$ domestic bonds are closer substitutes for foreign assets than for money and the impact of i is bigger on the foreign assets market than on the money market. In this case de increases.[29] A positive shock to the foreign interest rate is completely offset by an opposite variation of de, so that the overall rate of return on foreign assets stays constant.

We now turn to the analysis of dynamics and comparative statics. To do this we need Equation 2.16, 2.17 and 2.18 only. The state–space form of the model is defined as follows.

$$X_9 = E_3 X_{10} + E_4 X_{11}$$

where:

$$X_9' = (de, dF)$$

$$X_{10}' = (e, F)$$

$$X_{11}' = (M, B, i^*)$$

$$E_3 = \begin{bmatrix} [\phi_6 w_2 + (1 - w_2)\phi_1]/\phi^* & [\phi_6 w_2 + (1 - w_2)\phi_1/\phi^*] \\ \beta_1 & i_0^* \end{bmatrix}$$

where

$$\phi^* = (\phi_1 \phi_5 + \phi_2 \phi_6)$$

$$E_4 = \begin{bmatrix} 0 & \dfrac{-[\phi_6(w_1 + w_2) + (1 - w_1 - w_2)\phi_1]}{\phi^*} & \left[\dfrac{w_1(\phi_6 - \phi_1)}{\phi^*}\right] & -1 \\ 1 & 0 & 0 & F_0 \end{bmatrix}$$

The roots of the characteristic equation are:

$$\theta_s = 0.5\{[\phi_6 w_2 + (1 - w_2)\phi_1]/(\phi_1\phi_5 + \phi_2\phi_6) + i^*\}$$
$$- 0.5\{[\phi_6 w_2 + (1 - w_2)\phi_1]^2/[\phi_1\phi_5 + \phi_2\phi_6]^2$$
$$+ 4(\beta_1 - i_0^*)\}^{-1/2}$$

$$\theta_u = 0.5\{[\phi_6 w_2 + (1 - w_2)\phi_1]/(\phi_1\phi_5 + \phi_2\phi_6) + i^*\}$$
$$+ 0.5\{[\phi_6 w_2 + (1 - w_2)\phi_1]^2/[\phi_1\phi_5 + \phi_2\phi_6]^2$$
$$+ 4(\beta_1 - i_0^*)\}^{-1/2}$$

The system is saddlepath stable if $\beta_1 > i_0^*$; in other words the impact of a unit change of the exchange rate on the trade balance must be larger than the change in returns on foreign investment caused by a unit variation of F. According to Branson, this requirement is likely to be met in practice, given the existing empirical evidence about interest rates and trade elasticities.

Consider now exchange rate and foreign assets dynamics. At any point in time the relation between current and equilibrium values of the endogenous dynamic variables is defined as follows.

$$e_t = e_\infty + C exp(\theta_s t)$$

$$F_t = F_\infty + C u_s exp(\theta_s t)$$

where $(1, u_s)$ is the right eigenvector associated with the stable root $u_s = -\beta_1/(i^* - \theta_s)$ is negative, thus $C = (F_0 - F_\infty)/u_s$ is negatively related to $F_0 - F_\infty$.

This resembles closely the pattern of exchange rate dynamics outlined in Dornbusch and Fischer's model. Whenever a shock occurs implying a long-term increase in foreign assets the exchange rate instantaneously depreciates. From there it steadily appreciates, while domestic holdings of foreign assets increase. Once again, current account surpluses are associated with exchange rate appreciation. For instance, consider the effect of an increase in money supply. The Equations representing combinations of e and F that yield $de = dF = 0$ are as follows:

$$de = 0: \quad e = -F + G_1 \tag{2.20}$$

$$dF = 0: \quad e = -(i^*/\beta_1)F + G_2 \tag{2.21}$$

where G_1 and G_2 represent the exogenous variables and the selected parameters. Locus aa in Figures 2.5 and 2.6 describes Equation 2.20. It is negatively sloped because a fall in foreign assets must be compensated for by an exchange rate devaluation, so that the valuation of wealth in domestic currency stays constant.[30] Points above the aa locus represent a level of foreign wealth which is above equilibrium. This requires the expectation of a devaluation. Locus FF, corresponding to Equation 2.21, is negatively sloped because only a depreciation in the exchange rate can compensate for the fall in F; points above FF are associated with a current account surplus and vice versa. The necessary and sufficient condition for saddlepath stability, $\beta_1 > i^*$, implies that the locus $de = 0$ is steeper. In other words, this means that if F is initially too low, the devaluation necessary to generate a current account surplus and to restore the equilibrium value of foreign wealth must not raise the domestic valuation of foreign wealth above its equilibrium value. In fact, if the current account surplus can only be generated by a level of the exchange rate which raises the domestic valuation of foreign wealth above equilibrium, the surplus is associated with a further devaluation and the system becomes unstable. Agents in the financial markets cannot select a jump in the exchange rate which leads to convergent dynamics (Figure 2.6). On the other hand, if $\beta_1 > i^*$, a devaluation may be consistent with a

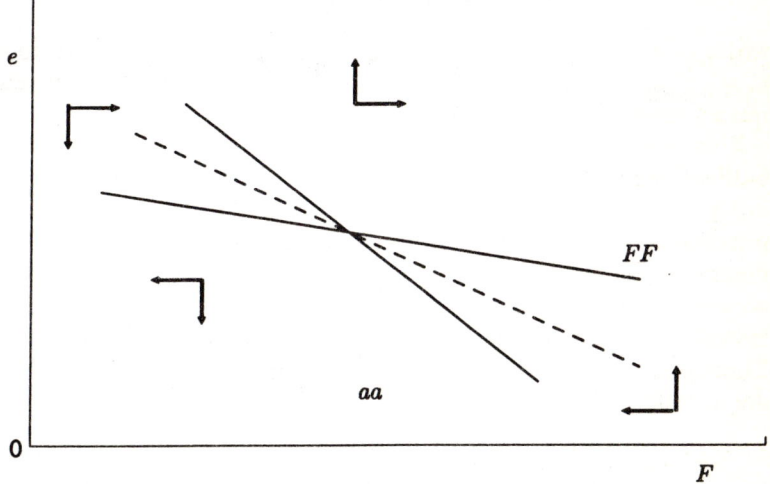

Figure 2.5   Branson model: the stable case

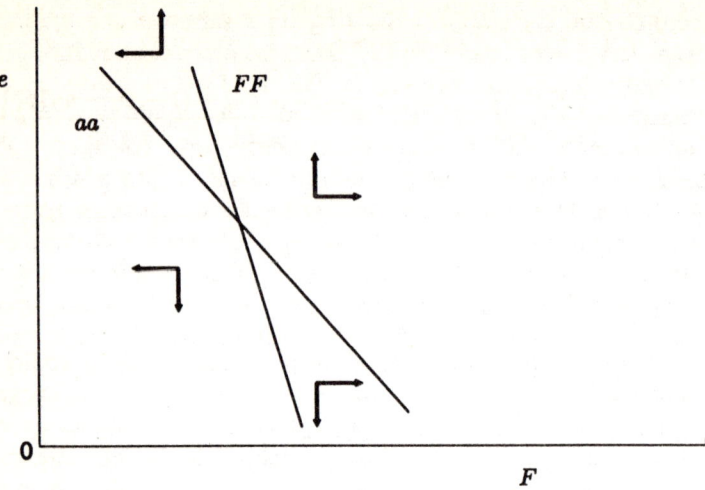

Figure 2.6   Branson model: the unstable case

gradual process of wealth accumulation and exchange rate appreciation as long the initial level of $(e + F)$ is below equilibrium. In this
case agents may choose the exchange rate jump which is consistent with
convergent dynamics (Figure 2.5).

This result shows that continuous equilibrium in the financial
markets may correspond to global instability once wealth accumulation is taken into account. In the next chapter it will be shown how
instability becomes more likely in a more general model of exchange
rate determination.

2.3.1   Comparative statics

$$e = - i_0^* i^* \left\{ \frac{(\beta_1 - i_0^*)[\phi_6 w_2 + (1 - w_2)\phi_1]}{(\phi_1 \phi_5 + \phi_2 \phi_6)} \right\}^{-1}$$

$$\frac{-F_0 i^*}{\beta_1 - i_0^*} \left\{ \frac{(\beta_1 - i_0^*)[\phi_6(w_1 + w_2) + (1 - w_1 - w_2)\phi_1]}{[\phi_6 w_2 + (1 - w_2)\phi_1]} \right\}^{-1}$$

$$(-i^* M) \left\{ \frac{(\beta_1 - i_0^*) w_1 [\phi_6 - \phi_1]}{[\phi_6 w_2 + (1 - w_2)\phi_1]} \right\}^{-1} i^* B - \frac{H^*}{(\beta_1 - i_0^*)}$$

$$F = \left\{ (\beta_1 - i_0^*) \frac{[\phi_6 w_2 + (1 - w_2)\phi_1]}{(\phi_1\phi_5 + \phi_2\phi_6)} \right\}^{-1} \beta_1 i^*$$

$$+ \frac{F_0 i^*}{\beta_1 - i_0^*} \left\{ (\beta_1 - i_0^*)^{-1} \frac{[\phi_6(w_1 + w_2) + (1 - w_1 - w_2)\phi_1]}{[\phi_6 w_2 + (1 - w_2)\phi_1} \right\}$$

$$(\beta_1 M)\left\{ (\beta_1 - i_0^*)^{-1} w_1 \frac{(\phi_6 - \phi_1)}{[\phi_6 w_2 + (1 - w_2)\phi_1]} \right\}^{-1} (-\beta_1 B)$$

$$+ H^*/(\beta_1 - i_0^*)$$

The term $(\beta_1 - i_0^*)$, whose sign is decisive for saddlepath stability, also determines the direction of changes in e and F after the exogenous variables have shifted. We shall analyse comparative statics under the assumption that $\beta_1 > i_0$. A comparison with the Dornbusch and Fischer model is problematic since the two models differ in so many respects. However, it must be emphasised that while in Dornbusch and Fischer the current account is in equilibrium when W equals its target value, Branson's model requires e and F, and implicitly the stock of financial wealth, to adjust to a level which ensures that, for given values of β_1 and i_0, the trade balance exactly offsets returns on foreign investment. Also, $e + F$ must ensure that portfolio equilibrium obtains jointly with $de = 0$. When discussing comparative statics we shall look first at the values of e and F which are required for exchange rate and current account dynamics to be nil, then we shall consider the change in the composition of wealth determined by the shifts in e and F.

A variation in the foreign interest rate has two effects. The first is to raise the relative profitability of foreign assets, which should therefore increase.[31] As a consequence current account equilibrium requires an exchange rate appreciation and a worsening of the trade balance. The second effect is linked directly to the initial net external position of the country. Therefore it is not possible to say a priori whether an increase in i^* has a positive or negative effect on F and e. However, the change in the valuation of foreign assets in domestic currency is positive:

$$d(e + F) = \{[\phi_6 w_2 + (1 - w_2)\phi_1/(\phi_1\phi_5 + \phi_2\phi_6)\}^{-1} i^*$$

An increase in domestic demand for foreign goods is matched by an exchange rate appreciation and a higher stock of foreign assets. Portfolio equilibrium requires the valuation of foreign assets to remain constant because the relative rates of returns on domestic and foreign assets have not changed.

A rise in the money supply causes an increase in F and an appreciation in the exchange rate is therefore required for the current account to be in equilibrium. The model exhibits non-neutrality, variations of M must alter portfolio composition and the differential between rates of return because, apart from induced changes in $e + F$, the supply of foreign bonds is fixed.

$$d(e + F)/dM = \{1 + [w_1(\phi_6 - \phi_1)/\phi_6 w_2 + (1 - w_2)\phi_1\}$$

The valuation of foreign wealth is positively linked to the level of the money supply; $d(e + F)/dM$ will be more or less than unity according to the sign of $\phi_6 - \phi_1$. In equilibrium the higher stock of money will be held only if the domestic interest rate is lower. This means that demand for foreign assets will be pushed up and will have to be matched by an increase in the value of foreign wealth in domestic currency. To the extent that bonds are better substitutes for money than for foreign assets, the fall of i will have smaller effects in the foreign assets market than in the money market, $d(e + F)/dM < 1$. Non-neutrality of the money supply originates directly from the assumption of imperfect capital mobility and from the explicit inclusion of the supply of bonds. Comparison with Dornbusch and Fischer's results confirms such a conclusion. In fact, according to their model

$$d(e + F)/dM = 1$$

$$di/dM = dF/dM = 0$$

The expansion of B requires a change in $e + F$ in order to offset the effect of dB on e in the current account. The sign of $d(e + F)$ depends on the patterns of substitutability between assets. If $\phi_6 > \phi_1$, domestic bonds are closer substitutes for foreign assets than for money, so $d(e + F)$ must be negative. Given the constraint of portfolio equilibrium, current account equilibrium implies that if $\phi_6 > \phi_1$, the exchange rate depreciates and domestic holdings of foreign assets are reduced.

2.4 CONCLUSIONS

In this chapter we have reviewed the basic elements of the theory of flexible exchange rates according to the macroeconomic approach. It is now widely recognised[32] that open economy macromodels should account for three key factors: continuous market clearing in the financial sector, price stickiness in the real sector, and wealth effects in aggregate demand. However, the literature on the subject still lacks attempts to 'nest' into the same model sluggish price adjustment, imperfect capital mobility, wealth effects in the consumption function,[33] and the current account. A more general model of this kind will be set out and analysed in detail in the next chapter.

3 Monetarist Macroeconomic Policy Rules in a Small Open Economy Model

INTRODUCTION

This chapter presents a small open economy model where it is assumed that the policymaker is following an orthodox monetarist rule. In the models considered so far, the exchange rate is determined by the following factors: price dynamics, wealth accumulation and the degree of capital mobility. It is also apparent that government intervention affects the exchange rate through fiscal and monetary policy. A great deal of research has focused on some specific aspects of the points outlined above, but attempts at integrating these three strands of the literature into a more general model of exchange rate determination are far less frequent[1] and usually no attention is paid to the instability potentially arising when a textbook Dornbusch model is extended to account for the current account equation and a specification of aggregate demand that considers wealth effects. According to the models analysed in the previous chapter, stability obtains anyway, as in Dornbusch, and Dornbusch and Fischer, or depends on a restricted set of parameters about whose 'normal' values a widespread consensus in the economic profession seems to have emerged, as in Branson. This chapter will show that the risk of instability is potentially more serious.

Following Dornbusch and Fischer, wealth effects will be included by assuming a life-cycle consumption function. Blanchard (1985) investigates the issue in a model with microfoundations.[2] He shows that current account dynamics converge if the propensity to spend out of wealth is greater than the rate of return on foreign assets. I shall argue that this is a necessary but not a sufficient condition for stability to hold. If the model accounts for output fluctuations, the impact of a change in domestic holdings of foreign wealth on the current account depends on the relative size of the corresponding variations in imports

46

and foreign interest payments. If a decrease in foreign wealth improves the current account, the system is stable. But this is not necessary for stability to obtain. When a fall in foreign wealth worsens the current account, the exchange rate must be devalued in order to bring about the required current account surplus. It will be shown that in this case stability obtains if devaluation of the exchange rate does not raise output above its natural level.

The rest of this chapter is laid out in four sections, the first and second of which present the behavioral equations and the reduced form of the model, respectively. The third section explains why instability might occur, and the final section outlines some implications for comparative statics and exchange rate dynamics which are not accounted for by simpler models.

3.1 THE MODEL

First of all the financial sector will be described:[3]

$$aF_0 + F = \phi[i^* + da - (i - dp)] \tag{3.1}$$

$$a = e - p \tag{3.2}$$

where a = real exchange rate; p = domestic price level; e = nominal exchange rate; F = domestic holdings of foreign assets (denominated in foreign currency and normalised with respect to equalibrium output); i = domestic interest rate; and i^* = foreign interest rate.

In Equation 3.1 it is assumed that assets denominated in different currencies are imperfect substitutes. In order to keep the model as simple as possible the full portfolio specification of the Branson model has not been introduced. Demand for domestic bonds is not explicitly modelled and the quantity of money does not appear in the definition of financial wealth. This inevitably causes a loss of generality: the model does not account for the long term non-neutrality of money supply changes when agents hold a fixed stock of non-indexed domestic bonds, an effect discussed at length in Branson (1983) and in Eaton and Turnovsky (1983). On the other hand, the simple portfolio structure adopted here makes it easier to model the dual role of money – whose demand is determined by portfolio optimisation as well as by the level of real income – and to keep the model small enough to be analytically manageable. Equation 3.1 states that real demand for foreign assets is always equal to the real value in domestic currency of the outstanding stock of foreign assets. Demand for financial wealth is expressed as a positive function of (a) the differential between foreign and domestic real interest rates[4] and (b) the expected variation of the real exchange rate, set equal to its actual rate of change under the familiar assumption of perfect foresight in the financial markets. Perfect flexibility of the exchange rate ensures continuous clearing in the market of foreign assets. Parameter ϕ in Equation 3.1 represents the impact of a change in the relative rates of return on demand for foreign assets. A more general, non-linear specification of Equation 3.1 might be obtained referring to microeconomic models where agents optimise portfolio choices for given combinations of risk and return. More properly, ϕ should be expressed as a function of the expected variances of relative prices as well as of the expected rates of return on domestic and foreign assets. In order to maintain the linear form it is assumed that the variances of the terms of trade and of the exchange rate are constant; the effect of changes of i and i^* on ϕ are ignored. Equation 3.1 can be rearranged as follows:

$$da = (i - dp) - i^* + (aF_0 + F)/\phi \tag{3.1b}$$

$(aF_0 + F)/\phi$ is the risk premium, that is, the compensation agents require for holding assets denominated in foreign currency. It grows with the size of the outstanding stock of foreign assets. On the other hand, the more sensitive the demand for foreign assets to changes in the relative returns on assets the bigger ϕ becomes, so that the risk premium becomes less relevant. When $\phi \to \infty$ agents in the financial markets are risk neutral, Equation 3.2 becomes the uncovered interest parity condition that is assumed to hold in the Dornbusch model.

$$m - p = k_1 y - k_2 i \tag{3.3}$$

Equation 3.3 is a standard demand for money function where m is the domestic money supply and y represents output deviations from the natural rate.

$$y = x^* + \beta a + \tau(aF_0 + F) - \sigma(i - dp) - \delta s \tag{3.4}$$

Equation 3.4 states that output deviations from the natural rate, are demand-determined. The country is assumed to be small in the market for foreign inputs, so that domestic demand does not influence foreign prices. On the other hand it is assumed that domestic firms face a downward sloped demand curve in the world markets: exports rise only if the real exchange rate is devalued. Therefore foreign demand for domestic goods depends on the terms of trade and an exogenous shift factor, x^*. Domestic consumption depends on disposable income, financial wealth and the real interest rate. Investment also depends on the current real interest rate. The description of domestic demand is completed by the inclusion of a shift factor, which represents domestic fiscal policy, in the form of a tax rate.[5]

Price stickiness is the first source of disequilibrium in the model.

$$dp = \epsilon y + dm \tag{3.5}$$

In Equation 3.5 it is assumed that domestic inflation responds to deviations of current output from the natural rate, and the rate of change of the money supply. The price level is predetermined but Equation 3.5 implies that inflation instantaneously responds to shocks and embeds some kind of forward-looking behaviour through the link with the rate of growth of the money supply, although this direct connection might be regarded as too simplistic.[6] Although a more sophisticated representation of the sluggish adjustment of both prices and wages, possibly including forward-looking behaviour, would be desirable, the need to simplify the algebraic analysis of the model has led to the choice of Equation 3.5. It has been argued elsewhere[7] that the selected form of price dynamics within the class of predetermined price equations is of secondary importance. Therefore the choice of Equation 3.5 should not undermine the relevance of the model. However, a more satisfactory description of wage–price dynamics will be presented in later chapters.

$$dm = 0 \tag{3.6}$$

In Equation 3.6 it is assumed that the government adopts a fixed money supply rule.[8]

The second source of disequilibrium in the model, wealth accumulation, is defined as follows.

$$dF = x^*/\alpha + \beta_1 a - \mu y + i^* F_0 + i_0^* F \tag{3.7}$$

Foreign wealth accumulation is equal to the current account balance. This in turn is determined by the trade balance and by returns on foreign investment; this has been linearised around equilibrium in order to evaluate the effects of a foreign interest rate shock.[9] The trade balance depends on foreign demand for domestic goods[10] and on imports, which are linked to the level of output.

3.2   THE REDUCED FORM OF THE MODEL

From Equations 3.3 and 3.4 we obtain 'reduced form' equations for the endogenous non-dynamic variables, y and i, in terms of a, F, p, m, s, i^*, x^*.

$$y = \pi[x^* + (\beta + \tau F_0)a + \tau F - \delta s - (\sigma/k_2)(p - m)] \tag{3.8}$$

$$i = (k_1/k_2)\pi[x^* + (\beta + \tau F_0)a + \tau F - \delta s] \\ - (m - p)[1 - \epsilon\sigma]k_2[1 - \sigma(\epsilon - k_1/k_2)]\}^{-1} \tag{3.9}$$

i and y depend on foreign demand for domestic goods, the tax rate, real financial wealth and real money balances.

$$\pi = 1/[1 - \sigma(\epsilon - k_1/k_2)]$$

π is equivalent to the familiar total multiplier of the IS-LM model, where the real interest rate is taken into account instead of the nominal interest rate. $1 - \sigma(\epsilon - k_1/k_2)$ shows the feedback effects of output changes on aggregate demand, which operate through the real interest rate. The term k_1/k_2 describes the impact of output changes on the nominal rate, determined in the money market. ϵ measures the effect of output variations on inflation. ϵ and k_1/k_2 work in opposite directions. An increase in output raises both the demand for money and the interest rate. On the other hand higher inflation lowers the real interest rate and stimulates aggregate demand. The former effect should be considered an endogenous 'controller' of output and inflation, the latter is unambiguously destabilising.[11]

Throughout this chapter it shall be assumed that an increase in output raises the real interest rate, that is,

$$(\epsilon - k_1/k_2) < 0$$

It is now clear that increases in a, F, x^* raise output and the interest rate, whereas higher taxes depress output and lower the interest rate. The influence of real money balances on i cannot be defined a priori. Suppose that monetary policy takes an expansionary stance. The real interest rate then falls:

$$d(i - dp)/dm = -[1 - \sigma(\epsilon - k_1/k_2)]^{-1}$$

This in turn stimulates output and raises real demand for money and the interest rate. The condition $1 - \epsilon\sigma < 0$ means that if an increase in the money supply causes a more than proportional increment of inflation[12] the expansion of output is so strong that the interest rate eventually rises.

Let us now turn to the reduced form of the full model. Substituting Equations 3.6, 3.8 and 3.9 into Equations 3.1, 3.5 and 3.7:

$$
\begin{aligned}
dp =& (\epsilon\pi\sigma/k_2)(m - p) + [\epsilon\pi(\beta + \tau F_0)]a + (\epsilon\pi\tau)F \\
& - (\epsilon\pi\delta)s + (\epsilon\pi)x^*
\end{aligned}
\tag{3.10}
$$

$$
\begin{aligned}
da =& (p - m)/k_2[1 - \sigma(\epsilon - k_1/k_2)] \\
& + \{\phi_{-1} - [(\epsilon - k_1/k_2)\pi(\beta + \tau F_0)]\}a \\
& + \{\phi^{-1} - (\epsilon - k_1/k_2)\pi\tau\}F \\
& - [(\epsilon - k_1/k_2)](x^* - \delta s) - i^*
\end{aligned}
\tag{3.11}
$$

$$
\begin{aligned}
dF =& (\mu\pi\sigma)(p - m) + [\beta_1 - \mu\pi(\beta + \tau F_0)]a \\
& + (i_0^* - \mu\pi\tau)F + (\mu\pi\delta)s + x^*/\alpha - \mu\pi x^* + F_0 i^*
\end{aligned}
\tag{3.12}
$$

From Equation 3.10 it is clear that a devaluation, an exogenous increase in foreign demand for domestic goods, an expansion in real money balances and an expansion in foreign wealth spur inflation, whereas fiscal policy has a deflationary impact.

Positive variations of a, F, x^*, raise the real interest rate. This in turn requires the expectation of a devaluation if demand and supply of foreign assets are to be in equilibrium (Equation 3.11). On the other hand, an expansion in real money balances and a fiscal contraction lower the real exchange rate and require the expectation of an appreciation.

It could be reasonably expected that $\beta_1 - \mu\pi\beta > 0$. This means that the export growth generated by a devaluation should be stronger than the import flow generated by the export-led increase in income. The model accounts for a second terms-of-trade effect on aggregate demand: the capital gains, in real terms, on domestic holdings of foreign assets which are caused by a devaluation of relative prices. If $F_0 > 0$ this effect weakens the total impact of a terms-of-trade devaluation on the current account. Nevertheless it shall be assumed that a devaluation actually improves the current account balance.[13] Furthermore, there is some theoretical[14] and empirical[15] support to believe that τF_0 is rather small.[16]

The size of $\mu\pi\tau$ is very important in determining the effect on the current account of changes in foreign assets. An increase in foreign assets expands aggregate demand and sucks in more imports, thereby worsening the current account. On the other hand higher interest payments on foreign investment improve it. Although one would expect that $\tau > i_0^*$, the net effect on wealth accumulation cannot be determined a priori because there is a presumption that $\mu\pi < 1$. If $\mu\pi\tau$ is big enough a negative deviation of F from equilibrium causes a reduction of imports greater than the corresponding fall in interest payments on foreign investment, therefore the current account improves and F is pushed back to equilibrium. $i_0^* - \mu\pi\tau$ will be considered as undetermined, and indeed the discussion of stability will focus on this aspect.

3.3 STABILITY ANALYSIS

The analysis of the conditions which are necessary and sufficient for stability to obtain is rather complex once the standard framework of the second order dynamic system is abandoned and the model becomes third order. To facilitate the interpretation of the stability condition of the full system it will be assumed that the price level is fixed. In this case the model may be regarded as a combination of two simpler models. In the first, output is fixed and wealth and exchange rate dynamics interact because foreign and domestic assets are imperfect substitutes, as in the Branson model. In the second, uncovered interest parity holds but output fluctuates. The stability conditions of these two simpler models will be discussed separately, and then their implications for the stability of the full model will be analysed.

3.3.1 The stability condition for the fixed price, fixed output model

If $dp = y = 0$ the model becomes:[17]

$$da = (aF_0 + F)/\phi - i^* \tag{3.13}$$

$$dF = \beta_1 a + i_0^* F + x^*/\alpha \tag{3.14}$$

Equations 3.13 and 3.14 are indeed qualitatively identical to the reduced form of the Branson model. The roots of the characteristic equation of this system are:

$$\theta_1 = \{-(i_0^* + 1/\phi) - [(i_0^* + 1/\phi)^2 + 4(\beta_1 - F_0 i_0^*)/\phi]^{-\frac{1}{2}}\}0.5$$

$$\theta_2 = \{-(i_0^* + 1/\phi) + [(i_0^* + 1/\phi)^2 + 4(\beta_1 - F_0 i_0^*)/\phi]^{-\frac{1}{2}}\}0.5$$

For the system to be saddlepath stable $(\beta_1 - F_0 i_0^*) > 0$ is required. This is similar to the stability condition derived for the Branson model. To grasp the economic intuition behind this result use will be made of the familiar state–space diagram.

$$da = 0: \quad a = [-F + i_0^*/\phi]/F_0 \tag{3.15}$$

$$dF = 0: \quad a = -(i_0^*/\beta_1)F - x^*/\beta\alpha \tag{3.16}$$

Locus aa in Figures 3.1 and 3.2 corresponds to Equation 3.15 under the assumption that $F_0 > 0$. It is negatively sloped because a fall in foreign assets must be offset by depreciation of the exchange rate, so that the valuation of wealth in domestic currency stays constant. This is the necessary condition for the financial market to be in equilibrium when $da = 0$.

Locus FF, describing the combinations of a and F which are consistent with current account equilibrium (Equation 3.16), is also negatively sloped. This is because after a fall in F depreciation of the exchange rate is necessary to balance the current account.

The economic interpretation of the stability condition may be stated as follows. Suppose that the stock of foreign assets is initially below its equilibrium level. A devaluation is therefore necessary to generate the current account surpluses which will bring foreign wealth back to equilibrium.

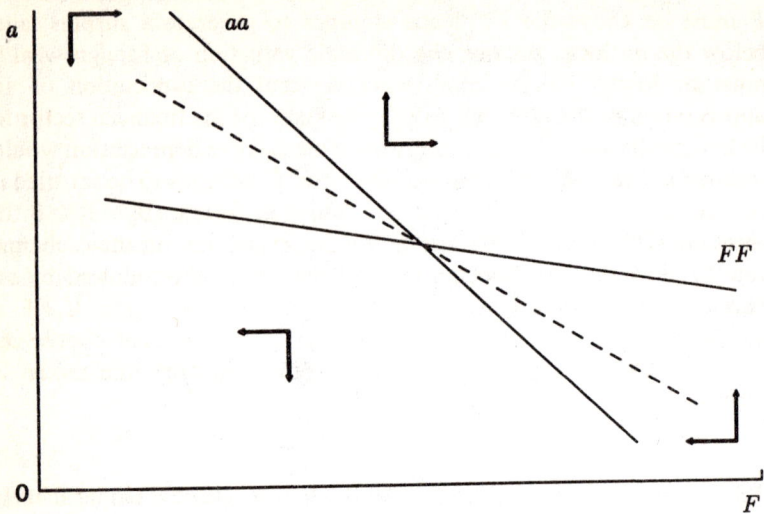

Figure 3.1 Branson-type model: the stable case

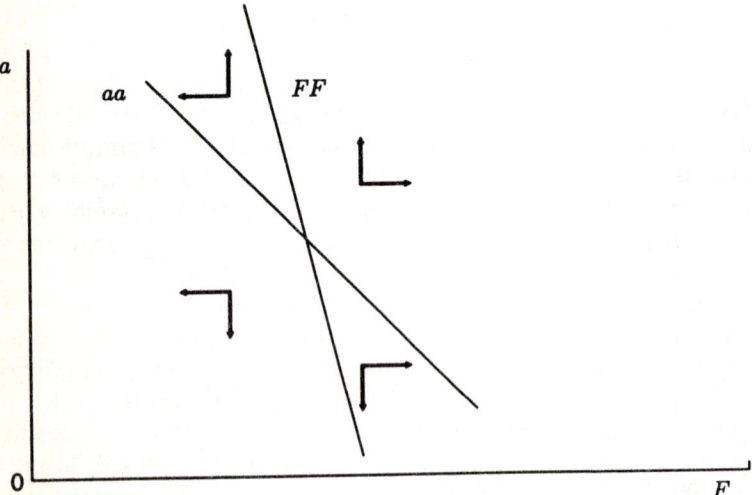

Figure 3.2 Dynamics in the Branson type model: the unstable case

After the jump in the exchange rate the initial combination of a and F must lie above the FF locus in order to generate a surplus, and below the aa locus because the domestic valuation of foreign wealth must be lower than in equilibrium, so that the expectation of an appreciation of the exchange rate is necessary for the financial sector to be in equilibrium. If it were otherwise, a cumulative depreciation would follow the initial devaluation. For these two conditions to be satisfied it is necessary that locus aa be steeper than FF, that is, $(\beta_1 - i_0^*) > 0$. In this case (Figure 3.1) it is possible for the initial jump in the exchange rate to generate a current account surplus and to be followed by an exchange rate appreciation, so that dynamics may converge. If FF is steeper than aa (Figure 3.2) the financial market cannot choose an initial exchange rate level so that dynamics converge: the model is unstable.

3.3.2 The stability condition for the fixed price, flexible output model under the assumption of perfect capital mobility

Let us now turn to an analysis of a model where p is fixed, uncovered interest parity holds and output fluctuates. Its reduced form is:

$$da = [(k_1/k_2)\pi_1(\beta + \tau F_0)]a + [(k_1/k_2)\pi_1\tau]F + G_1 \qquad (3.17)$$

$$dF = [\beta_1 - \mu\pi_1(\beta + \tau F_0)]a + (i_0^* - \mu\pi_1\tau)F + G_2 \qquad (3.18)$$

where G_1 and G_2 represent the forcing variables and the related parameters. $\pi_1 = 1/(1 + \sigma k_1/k_2)$ is the equivalent of π under the assumption that the price level is fixed. The roots of the characteristic equation are

$$\theta_1 = 0.5[L + (L^2 + 4T)^{1/2}]$$

$$\theta_2 = 0.5[L - (L^2 + 4T)^{1/2}]$$

where

$$L = [(k_1/k_2)(\beta + \tau F_0)/\pi_1] + i_0^* - \mu\tau/\pi_1$$

$$T = (k_1/k_2)[(\beta_1\tau - \beta i_0^*) - F_0\tau i_0^*]/\pi_1]$$

For the system to be saddlepath stable:

$$(\beta_1 \tau - \beta i_0^*) - F_0 \tau i_0^* > 0 \qquad (3.19)$$

but that is not guaranteed.

Consider the familiar state–space diagram. The loci representing combinations of a and F such that no terms of trade or wealth dynamics occur are defined as follows.

$$da = 0: \quad a = -[\tau/(\beta + \tau F_0)]F + G_1 \qquad (3.20)$$

$$dF = 0: \quad a = -\{(i_0^* - \mu \pi_1 \tau)/[\beta_1 - \mu \pi_1 (\beta + \tau F_0)]\}F + G_2 \qquad (3.21)$$

Locus aa (Equation 3.20) is negatively sloped. When F is below equilibrium, the low level of wealth has a deflationary impact on aggregate demand so that the interest rate falls. Thus, the covered interest parity condition would require the expectation of an appreciation of the exchange rate. To avoid this the depreciation of the exchange rate must offset the negative impact of lower foreign wealth in aggregate demand, stabilising output. In fact, along aa, output is constant at the natural rate. When output and interest rates are above equilibrium[18] the exchange rate must depreciate, while in a recession[19] covered interest parity requires an appreciation. Let us now consider locus FF, representing combinations of a and F that are consistent with current account equilibrium. Its slope can be either positive or negative, according to the sign of $i_0^* - \mu \tau/\pi_1$. For the moment it is assumed that:

$$i_0^* - \mu \pi_1 \tau < 0$$

The FF curve is positively sloped (Figure 3.3). Shocks to F trigger a self-stabilising dynamic process of wealth accumulation because the variation of imports is bigger than the corresponding change in interest payments on foreign investment. In this case the model is saddlepath stable. A negative shock to wealth lowers both output and the interest rate. This requires the expectation of an appreciation: the exchange rate must overshoot. The combination of a and F after the jump in the exchange rate must be represented by a point lying below the aa locus to avoid cumulative depreciation. As long as $i_0^* - \mu \pi_1 \tau < 0$ this point will certainly be associated with a current account surplus.[20]

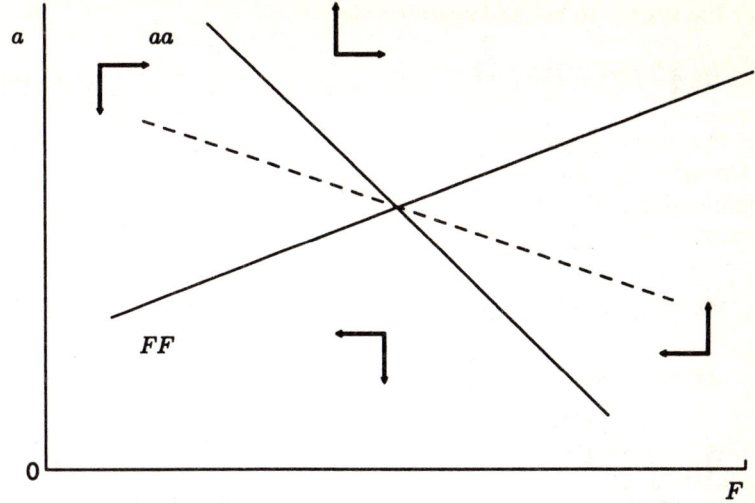

Figure 3.3 Dynamics when wealth is self-correcting

Let us now discuss the case where:

$$i_0^* > \mu\pi_1\tau$$

The FF locus is negatively sloped. Combinations of F and a represented by points above the FF locus are associated with surpluses; points to the left of FF correspond to deficits. After a fall in F the change in foreign payments originating from a deviation of foreign wealth from equilibrium always dominates the corresponding variation of imports. Thus a devaluation is necessary to bring wealth back to equilibrium; the initial combination of F and a must lie above locus FF, and to the left of aa. But this may happen if aa is steeper than FF. Figures 3.4 and 3.5 give a diagrammatic exposition of the two alternative outcomes.

The algebraic condition ensuring that aa is steeper than FF is:

$$\tau/(\beta + \tau F_0) > (i_0^* - \mu\pi_1\tau)/[\beta_1 - \mu\pi_1(\beta + \tau F_0)]$$

which corresponds to:

$$(\beta_1\tau - \beta i_0^*) - F_0\tau i_0^* > 0 \tag{3.19}$$

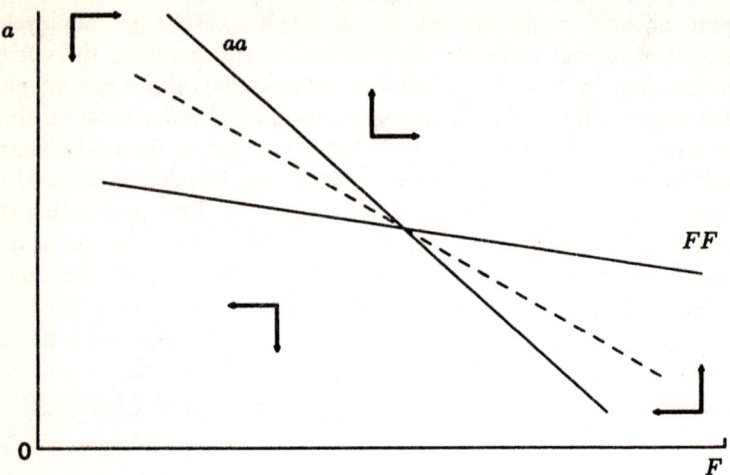

Figure 3.4   Dynamics when wealth is not self-correcting: the stable case

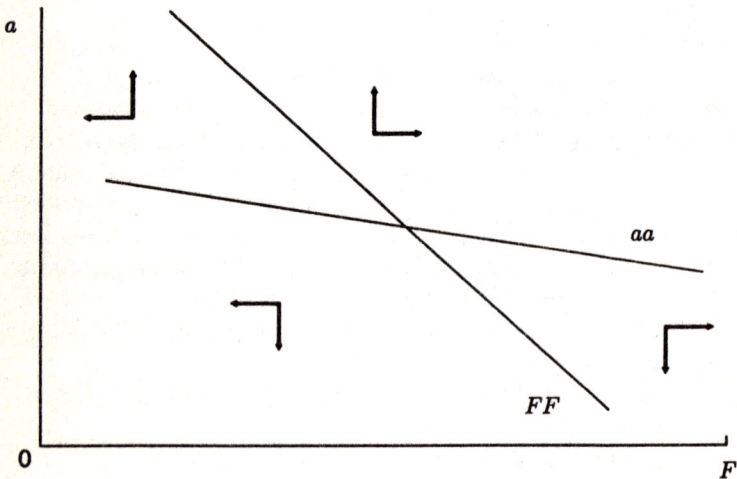

Figure 3.5   Dynamics when wealth is not self-correcting: the unstable case

If $i_0^* > \mu\pi_1\tau$, only a devaluation of the exchange rate may generate converging wealth dynamics. But if condition 3.19 is not satisfied, agents in the financial markets cannot select an exchange rate level. If the initial overshooting is followed by an appreciation, the current account remains in deficit. On the other hand, if the initial jump generates a surplus, the initial combination of F and a must lie above the aa curve. This implies that the improvement in the trade balance must be so strong that output will rise above the natural rate and the interest rate will increase. As a result, equilibrium in the financial markets will require further devaluation. Indeed the whole issue of stability eventually boils down to the requirement that after the jump in the exchange rate the current account surplus may be associated with an output level which is below the natural rate, despite the positive influence of the devaluation. In this case the interest rate falls and the gradual appreciation drives the exchange rate back to equilibrium.

3.3.3 The stability condition of the full model

The state–space form of the full model is defined as follows.

$$H = AZ + BG$$

where

$$H' = (dp, da, dF); \quad Z = (p, a, F); \quad G = (M, s, x^*, i^*)$$

$$A = \begin{bmatrix} -\dfrac{\epsilon\sigma}{k_2\pi} & \dfrac{\epsilon(\beta+\tau F_0)}{\pi} & \epsilon\tau\pi \\[2ex] \dfrac{1}{k_2\pi} & \left[-\dfrac{(\epsilon-k_1/k_2)(\beta+\tau F_0)}{\pi}\right]+\dfrac{1}{\phi} & \dfrac{1}{\phi}-(\epsilon-k_1/k_2)\tau\pi \\[2ex] \mu\sigma\pi & \beta_1-\mu(\beta+\tau F_0)\pi & i_0^*-\mu\tau\pi \end{bmatrix}$$

$$B = \begin{bmatrix} \dfrac{\epsilon\sigma\pi}{k_2} & -\epsilon\delta\pi & \epsilon\pi & 0 \\[2ex] \dfrac{\pi}{k_2} & \left[\dfrac{(\epsilon-k_1/k_2)\delta}{\pi}\right]+\dfrac{1}{\phi} & \dfrac{1}{k_2\pi} & -1 \\[2ex] -\mu\sigma\pi & \mu\delta\pi & \dfrac{1}{\alpha}-\mu\pi & F_0 \end{bmatrix}$$

The sign of the roots of the characteristic equation $|A - \theta I| = 0$ cannot be analytically determined. Nevertheless it is possible to draw some meaningful conclusions from the coefficients of the characteristic equation

$$|A - \theta I| = \theta_3 + b_1 \theta_2 + b_2 \theta_1 + b_3 = 0$$

It can be shown that

$$-b_1 = \theta_3 + \theta_2 + \theta_1 = a_{11} + a_{22} + a_{33}$$
$$b_2 = \theta_3 \theta_2 + \theta_3 \theta_1 + \theta_1 \theta_2$$
$$= a_{11}a_{33} - a_{13}a_{31} + a_{22}a_{11} - a_{12}a_{21} + a_{22}a_{33} - a_{32}a_{23}$$
$$b_3 = -|A|$$

If the determinant of the dynamic matrix is negative the system cannot be saddlepath stable. In fact, if $|A| < 0$ the characteristic equation has either one or three roots with negative real parts. Saddlepath stability requires the number of non pre-determined variables to equal the number of roots with positive real parts.[21] This model allows for one non-predetermined variable, hence saddlepath stability is precluded when $|A| < 0$. In this case the model must be either unstable (two roots with positive real parts) or globally stable (three negative roots) and undetermined in its dynamics. Saddlepath stability requires:

$$|A| = [(\beta_1 - F_0 i_0^*)/\phi + \beta_1 \tau - \beta i_0^* - F_0 \tau i_0^*] \epsilon \pi / k_2 > 0 \qquad (3.22)$$

Equation 3.22 is a combination of the two conditions necessary for stability to hold in the simpler models discussed above. Provided that 3.22 holds, coefficient b_2 might provide some further information on the roots of the characteristic equation.

$$b_2 = - (\epsilon \pi / k_2)[(i_0^* + \phi^{-1})\sigma + \beta + \tau F_0] + (i_0^* - \beta_1 + \mu \beta \pi)\phi^{-1}$$
$$+ [(k_1/k_2 - \epsilon)\pi][\tau(F_0 i_0^* - \beta_1) + \beta i_0^*]$$

$b_2 < 0$ rules out the possibility that the roots of the characteristic equation have the same sign. If $b_2 < 0$ the system is either unstable, when $|A| < 0$, or saddlepath stable, when $|A| > 0$. We maintain that $(k_1/k_2 - \epsilon) > 0$. If $|A| > 0$ it may be shown that[22]

$$i_0^* - \beta_1 < 0$$

and

$$\tau(i_0^* F_0 - \beta_1) + \beta i_0^* < 0$$

or very close to 0. Therefore it could be reasonably argued that in this case $b_2 < 0$ and the system is stable.

This analysis of stability points out that a standard Dornbusch model is unable to highlight the risk of instability inherent to open economies where the policy rule follows the orthodox monetarist prescriptions. Nor can the Dornbusch and Fischer model give more helpful insights. The Branson model points at the real exchange rate trade balance elasticity and at the foreign interest rate as the determinants of stability. The Blanchard model simply requires the propensity to spend out of wealth to be bigger than the foreign interest rate. I show that the potential risk of instability can be assessed only when a proper description of the current account is introduced and output fluctuations are considered. The model may be unstable if the wealth effect on import spending is dominated by the corresponding influence of wealth on foreign interest payments. In this case only an exchange rate adjustment may restore wealth equilibrium, but stability requires the terms of trade effect on output to be modest relative to its influence on the current account.

3.4 COMPARATIVE STATICS AND DYNAMIC ADJUSTMENT

Equilibrium values of the endogenous variables are obtained from the state–space form of the model setting $dp = da = dF = 0$.

$$\begin{aligned}
p =\ & m - \{k_2\delta(\beta_1 - F_0 i_0^*)/\phi\sigma[(\beta_1 - F_0 i_0^*)/\phi + \beta_1\tau - \beta i_0^* - F_0\tau i_0^*]\}s \\
& + \{k_2[(\beta_1 - F_0 i_0^*) - F_0\tau i_0^* - \beta_1 F_0]/\sigma[(\beta_1 - F_0 i_0^*)/\phi \\
& + \beta_1\tau - \beta i_0^* - F_0\tau i_0^*]\}i^* \\
& + \{k_2[\beta_1 - F_0 i_0^* - \beta/\alpha]\phi\sigma[(\beta_1 - F_0 i_0^*)/\phi + \beta_1\tau - \beta i_0^* - F_0\tau i_0^*]\}x^*
\end{aligned}$$

$$\begin{aligned}
a =\ & - \delta i_0^* s/[(\beta_1 - F_0 i_0^*)/\phi + \beta_1\tau - \beta i_0^* - F_0\tau i_0^*] \\
& - \{\sigma i_0^* + (\tau + 1/\phi)F_0/[(\beta_1 - F_0 i_0^*)/\phi + \beta_1\tau - \beta i_0^* - F_0\tau i_0^*]\}i^* \\
& - \{[(1/\phi + \tau)/\alpha - i_0^*)/[(\beta_1 - F_0 i_0^*)/\phi + \beta_1\tau - \beta i_0^* - F_0\tau i_0^*]\}x^*
\end{aligned}$$

$$\begin{aligned}
F =\ & + \delta\beta_1 s/[(\beta_1 - F_0 i_0^*)/\phi + \beta_1\tau - \beta i_0^* - \tau i_0^*] + \{\sigma\beta_1 \\
& + (\beta + \tau F_0 + 1/\phi)F_0/[(\beta_1 - F_0 i_0^*)/\phi + \beta_1\tau - \beta i_0^* - F_0\tau i_0^*]\}i^* \\
& + \{[-\beta_1 + (F_0/\phi + \beta + F_0\tau)/\alpha]/[(\beta_1 - F_0 i_0^*)/\phi \\
& + \beta_1\tau - \beta i_0^* - F_0\tau i_0^*]\}x^*
\end{aligned}$$

The money supply has no permanent effect on real variables: in equilibrium monetary shocks affect the price level only. But in the short term, dynamics involve both the exchange rate and the current account. The initial jump in the exchange rate can be expressed as a function of the deviation of predetermined variables from their equilibrium values.

$$a(0) - a_\infty = T_1(p_0 - p_\infty) + T_2(F_0 - F_\infty)$$

where $(x_0 - x_\infty)$ is the initial deviation of each endogenous dynamic variable from its equilibrium value, $a(0)$ is the level of the real exchange rate after its initial jump, $(1, T_1, T_2)$ is the left eigenvector associated with the unstable root. The system is far too complex for an analytical determination of the signs of T_1 and T_2. Analysis of simpler models and numerical simulations[23] has shown that when the money supply increases the terms of trade must initially overshoot. This result cannot be guaranteed for more complex models like the present one. However, it must be emphasised that terms of trade deviations from equilibrium will necessarily generate wealth accumulation/reduction which must be reversed later on, given that monetary shocks are neutral in the long term[24]. This contradicts one of the basic and most widely accepted results of the Dornbusch model: the fact that after a monetary shock adjustment is monotonic and both the exchange rate and the price level smoothly adjust to their long-term values.

After a fiscal shock[25] terms of trade and foreign assets move in opposite directions[26]. An increase in real taxation leads to a permanently higher stock of foreign assets. Current account equilibrium requires that higher interest payments on foreign debt be matched by lower net exports: terms of trade must appreciate. The model contradicts the popular wisdom that after a fiscal contraction a depreciation is necessary to keep aggregate demand in equilibrium. Higher real taxation will also permanently alter the interest rate differential because of the higher risk premium commanded by increased holdings of foreign assets; the lower ϕ the more powerful the effect of fiscal policy on i. In the money market the fall in i raises demand for money, so that in equilibrium the domestic price level is lower. After an exogenous rise in foreign demand for domestic goods, holdings of foreign assets should increase and the exchange rate should appreciate. The valuation of foreign wealth in domestic currency increases if $\beta > \beta_1$:

$$aF_0 + F = [F_0 i_0^* + \beta - \beta_1]x^* / [\beta_1\tau - \beta i_0^* + (\beta_1 - F_0 i_0^*)/\phi - F_0\tau i_0^*]\alpha$$

As a consequence, the domestic interest rate must fall because the risk premium is higher. In the goods market the appreciation in the terms of trade offsets both the initial shock and the inflationary pressures originating from higher wealth and lower i.

An increase in the foreign interest rate affects the financial markets and the current account. The portfolio reallocation following the foreign interest rate shock raises domestic holdings of foreign assets as well as interest payments on foreign investment. The domestic interest rate will change as well, in order to keep aggregate demand at its equilibrium level. Under perfect capital mobility $\Delta i = \Delta i^*$. If capital is not perfectly mobile the change of i should be lower than the change in i^*. On the other hand, if $F_0 > 0$ domestic holdings of foreign assets increase and the exchange rate appreciates. The valuation of foreign wealth in domestic currency must rise:

$$d(aF_0 + F)/di^* = \beta_1 F_0$$

As a consequence the risk premium increases and the domestic interest rate falls correspondingly. Equilibrium in the money market requires higher real money balances so that the price level is reduced. Thus, the overall impact of a foreign interest rate change on endogenous variables is ambiguous.

3.5 CONCLUSIONS

We have considered an extended Dornbusch model, which accounts for imperfect capital mobility and wealth effects.

Comparative statics. The standard Fleming–Mundell–Dornbusch result about the effect of a permanent fiscal change is reversed once wealth effects and the current account identity are considered. In the long term a fiscal expansion, or any positive domestic demand shock, depreciates the terms of trade in order to restore current account equilibrium at a lower level of return from foreign investment. When a monetary 'surprise' occurs the model shows that, if the money supply is to be neutral in the long term, the dynamic path towards equilibrium cannot be monotonic. Temporary current account imbalances must be reversed in the future.

Stability analysis. Under the assumption of perfect capital mobility the model shows that instability occurs when the devaluation which is needed to improve the current account must be so strong that output rises above the natural rate. On the other hand, the lower the degree of capital mobility the more likely it is that the system will be stable.

By and large, the model casts serious doubts on the desirability of monetarist policies which rely on a priori assumptions about the self-stabilising properties of the economic system.

The amplitude of the necessary shifts in the equilibrium position of the system is inherently connected to the stability condition. The lower $\beta_1 \tau - \beta i_0^* - F_0 \tau i^*$ and the higher the degree of capital mobility, the wider the necessary adjustments of endogenous variables to shocks. Therefore, even assuming that the model is stable, the policy rule might be inefficient in the face of real shocks.

4 Simple Policy Rules for the Open Economy: Evaluating Alternative Proposals

INTRODUCTION

The design of macroeconomic stabilisation policies has undergone thorough revision over the last few years. After the collapse of monetarism as a philosophy of economic policymaking, many scholars have suggested the abandonment of open-loop rules in favour of more interventionist policies. However, an important legacy of monetarism is the emphasis on the need for rules that stabilise the economy because they are known to the private sector and perceived as credible.

To some extent the debate on macroeconomic stabilisation has been concerned with the choice between fully optimal policies and simple feedback rules. For reasons stated in Chapter 1 I have chosen not to implement a fully optimising rule. Optimal policies are shock contingent and their dynamic structure is usually very complex and difficult to understand and implement. Over the last few years more work has been devoted to the search for simple, linear feedback rules which, albeit sub-optimal, may be more easily understood and implemented, thereby enhancing the sustainability of the policy stabilisation process. In this context simplicity means that the policy rule must have a simple dynamic structure *and* that it should respond to a restricted set of variables. Within this class fall the so called 'decoupled' control rules which assign each instrument to a single target variable (Vines *et al.*, 1983) Following this approach, we will explore the implications that some proposals have in terms of (a) the stability of the system and (b) the permanent effects of shocks on some variables which are not directly controlled but whose evolution might well be objects of legitimate concern for governments. In general no single feedback rule will dominate others for all the shocks, however the following investigation might be useful in the search for rules that perform reasonably well and are robust.

The first rule we consider is akin to the standard monetarist policy, as it is concerned only with monetary control of domestic inflation. It involves a real interest rate feedback on a nominal income target, instead of the traditional fixed rate of growth of the money supply.

The second rule adds fiscal control of a foreign wealth target to the assignment of monetary policy to the nominal income target, as proposed by Boughton (1989), Genberg and Swoboda (1988) and Weale *et al.* (1989). It has often been called the reversed assignment in comparison with the early Mundell proposal, which we consider next.

Rule three, the Mundell Assignment, works in the opposite way: fiscal policy is concerned with the domestic objective and monetary policy controls the foreign wealth target.

The fourth rule implements the target zones proposal as it has been spelled out in Williamson (1987) and Edison, Miller and Williamson (1987).

Finally, numerical simulations of a small theoretical model will give some insights into the dynamic performance of the economy under the alternative assignments.

The main conclusions of this chapter are summarised as follows. First, algebraic analysis of the model shows that the monetarist rule is prone to the same risk of instability discussed in Chapter 3, whereas this does not happen under the other assignments. Second, Assignments (3) and (4), involving fiscal control of the domestic objective, are relatively more effective than Assignment (1) when policy is concerned, along with the traditional inflation target, with the stabilisation of foreign wealth and the exchange rate. However, both rules require great reliance on the fiscal instrument. Third, when permanent real demand shocks hit the economy the necessary permanent variations of foreign wealth and the exchange rate are substantially larger under a monetarist policy. Fourth, under each assignment disinflation policy requires an output loss, but the target zone rule also requires a permanent redistribution of foreign wealth and a corresponding permanent variation of the equilibrium exchange rate. Fifth, Assignment (2) avoids the danger of instability inherent to a monetarist rule, substantially limits permanent changes of foreign wealth and the exchange rate, does not require wide swings of fiscal policy. This conclusion obtains irrespective of the shock considered.

The rest of this chapter is organised as follows. The first section discusses the rationale for adopting each policy assignment. In the second section the model is set out. This model is a modified version of the one presented in Chapter 3. The third section investigates the necessary stability conditions under each assignment. The fourth section considers the long-term implications of permanent shocks and evaluates the dynamic performance of the model by means of numerical simulations.

4.1 PROPOSALS FOR MACROECONOMIC STABILISATION IN OPEN ECONOMIES

The first proposal under consideration suggests that governments should focus on the internal objective, neglecting the evolution of the current account, whose balance is regarded as the result of optimising saving–consumption decisions by the private sector. This proposal is deeply rooted in the monetary approach to the balance of payments.[1] Typically its advocates assert that, as long as the budget is balanced, governments should not be concerned with external disequilibria simply because the private sector will not run a permanent deficit. This proposal is labelled 'monetarist', although it departs from the standard monetarist orthodoxy by setting a closed loop rule; it is restricted to the use of monetary policy only and completely overlooks fiscal policy as a viable instrument for stabilisation purpose. This approach seems open to criticism for the reasons already discussed in Chapter 1, which will be briefly restated here.

First, external deficits increase the consumption of current generations at the expense of future ones (Cooper, 1986). In an economy where consumption decisions follow a life-cycle model, and there is a lack of effective intergenerational linking of preferences, future generations are not represented in current capital formation decisions.[2] Boughton emphasised this point and argued that legitimate governmental concern with intergenerational wealth transfer should find a logical counterpart in the setting of foreign wealth targets.

Second, the danger of withdrawal on short notice might turn external debt into a serious threat to national independence (Dornbusch and Park, 1987), hence governments might prefer to avoid the piling up of excessive external debt. It is also possible that, in a world where markets are riddled with imperfections, excessive profligacy today would require severe constraints on future consumption, which may be wise to avoid.[3]

The second rule, the Reversed Assignment, has been advocated, in a broad form, by Genberg and Swoboda (1988), Boughton (1989) and

Weale *et al.* (1989). It combines monetary control of the domestic
objective with the assignment of the fiscal feedback to the current
account. There are two intuitions underlying this assignment. The first
is that neglecting the current account balance is dangerous, partly
because of the reasons stated above, partly because in the long term
cumulating external imbalances require a real exchange rate adjustment and this is likely to complicate the task of controlling domestic
inflation. In the context of the simple model used here, setting a foreign
wealth target is equivalent to the choice of a long-term real exchange
rate target.

The second intuition is that fiscal policy has a comparative
advantage over monetary policy when controlling the current
account. Boughton (1989) has argued that whenever monetary policy
becomes expansionary in order to depreciate the exchange rate and
improve the trade balance, the gains from the terms of trade
devaluation are at least partly offset by the higher volume of imports
which is the direct consequence of the positive stimulus that lower
interest rates exert on domestic demand.

To assess the relevance of this claim I have chosen to consider
Assignment (3): fiscal control of domestic inflation and assignment of
monetary policy to the external objective.

Finally, Assignment (4) describes stabilisation policy under a target
zone regime. Advocates of this proposal have suggested that fiscal
policy should target domestic inflation, whereas monetary policy
should be left as a 'reserve weapon' against speculative bubbles in the
foreign exchange markets.

Edison, Miller and Williamson (1987) evaluated this proposal in a
two-country model, but their exercise suffered from two serious
shortcomings. First, they did not model the current account, nor did
they allow for wealth effects. Secondly, they considered an inflationary
shock only, completely overlooking the implications of 'real' shocks.

Comparative studies of the performance of such rules already exist.
This chapter aims to add to that work. So far investigations have
mainly been carried out with the aid of large econometric models
(Currie and Wren-Lewis, 1989; Frenkel, Masson and Goldstein, 1988,
1989). But simulation exercises on large models are not always easy to
interpret. Also those studies do not focus on a key feature of the
working of the international economic system: the link between
cumulating current account imbalances, foreign interest payments and
wealth effects in domestic demand. This book therefore aims to add to
the simple-rules-evaluation literature, and to clarify the crucial current

account issue, by using a simple transparent model of a small open economy.

4.2 THE MODEL

This is a more complex version of the model discussed in Chapter 3. Following Dornbusch price stickiness will be assumed, but a more sophisticated description of inflation dynamics will be introduced. Also considered are current account and wealth effects on aggregate demand. The model's behavioural equations are defined as follows:[4]

$$y = \beta a + \tau(aF_0 + F) - \sigma r - \delta s + \alpha x^* + x_d \tag{4.1}$$

$$dp = \epsilon y + \pi + \mu da \tag{4.2}$$

$$d\pi = \phi(dp - \pi) \tag{4.3}$$

$$dF = \beta_1 a - \mu y + x^* + r^* F \tag{4.4}$$

$$da = r - r^* \tag{4.5}$$

Output, y, is demand-determined (Equation 4.1). Its deviations from the natural rate depend on the real exchange rate, a, net foreign wealth, $(aF_0 + F)$, the *real* interest rate, r, and a fiscal policy index, s. In Equation 4.2 the rate of change of consumption prices,[5] dp, depends on the real exchange rate and domestic wage inflation, linked to current output and core inflation, π. Core inflation adjusts slowly to actual inflation[6] (Equation 4.3). The increase in real foreign wealth equals the trade surplus ($\beta_1 a - \mu y$) plus interest receipts on (net) foreign wealth holdings (Equation 4.4). The foreign interest rate[7] is r^*. Finally, Equation 4.5 describes real exchange rate dynamics under perfect foresight when domestic and foreign currencies are perfect substitutes. The term x_d denotes a demand shock, x^* is a foreign demand shock, which influences both domestic output and the current account balance.

Following Miller, (1985), from Equations 4.3 and 4.2 we get

$$\pi = \phi\epsilon z + \phi\mu a + x_p \tag{4.6}$$

$$dz = y \tag{4.7}$$

Core inflation is determined by the real exchange rate and by

$$z = \int_0^t y\,dt$$

which is the integral of output deviations from the natural rate. x_p is a shock to the level of inflation. The model may then be written as three equations in the three endogenous variables z, F and a.

$$dz = y = \beta a + \tau(aF_0 + F) - \sigma r - \delta s + \alpha x^* + x_d \tag{4.8}$$

$$dF = \beta_1 a - \mu dz + r^* F + x^* \tag{4.9}$$

$$da = r - r^* \tag{4.10}$$

To close the model we need to endogenise the fiscal and monetary[8] instruments according to the policy rules discussed above. The alternative proposals may be represented as

(1) **Monetarist rule:**

$$r = k_1 \pi \tag{4.11a}$$

$$s = 0 \tag{4.12a}$$

(2) **Reversed Assignment:**

$$r = k_1 \pi \tag{4.11b}$$

$$s = -k_2 F \tag{4.12b}$$

(3) **Mundell Assignment:**

$$s = n_1 \pi \tag{4.11c}$$

$$r = n_2 F \tag{4.12c}$$

(4) **Target zone rule:**

$$s = n_1 \pi \tag{4.11d}$$

$$r = r^* \tag{4.12d}$$

4.3 STABILITY ANALYSIS

For each assignment the appropriate versions of Equation 4.11 and 4.12 into Equations 4.6–4.9. As a result variable π is eliminated, obtaining a third-order dynamic system. Saddlepath stability requires one unstable and two stable roots. A necessary condition for this is that $|A|$, the determinant of the relevant transition matrix defined below, be positive. The main focus is on this necessary condition,[9] which yields interesting insights even in a rather complex third-order system.

4.3.1 The monetarist rule and the reversed assignment

Under the monetarist rule the real interest rate is targeted on the internal objective. The reversed assignment adds the use of fiscal policy to target the current account. The two assignments may be nested into a third order dynamic system, but the economic interpretation of the stability condition is rather difficult. Therefore the analysis of stability will be undertaken in stages. Since it is assumed that the domestic price of foreign imports instantaneously adjusts to exchange rate 'surprises',[10] core inflation is immediately affected by jumps in the exchange rate (Equation 4.6). As a preliminary step it is assumed that the core, underlying rate of inflation is determined only by cumulated past deviations of output from equilibrium:

$$\pi = \Phi \epsilon z$$

In this case the dynamic system is defined as follows:

$$dx = Ax + Bv$$

where

$$x = \begin{bmatrix} z \\ f \\ a \end{bmatrix} \qquad v = \begin{bmatrix} x_p \\ x_d \\ x^* \end{bmatrix}$$

$$A^* = \begin{bmatrix} -\sigma k_1 \phi \epsilon & (\tau + \delta k_2) & (\beta + F_0 \tau) \\ \mu \sigma k_1 \phi \epsilon & r^* - \mu(\tau + \delta k_2) & \beta_1 - \mu(\beta + F_0 \tau) \\ k_1 \phi \epsilon & 0 & 0 \end{bmatrix}$$

$$B = \begin{bmatrix} 1 & \alpha & -\sigma k_1 \\ -\mu & 1 - \mu\alpha & \mu\sigma k_1 \\ 0 & 0 & k_1 \end{bmatrix}$$

The stability condition of this simplified system is remarkably similar to the one discussed in Chapter 3, under a standard monetarist rule:[11]

$$|A^*| = k_1\Phi\epsilon\{[\beta_1 - \mu(\beta + F_0\tau)](\tau + \delta k_2) \\ - [r^* - \mu(\tau + \delta k_2)](\beta + \tau F_0)\} \tag{4.13}$$

An intuitive interpretation of Equation 4.13 can be given as follows. First we make the plausible assumption that the net effect of a devaluation on the current account is positive.[12] When $r^* > \mu(\tau + \delta k_2)$, that is, when a loss of foreign assets worsens the current account, a devaluation is necessary to generate a current account surplus and to restore the equilibrium stock of foreign wealth. In the domestic goods market loss of wealth weakens demand and output, whereas devaluation exerts the opposite effect. If the depreciation dominates the effect of the loss of wealth and raises output above the natural rate the model becomes unstable. In fact the output expansion triggers a rise in inflation. This in turn will cause an increase in the domestic interest rate and a further depreciation: wealth and the exchange rate will take an ever-increasing path. The stability condition simply requires that the necessary depreciation be associated with a current account surplus and with a level of output which is below the natural rate. From the transition matrix the combinations of a and F may be derived which leave output and the current account in equilibrium.[13]

$$y = 0: \qquad a = -[(\tau + \delta k_2)/(\beta + F_0\tau)]F \tag{4.14}$$

$$dF = 0: \qquad a = -\{[r^* - \mu(\tau + \delta k_2)]/[\beta - \mu(\beta + F_0\tau)]\}F \tag{4.15}$$

In Figure 4.1 locus yy represents the combinations of wealth and the exchange rate which leave output at the natural rate. Locus FF represents the combinations of wealth and the exchange rate which are consistent with current account equilibrium.[14] Stability requires that the initial combination of wealth and the exchange rate be set above FF to generate a current account surplus, and below yy so that output does not exceed the natural rate. This may happen only if yy is steeper than FF, that is:

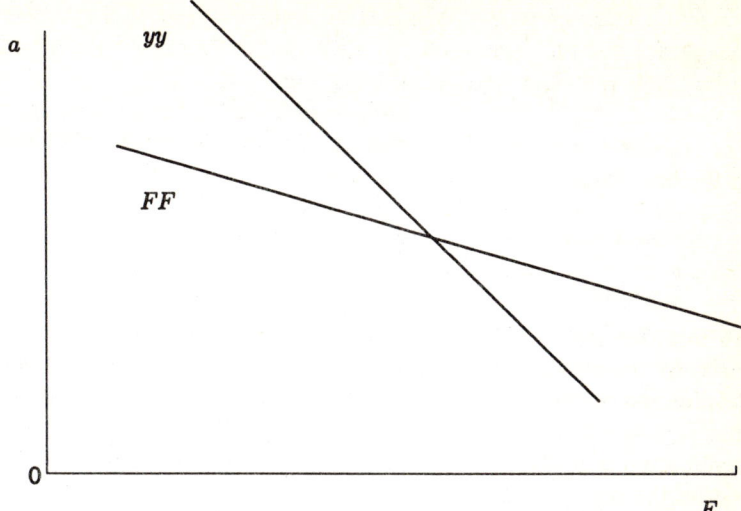

Figure 4.1 The combinations of wealth and the real exchange rate which are consistent with output and current account equilibrium in the stable case

$$(\tau + \delta k_2)/(\beta + F_0\tau) > [r^* - \mu(\tau + \delta k_2)]/[\beta_1 - \mu(\beta + F_0\tau)] \quad (4.16)$$

Condition 4.16 holds when 4.13 is satisfied.

On the other hand, when $r^* < \mu(\tau + \delta k_2)$, that is, when a loss of foreign wealth improves the current account, the depreciation is no longer necessary to restore the equilibrium level of wealth and it is always possible for the initial combination of wealth and the exchange rate to be consistent with a current account surplus and a recession in the goods market. In fact condition 4.13 implies that when $r^* < \mu(\tau + \delta k_2)$ saddlepath stability is guaranteed.[15]

Let us now consider the case where:

$$\pi = \Phi \epsilon z + \Phi \mu a$$

The transition matrix becomes:

$$A = \begin{bmatrix} -\sigma k_1 \phi \epsilon & (\tau + \delta k_2) & (\beta + \tau F_0 - k_1 \phi \mu) \\ \mu \sigma k_1 \phi \epsilon & r^* - \mu(\tau + \delta k_2) & \beta_1 - \mu(\beta + \tau F_0 - k_1 \phi \mu) \\ k_1 \phi \epsilon & 0 & k_1 \phi \mu \end{bmatrix}$$

Inflation instantaneously responds to exchange rate 'surprises' and triggers an interest rate feedback. This, in turn, affects output, the current account and interest rate dynamics. A first fundamental difference between A^* and A is that the direct link between the interest rate and the exchange rate substantially dampens the expansionary effect of a devaluation on output because the depreciation is instantaneously followed by a monetary contraction. Furthermore, the interest rate feedback has a positive effect on the current account as the flow of imports associated to the devaluation is reduced. On the other hand the rise in the real interest rate has a destabilising effect on exchange rate dynamics: after the initial jump in the exchange rate the monetary contraction requires the expectation of a further devaluation.[16] Quite strikingly, the new stability condition is identical to 4.13:

$$|A| = k_1 \Phi \epsilon \{ [\beta_1 - \mu(\beta + F_0 \tau)](\tau + \delta k_2) - [r^* - \mu(\tau + \delta k_2)](\beta + F_0 \tau) \}$$

The stabilising influence of the interest rate on output and the current account is exactly offset by the effect of the rise in the interest rate on exchange rate dynamics.

If a negative shock occurs to F the monetary feedback is activated only to the extent that the change in domestic expenditure drives inflation away from the desired path, regardless of the need to achieve long-term equilibrium in the stock of wealth. Let us assume that, starting from an equilibrium where all variables are zero, foreign assets rise. If $r^* > \mu(\tau + \delta k_2)$ interest receipts increase more than import spending, and the current account improves. The exchange rate must instantaneously appreciate, so as to generate the necessary fall in foreign wealth. The appreciation reduces the cost of foreign imports and inflation, leading, via monetary policy, to a lower real interest rate, and inevitably causing a further gradual devaluation. But a turning point in exchange rate dynamics *must* be reached. At this stage, where $da = r = \pi = 0$, a is below its long-term value. For it to converge to equilibrium, it is necessary that r begins to rise. That requires[17] output to be positive. This, in turn, implies that F is still above equilibrium.[18] Since from now on the interest rate will be rising and the real exchange rate will be depreciating,[19] at this point the current account must be in deficit, otherwise foreign wealth will never converge to equilibrium. Condition 4.13 ensures that this will happen. It shows that when $F > 0$ and $r = da = 0$, an appreciated exchange rate can generate a current account deficit and yet set the output level above the natural rate. From the transition matrix, when $da = 0$, we obtain:

$$y = (\tau + \delta k_2)F + (\beta + F_0\tau)a$$

But if $y > 0$ then

$$a = -[(\tau + k_2)/(\beta + \tau F_0)]F + \Omega, \quad \Omega > 0$$

since at this point $F > 0$.

Thus the requirements for a current account deficit are as follows:

$$[r^*(\beta + F_0\tau) - \beta_1(\tau + k_2)]F < \Omega[\beta_1 - \mu(\beta + F_0\tau)]$$

Since F is positive, this requires that condition 4.13 holds.

The influence of the two assignments on stability is profoundly different. *Under the monetarist assignment*, when $k_2 = 0$, the necessary stability condition is independent from the policy control and may be ensured only by a favourable combination of the structural parameters which cannot be taken for granted. *Under the reversed assignment* stability may be ensured by an appropriate fiscal feedback. Note that a strong fiscal control may guarantee a condition which is sufficient for stability to obtain:[20]

$$tr A = -k_1\phi(\sigma\epsilon - \mu) + r^* - \mu(\tau + \delta k_2) < 0$$

4.3.2 The Mundell and the Target Zone Assignments

Under the target zone rule domestic and foreign real interest rates are equalised – to prevent real exchange rate dynamics – and fiscal policy controls inflation. The Mundell assignment retains fiscal control of inflation, and the monetary instrument is assigned to a foreign wealth target. Again, the two assignments may be nested into the same dynamic system.

$$dx = Ax + Bv$$

where

$$A = \begin{bmatrix} -\delta n_1\phi\epsilon & (\tau - \sigma n_2) & (\beta + \tau F_0 - \delta n_1\phi\mu) \\ \mu\delta n_1\phi\epsilon & r^* - \mu(\tau - \sigma n_2) & \beta_1 - \mu(\beta + \tau F_0 - \delta n_1\phi\mu) \\ 0 & n_2 & 0 \end{bmatrix}$$

$$B = \begin{bmatrix} 1 & \alpha & -\delta n_1 \\ -\mu & 1 - \mu\alpha & \mu\delta n_1 \\ 0 & 0 & 0 \end{bmatrix}$$

Under the *Mundell assignment* monetary control of foreign wealth exploits the exchange rate swings generated by differentials between domestic and foreign interest rates. The system is saddlepath stable. Suppose that the stock of foreign assets rises. The domestic real interest rate is then increased in order to appreciate the exchange rate. This certainly worsens the trade balance, but on the other hand the monetary contraction lowers domestic expenditure on imports. Boughton (1989) claimed that under this assignment the weak influence of monetary policy on the current account might generate instability. The analysis here shows that this is not so as long as the financial markets choose the proper initial jump in the exchange rate, since the determinant condition, $|A| > 0$, obtains anyway:

$$|A| = \delta n_1 \phi \epsilon \beta_1 n_2$$

Furthermore, the relative strength of the two policy feedbacks may be designed so as to satisfy a sufficient stability condition:[21]

$$tr A = -\delta n_1 \phi \epsilon + r^* - \mu(\tau - \sigma n_2) < 0$$

Boughton failed to take into account that the weak impact of monetary policy on the current account would simply require wider exchange rate swings,[22] instead of causing dynamic instability. To further clarify the issue we shall analyse the stability condition under the assumption that the government does not control inflation but sets a foreign wealth target. In this case the system has the following state–space form:

$$dF = [r^* - \mu(\tau - \sigma n_2)]F + [\beta_1 - \mu(\beta + F_0\tau)]a + G_1$$

$$da = n_2 F + G_2$$

where G_1 and G_2 represent the forcing variables we are not interested in at the moment. The roots of the characteristic equation are:

$$\theta_1 = 0.5\{[r^* - \mu(\tau - \sigma n_2)]\}$$
$$+ 0.5\{[r^* - \mu(\tau - \sigma n_2)]^2 + 4n_2[\beta_1 - \mu(\beta + F_0\tau)]\}^{1/2}$$

$$\theta_2 = 0.5\{[r^* - \mu(\tau - \sigma n_2)]\}$$
$$- 0.5\{[r^* - \mu(\tau - \sigma n_2)]^2 + 4n_2[\beta_1 - \mu(\beta + F_0\tau)]\}^{1/2}$$

The system is saddlepath stable provided that a devaluation improves the current account.[23] The destabilising influence of the policy feedback on domestic demand does not matter because it is always possible that an appropriate jump in the exchange rate will generate convergent wealth and exchange rate dynamics. This is shown with the aid of the familiar state–space diagram (Figure 4.2). Along locus *aa* domestic and foreign interest rates are equal. It is vertical on the foreign wealth target[24] because exchange rate changes do not trigger any interest rate feedback. For instance, when foreign assets are above equilibrium the real interest rate is increased, therefore equilibrium in the international financial markets requires an instantaneous appreciation followed by an expected devaluation.[25] Locus *FF* represents combinations of foreign wealth and the exchange rate which yield current account equilibrium. It is negatively sloped under the assumption that a loss of foreign assets worsens the current account because the corresponding reduction of the interest rate expands domestic demand and dominates the negative wealth effect caused by the fall in F.[26] Points above FF are associated with a current account surplus and vice versa. Suppose that foreign wealth falls below target. Monetary policy takes an expansionary stance, and the domestic real interest rate falls. As a result the exchange rate must depreciate.[27] Figure 4.2 shows that if a devaluation improves the current account the initial jump in the exchange rate can generate the necessary current account surplus. The gradual accumulation of foreign assets is then followed by an increase in the real interest rate and by appreciation in the exchange rate.

Under a *target zones rule* $r = r^*$, thus $|A| = 0$. But it is possible to solve the characteristic equation for A and determine algebraically the signs of its roots.

$$|A - \theta I| = \theta(\theta^2 + \alpha_1\theta + \alpha_2) = 0$$

Since $\alpha_2 = -r^*\delta n_1 \phi \epsilon < 0$ is the product of the two roots which are different from zero, the model is always saddlepath stable, the signs of the three roots being $\theta_1 = 0$; $\theta_2 > 0$; $\theta_3 < 0$.

The requirement of saddlepath stability has an important implication. Given the structure that this assignment imposes upon the dynamic matrix, swings in the real exchange rate cannot occur. Nevertheless the real exchange rate remains an endogenous variable because the model includes the current account equation. Equation 4.4 shows that in equilibrium, when $y = 0$, a permanent variation of the real

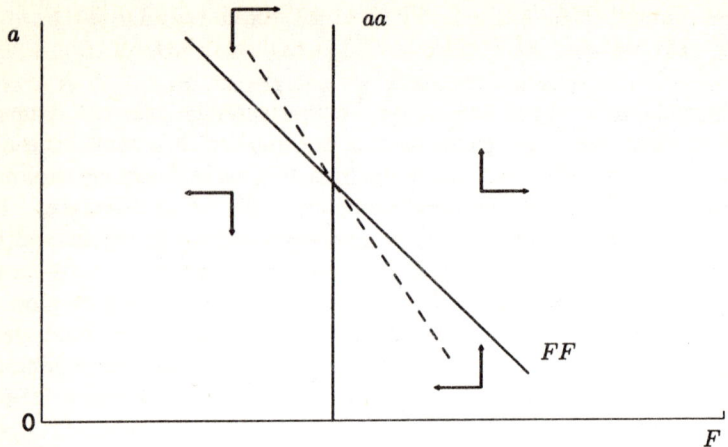

Figure 4.2   Dynamics under the Mundell assignment

exchange rate must offset permanent transfers of net foreign wealth. Due to the constraint that $r = r^*$, the real exchange rate must instantaneously jump into its new long-term value, after which the system converges to current account equilibrium at a new long-term level of wealth.[28]

The implication is that when fiscal policy is assigned to the domestic objective, monetary control of a foreign wealth target is not necessary to ensure stability, provided that the real exchange rate is allowed to adjust once and for all in the face of shocks which cause permanent variations of foreign wealth.

4.3.3 Summary

Open economy models which include wealth effects and the current account might be unstable. The danger of instability is a consequence of the presence of foreign investment service in the current account: if $r^* = 0$ stability would always obtain. The choice of the policy rule has important implications for stability. The adoption of an explicit foreign wealth target (Assignments 2 and 3) might ensure stability. By contrast, under a monetarist assignment the system might be inherently unstable, irrespective of the strength of the policy feedback. If the government adheres to a target zone rule, the exchange rate target must be revised whenever the nature of the shock requires permanent changes of net foreign wealth.[29]

4.4 COMPARATIVE STATICS AND ANALYSIS OF THE DYNAMIC ADJUSTMENT TO EQUILIBRIUM

The policy rules outlined above obviously imply different dynamic adjustment paths in response to shocks. To a certain extent this is also true for the required permanent changes of some endogenous variables. This section presents a detailed analysis of these differences. The dynamic performance of the model under each policy regime and the magnitude of long-term changes of z, F and a after permanent shocks are evaluated by means of numerical simulations.[30] Also presented are some algebraic results concerning the theoretical determination of these long-term changes. The standard method used to determine the consequences of permanent shocks requires the inversion of the transition matrix.[31] Such a procedure cannot be adopted under Assignment 4, because in that case $|A| = 0$, therefore I introduce an alternative solution method[32] which is original and has the merit of highlighting the interaction between dynamics and long-term equilibrium under a target zones regime.

4.4.1 Inflation shock

We now consider an increase of core inflation. In the simulations it is assumed that $x_p = 10$ per cent.

4.4.4.1 New equilibrium values

Under Assignments 1–3 disinflation has no permanent effects on foreign wealth and the exchange rate. From Equation 4.6 $\pi = 0$ if:

$$\phi \epsilon z = -(\phi \mu a + x_p)$$

Therefore, disinflation requires a cumulated output loss which is invariant to the dynamic path[33] implied by the policy rule and amounts to:

$$z_\infty = -x_p / \phi \epsilon$$

Exchange rate swings stabilise foreign wealth during the transition.

Under Assignment 4 the picture is substantially different: an inflation shock does have permanent effects.

$$a_\infty = -(x_p/\phi\epsilon)[(r^*/\beta_1) \times (v_1/v_2)]/\{1 + (v_1/v_2\delta n_1\phi\epsilon) \times$$
$$\times [\tau - r^*(\beta + \tau F_0 - \delta n_1\phi\mu)/\beta_1]\} < 0$$

$$F_\infty = (x_p/\phi\epsilon)^*(v_1/v_2)/\{1 + (v_1/v_2\delta n_1\phi\epsilon) \times$$
$$\times [\tau - r^*(\beta + \tau F_0 - \delta n_1\phi\mu)/\beta_1]\} > 0$$

$$z_\infty = -[x_p/\phi\epsilon]/\{1 + (v_1/v_2\delta n_1\phi\epsilon) \times$$
$$\times [\tau - r^*(\beta + \tau F_0 - \delta n_1\phi\mu)/\beta_1]\} < 0$$

The signs of long-term effects are as shown because:

$$\theta_2 > 0$$

$$v_1/v_2 = (\theta_2 + \delta n_1\phi\epsilon)/\beta_1 n_1\phi\epsilon$$
$$+ [\beta_1 - \mu(\beta + \tau F_0 - \delta n_1\phi\mu)]\theta_2 > 0$$

$$\tau > r^*$$

$(\beta + \tau - n_1\phi\mu)/\beta_1 < 1$ if the fiscal feedback is sufficiently strong.

Under a target zones regime, when fiscal policy controls domestic inflation and monetary policy is not activated, disinflation determines permanent changes of F and a. The fiscal contraction, necessary to control domestic inflation, reduces domestic demand for foreign goods and causes a permanent accumulation of foreign wealth. If the current account is to be in equilibrium in the long term, a permanent exchange rate appreciation is required.

Assignment 4 causes a permanent wealth redistribution because, unlike the other rules, it does not determine an exchange rate undershooting during the recession which is necessary to curb inflation. Under the other rules, exchange rate swings prevent the domestic output loss from permanently affecting foreign wealth. By contrast, under a target zones regime the exchange rate simply jumps onto the new equilibrium value, which accounts for the current account surpluses accumulated during the disinflation. Another interesting feature of this regime is that the permanent appreciation in the terms of trade reduces the necessary output loss (Table 4.1).

The numerical simulations confirm the algebraic analysis and imply that the size of the wealth transfer is positively related to the trade elasticities, especially to income elasticity. Although I do not make great claims of realism, this result suggests that the redistribution of wealth might be substantial. In a way it could be argued that a deflationary policy under this assignment could turn out to be another kind of beggar-thy-neighbour policy, as the renunciation to temporarily 'exporting' inflation abroad by means of a terms of trade appreciation[34] is matched by the permanent increase in national disposable income obtained by raising domestic holdings of foreign wealth. Further research should investigate whether this outcome would be more or less likely to induce retaliatory policies from the commercial partners of the country than would the fluctuation of the real exchange rate.

Table 4.1   Permanent effects of a disinflationary policy under a target zones regime when nominal income is the domestic target (simulations)

	Low interdependence %	*High interdependence* %
z	−39.6	−38.3
F	+3.5	+10.0
a	−1.2	−2.0

4.4.1.2 Dynamics

Let us now turn to an analysis of the dynamic performance of the model under the alternative rules. When monetary policy is activated (Assignments 1, 2 and 3) the real exchange rate initially appreciates. Later on it gradually depreciates toward its equilibrium value. Comparing Assignments 1 and 2 (Figures 4.3 and 4.4) we observe that the latter requires a more moderate initial jump in the exchange rate, probably because the fiscal control, which curbs domestic demand in order to achieve the wealth target, has a favourable side-effect on the domestic objective. Relative to the performance of Assignment 1 the fluctuations of financial wealth are dampened. If the model is simulated assuming lower values of the trade balance elasticities, wider fluctuations of the exchange rate and the monetary instrument occur under both rules.

Under Assignment 3 (Figure 4.5) the disinflation policy works as follows. The fiscal contraction reduces output, turning the current account balance into a surplus. External equilibrium requires a temporary appreciation in the exchange rate, which is achieved by increasing the domestic real interest rate. Again, as in the case of Assignment 2, exchange rate and fiscal and monetary policy exert a contractionary stimulus, but with a different mix, fiscal policy being more strongly activated than monetary policy. Also, appreciation in the terms of trade necessary to control the current account is milder than the revaluation required to bring down inflation under Assignments 1 and 2. If the trade balance elasticities are low, the deviation of the exchange rate from equilibrium are relatively smaller, whereas under Assignments 1 and 2 they are enhanced. This probably happens because the positive influence of the fiscal contraction on the current account is weaker, so that the necessary rise in the domestic interest rate is also weaker. It could be argued that Assignment 3 has the appealing implication of imposing less deflationary pressure upon the sector open to international competition relative to the one producing non-traded goods. Boughton's claim that under this rule current account control would be relatively more difficult than in the case of Assignment 2 does not seem to have been confirmed: wealth fluctuations are less wide than under Assignment 2. But this probably happens because it is the fiscal contraction necessary to bring inflation down which helps to keep wealth close to the target rather than the monetary policy rule.

Finally, Table 4.2 presents the cumulated deviations of policy instruments from equilibrium. The exchange rate is included because under Assignments 1, 2 and 3 fluctuations in the terms of trade are exploited for the purpose of target stabilisation. The implied costs in terms of interest rate and relative prices disequilibria are gradually reduced when moving from Assignment 1 to 4. The opposite conclusion holds when considering tax deviations from equilibrium. Compared to Assignment 1, Rule 2 cuts down deviations of the exchange rate from equilibrium by approximately one-third and requires a substantially more moderate use of the monetary instrument, −50 per cent, at the cost of a rather limited use of the fiscal weapon. By contrast, the assignment of fiscal policy to the domestic target requires fluctuations of the tax rate which are far wider than those necessary to control the current account. When weighing the relative merits of each rule this should be taken into account. It has been rightly claimed that disinflation policies exploiting the appreciation of the exchange rate might heavily alter the patterns of international trade, but on the other hand it should be borne in mind that the alternative rule which assigns fiscal control to the domestic objective might imply substantial deviations of the tax rate from the desired equilibrium level. Figure 4.7 shows that Assignments 3 and 4 require a tax rate hike that can be as high as 8 per cent and might simply not be feasible. Furthermore, an evaluation of Assignment 4 would require taking into account the permanent changes of wealth and the exchange rate that become necessary under this rule.

Table 4.2   Disinflation policy: cumulated squared deviations from equilibrium of policy instruments (percentage values)

	Assignment			
	1	*2*	*3*	*4*
Low interdependence:				
r	81.95	46.13	0.64	–
s	–	20.16	263.50	266.0
a	948.00	599.10	238.57	–
High interdependence:				
r	94.76	15.23	10.68	–
s	–	19.78	115.02	256.5
a	632.15	454.36	348.20	–

4.4.2   Domestic demand shock

4.4.2.1   New equilibrium values

We shall consider a permanent rise of domestic demand in real terms; in the numerical simulations x_d is set equal to 5 per cent.

Under Assignments 1 and 2 the system multipliers are:

$$z_\infty = -\mu r^* / [\beta_1(\tau + \delta k_2) - r^*(\beta + \tau F_0)]x_d$$

$$F = -\beta_1 x_d / [\beta_1(\tau + \delta k_2) - r^*(\beta + \tau F_0)]$$

$$a_\infty = r^* x_d / [\beta_1(\tau + \delta k_2) - r^*(\beta + \tau F_0)]$$

Consider the monetarist assignment, $k_2 = 0$. The policy control is activated only to the extent that excess demand raises inflation, regardless of the current account, which goes into deficit. Eventually, the real exchange rate must depreciate in order to ensure external equilibrium. Wealth effects in aggregate demand will compensate for

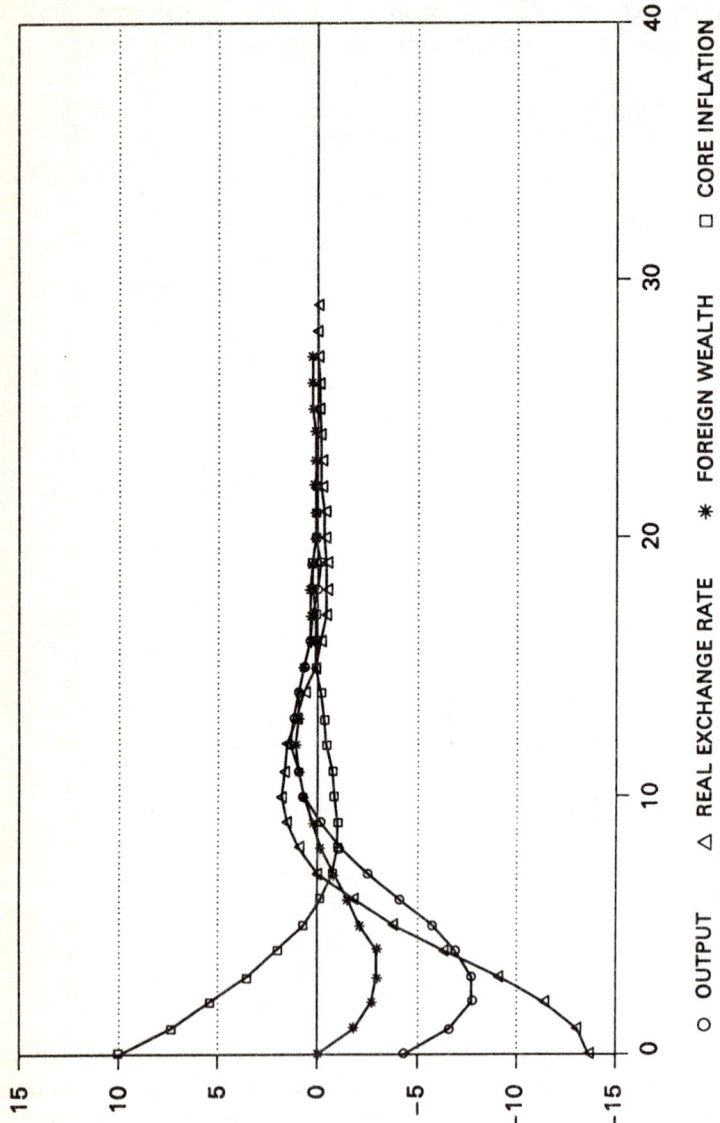

Figure 4.3 Disinflation policy: assignment 1: percentage deviations from equilibrium

○ OUTPUT   △ REAL EXCHANGE RATE   ✳ FOREIGN WEALTH   □ CORE INFLATION

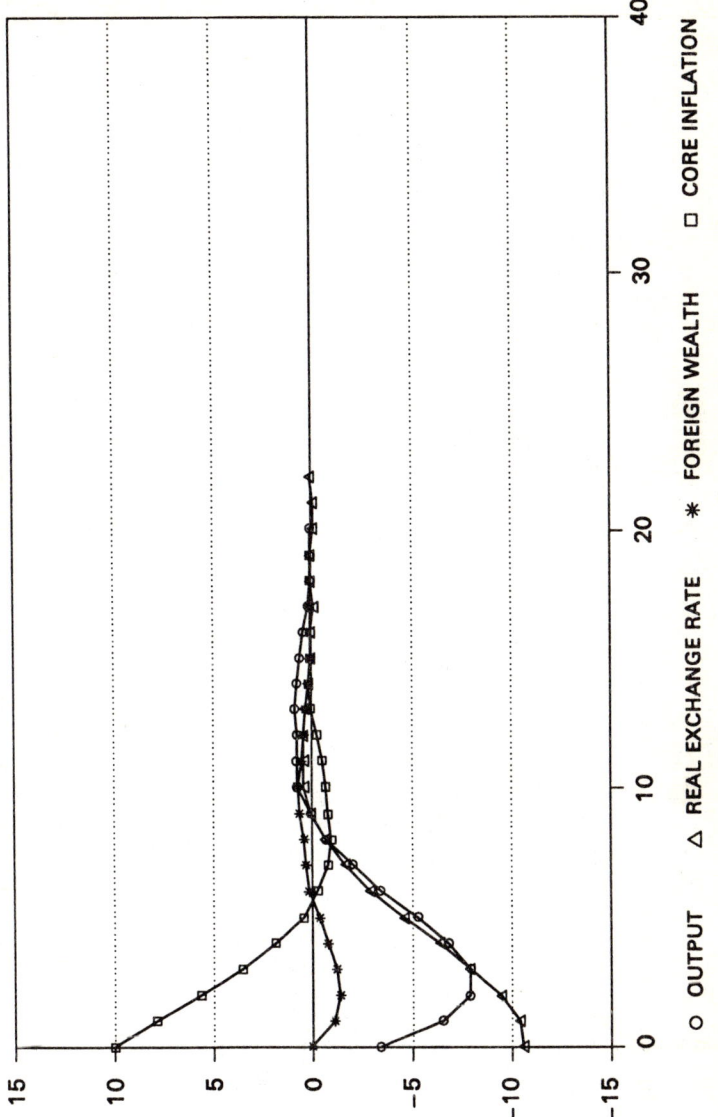

Figure 4.4 Disinflation policy: assignment 2: percentage deviations from equilibrium

○ OUTPUT   △ REAL EXCHANGE RATE   ✳ FOREIGN WEALTH   □ CORE INFLATION

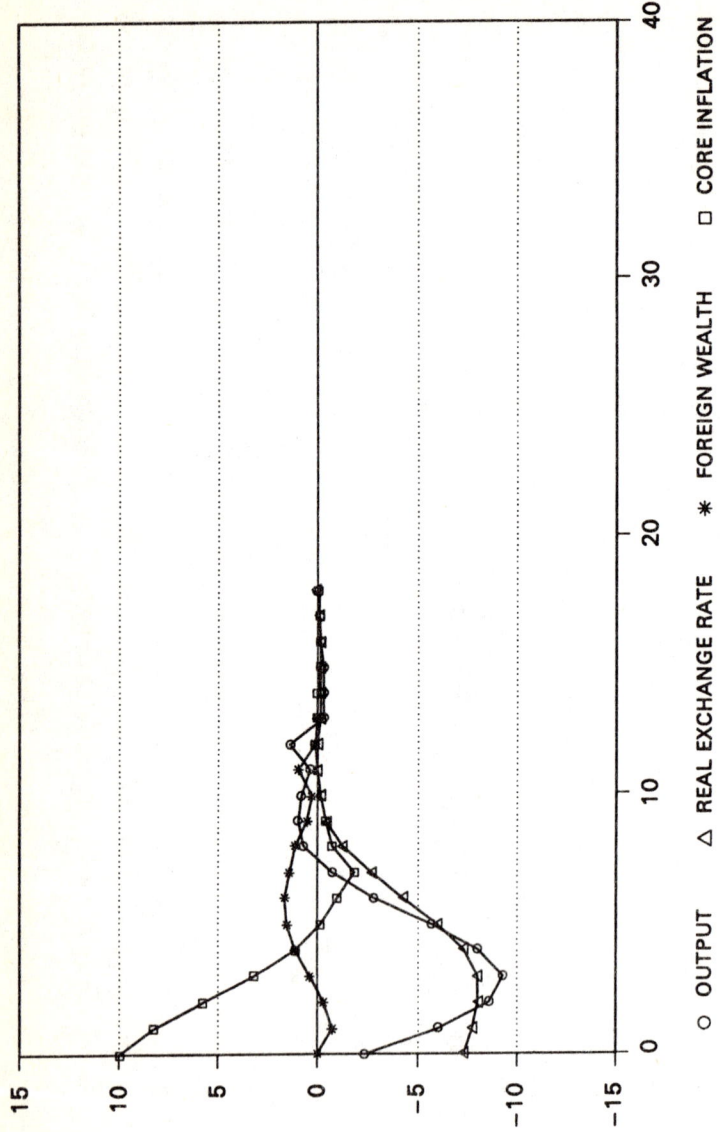

Figure 4.5 Disinflation policy: assignment 3: percentage deviations from equilibrium

○ OUTPUT   △ REAL EXCHANGE RATE   ✳ FOREIGN WEALTH   □ CORE INFLATION

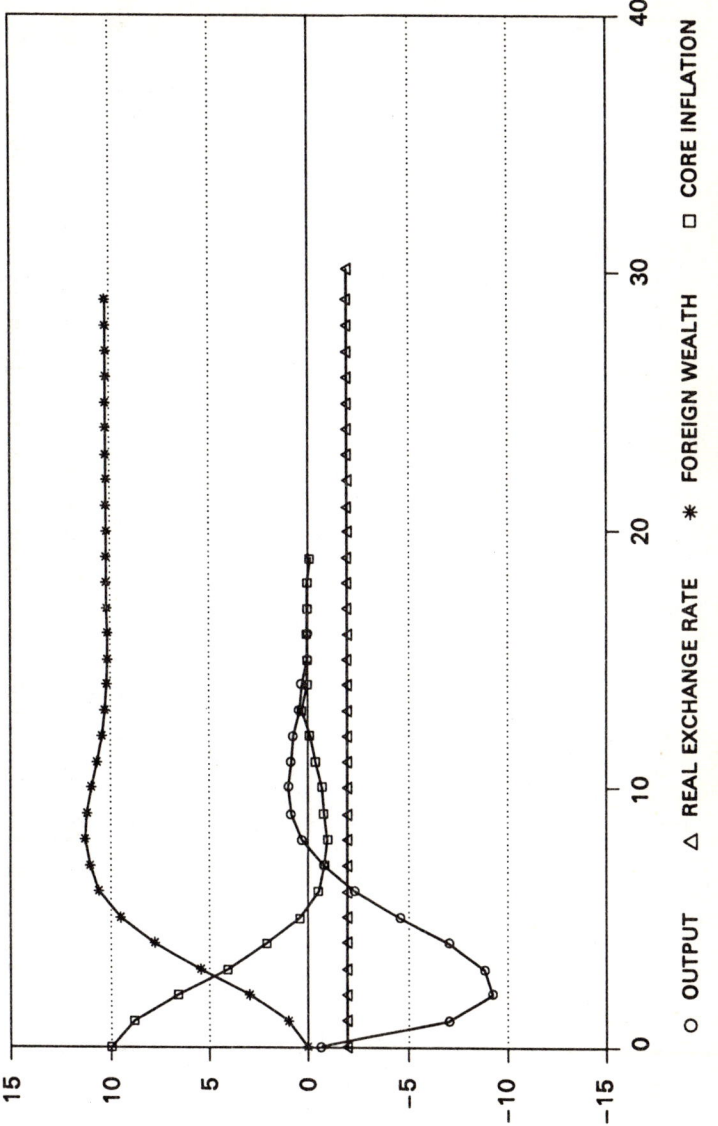

Figure 4.6 Disinflation policy: assignment 4: percentage deviations from equilibrium

○ OUTPUT   △ REAL EXCHANGE RATE   ✳ FOREIGN WEALTH   □ CORE INFLATION

88

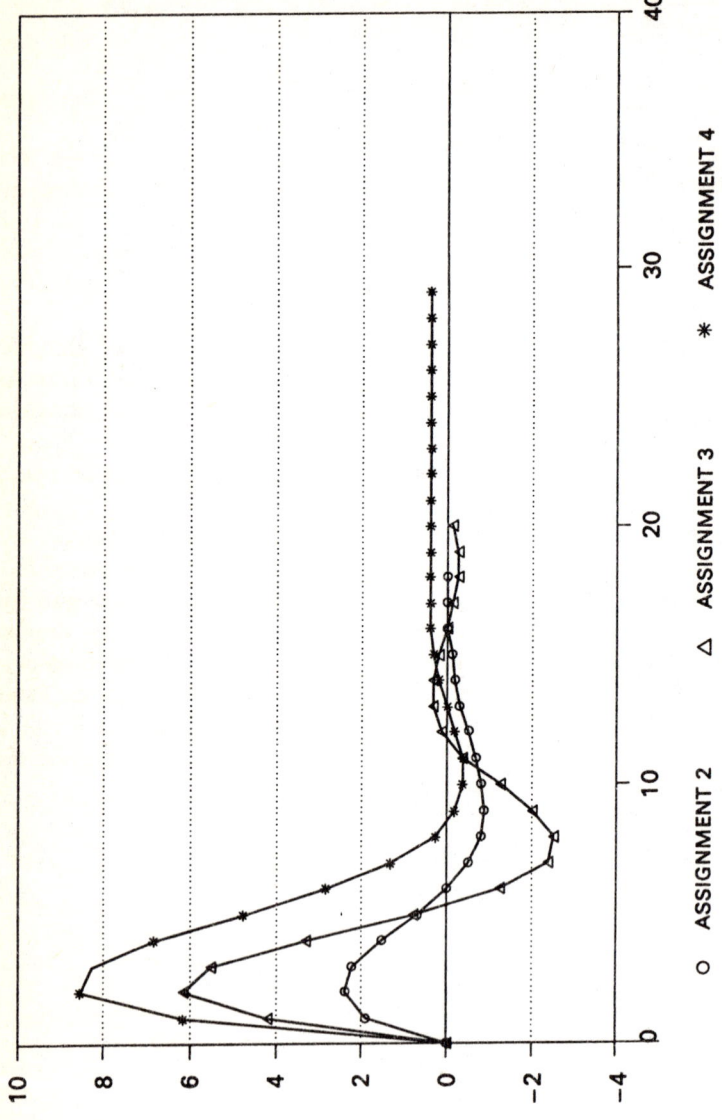

Figure 4.7 Disinflation policy: alternative paths of the tax variable (percentage deviations from equilibrium)

O ASSIGNMENT 2   △ ASSIGNMENT 3   * ASSIGNMENT 4

the initial shock, ensuring that $y_\infty = 0$. The foreign wealth loss is certainly bigger than the initial expansion of domestic demand. Notice that the stronger the wealth effects in aggregate demand, the smaller the necessary loss of financial assets and the smaller the required devaluation of the real exchange rate.

$$dF_\infty/d\tau = \beta_1(\beta_1 - r^*F_0)/[\beta_1(\tau + \delta k_2) - r^*(\beta + \tau F_0)]^2$$

If the model is to be stable[35] $(\beta_1 - r^*F_0) > 0$, hence $dF_\infty/d\tau > 0$. The stronger the wealth effects in aggregate demand, the smaller the necessary loss of financial assets.

$$da_\infty/d\tau = -r^*(\beta_1 - r^*F_0)/[\beta_1(\tau + \delta k_2) - r^*(\beta + \tau F_0)]^2 < 0$$

Stronger wealth effects require a smaller devaluation of the real exchange rate. In terms of domestic output the foreign wealth transfer is very likely to be stronger than the initial expansion of domestic demand. Our numerical simulations show that under this assignment the transfer of foreign wealth can be huge, but it substantially decreases when wealth effects are stronger.

Assignment of fiscal control to the external equilibrium $(k_2 > 0,$ Assignment 2) may substantially change the picture. To the extent that fiscal control is sufficiently strong, the wealth redistribution and the exchange rate devaluation are drastically reduced. Numerical simulations confirm this and show that fiscal policy acts far more quickly than wealth effects in curbing the excess of domestic demand (Table 4.3). However, under this rule, as well as under Assignments 3 and 4, only a permanent increase of the tax rate may compensate for the permanent shock to aggregate demand.[36]

Table 4.3   Simulation results: long-term effects of a domestic demand shock $(\tau = 0.15)$

	Assignment 1	Assignment 2
	(high trade elasticities)	
z	−6.3	−0.5
F	−39.0	−2.6
a	+7.9	+0.5

Note: Percentage deviations from initial equilibrium, z and F are 'normalised' with respect to equilibrium output.

Under Assignment 3, when monetary policy is assigned to a wealth target and fiscal policy controls domestic inflation:

$$z_\infty = x_d/n_1\phi\epsilon\delta$$

$$F = 0$$

$$a_\infty = 0$$

In contrast to Assignments 1 and 2, permanent changes in wealth and the exchange rate cannot occur. Monetary policy is assigned to the foreign wealth target, but in the long term the domestic interest rate is tied to the foreign one by perfect capital mobility, therefore F must be zero.

Under Assignment 4:

$$a_\infty = x_d[(r^*/\beta_1)^* v_1/v_2]/\{n_1\phi\epsilon \\ + (v_1/v_2)[\tau - r^*(\beta + \tau F_0 - n_1\phi\mu)/\beta_1]\}$$

$$F = - x_d(v_1/v_2)/\{n_1\phi\epsilon + (v_1/v_2)[\tau - r^*(\beta + \tau - n_1\phi\mu)/\beta_1]\}$$

$$z_\infty = + x_d/\{n_1\phi\epsilon + (v_1/v_2)[\tau - r^*(\beta + \tau F_0 - n_1\phi\mu)/\beta_1]\}$$

Domestic holdings of foreign assets decrease, the exchange rate depreciates and cumulated excess demand is positive. In fact simulations show that these permanent changes are negligible, always below 1 per cent, with the exchange rate variation being very close to zero.

4.4.2.2 *Dynamics*

Under a monetarist rule the model exhibits prolonged persistence and huge swings in the exchange rate. Excess demand impinges on core inflation and this stimulates a monetary contraction. As a result, the terms of trade must appreciate initially, by about 8 per cent using our standard parameters which show a high degree of interdependence in trade, by up to 20 per cent when trade volume and price parameters are smaller. However, equilibrium requires a permanent depreciation, which occurs slowly over time, along with the decumulation of foreign assets. The strength of the initial appreciation is clearly determined by the need to achieve a cumulated output loss, necessary to pin down inflation in spite of the permanent devaluation of the exchange rate.

Both the output loss and the exchange rate swings are caused by the relative weakness of wealth effects and by the absence of fiscal control. In contrast, under Assignment 2 both the transfer of wealth and the exchange rate swings are very limited, and convergence is certainly faster. Under Assignment 3 the excess demand initially spurs inflation and raises imports. The policy response involves a fiscal contraction and a fall in the domestic interest rate. The latter is necessary to bring about a temporary devaluation of the exchange rate and a reduction in the current account deficit. The early stages of the cycle show high output with inflation and a very moderate current account deficit, followed by a recession and wealth accumulation.

Dispensing with monetary policy altogether (Assignment 4) only marginally affects the fluctuations of inflation and output, with the desirable result of achieving almost complete exchange rate stability.

Analysis of the deviations from equilibrium of the policy instruments shows that Assignments 2 and 4 (Figures 4.9 and 4.11) are preferable to Assignments 1 and 3 respectively (Figures 4.8 and 4.10). Monetary control of the wealth target complicates the task of fiscal policy: Assignment 4 requires less fiscal intervention than Assignment 3. This is even more true when import propensities are high, because in that case the interactions between wealth accumulation and aggregate demand become stronger. For low trade elasticities the target zone rule seems preferable to Assignment 2, whereas when interdependence is high the choice between the two depends on the relative cost associated with fluctuations of the tax rate and of the terms of trade.

Table 4.4 Domestic demand shock: cumulated squared deviations from equilibrium of policy instruments (percentage values)

| | *Assignment* | | | |
	1	*2*	*3*	*4*
Low trade elasticities:				
r	11.10	7.05	0.31	–
s	–	18.32	13.6	9.8
a	2100.00	55.60	1.14	–
High trade elasticities:				
r	8.51	0.98	2.38	–
s	–	5.78	21.37	9.2
a	1960	10.10	7.36	–

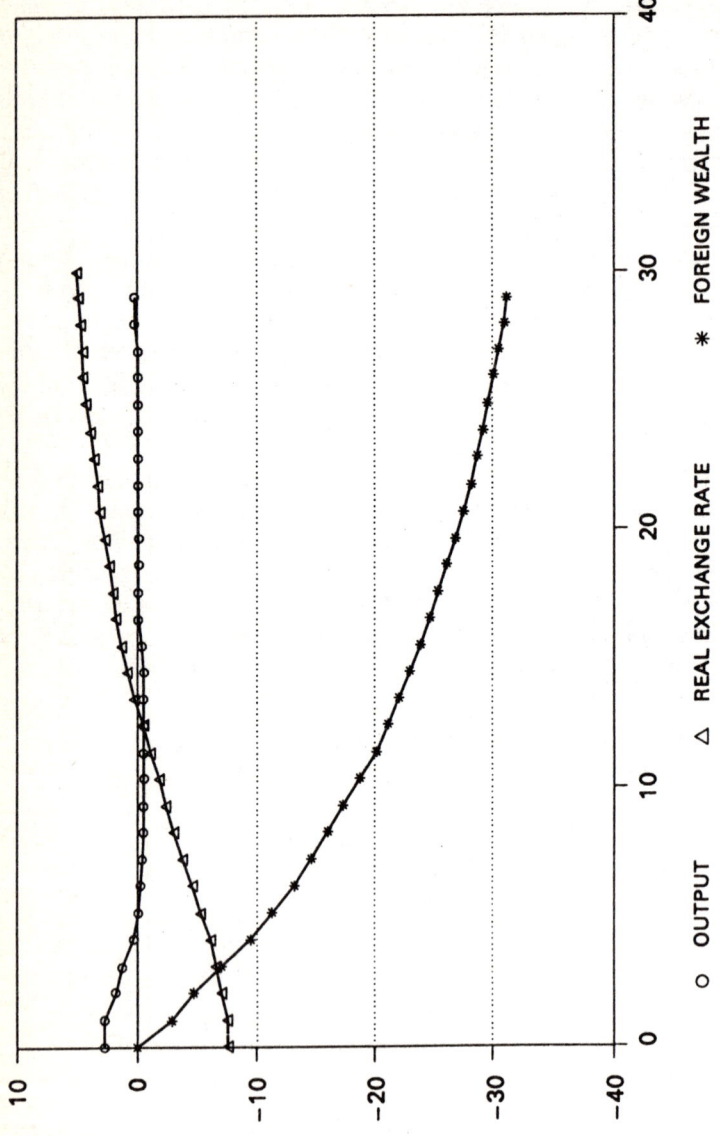

○ OUTPUT   △ REAL EXCHANGE RATE   * FOREIGN WEALTH

Figure 4.8   Domestic demand shock: assignment 1 (high interdependence) (percentage deviations from equilibrium)

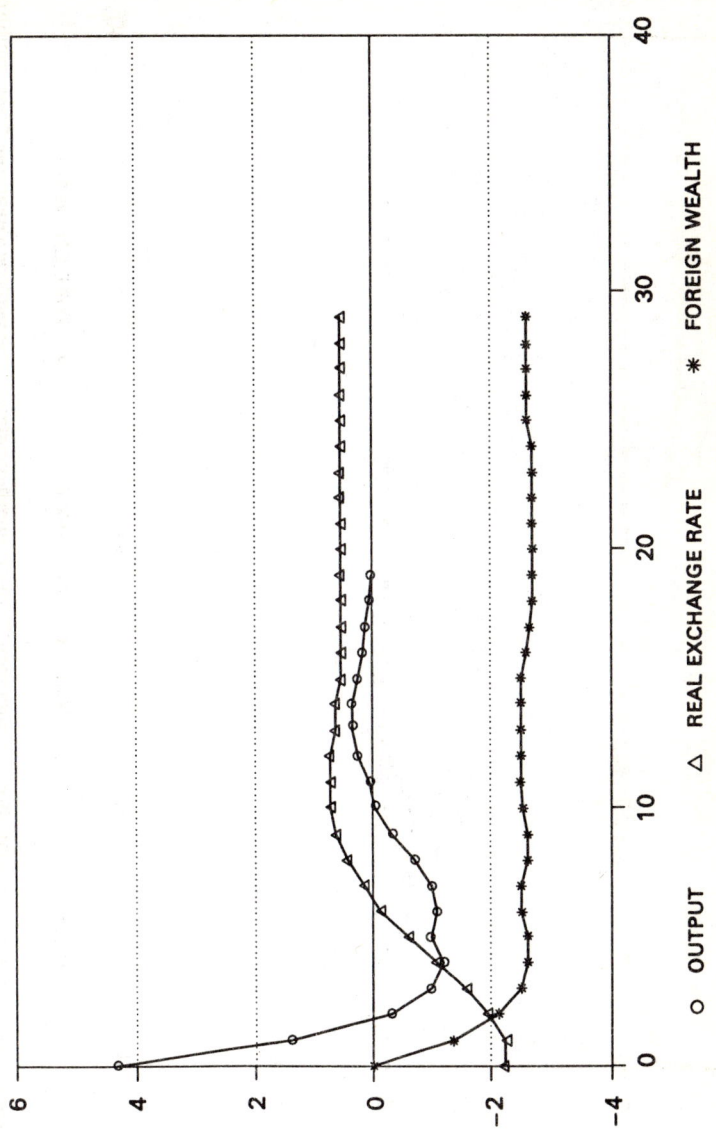

Figure 4.9   Domestic demand shock: assignment 2 (high interdependence) (percentage deviations from equilibrium)

o   OUTPUT   △   REAL EXCHANGE RATE   *   FOREIGN WEALTH

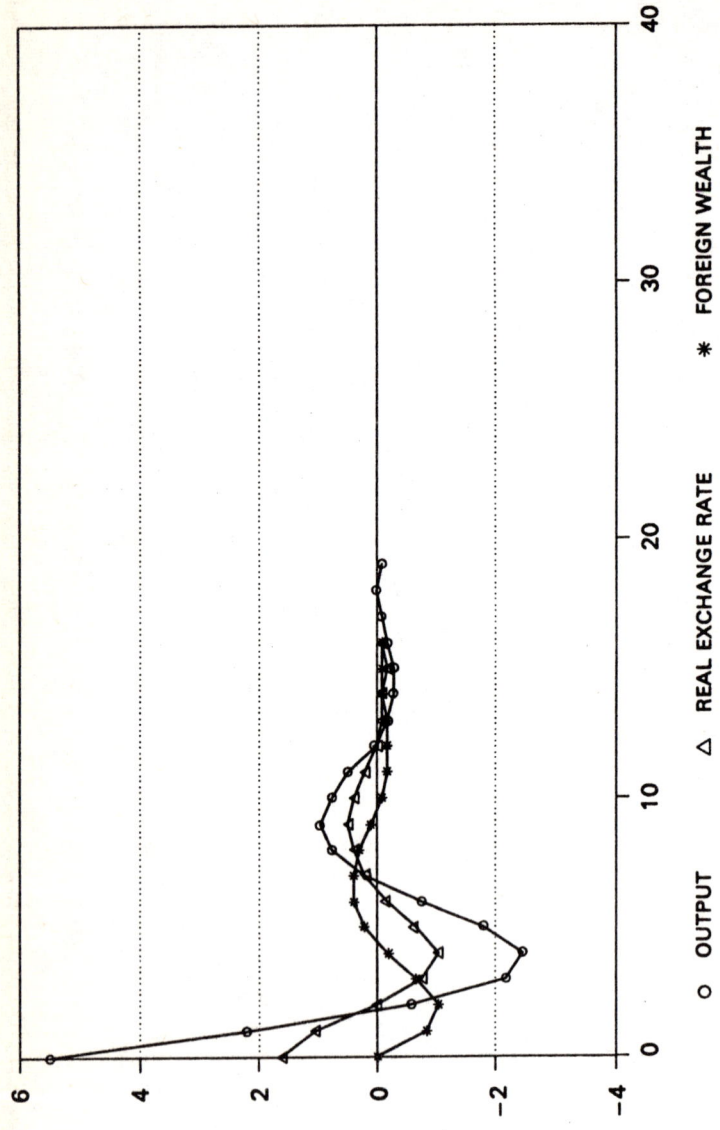

Figure 4.10 Domestic demand shock: assignment 3 (high interdependence) (percentage deviations from equilibrium)

○ OUTPUT   △ REAL EXCHANGE RATE   * FOREIGN WEALTH

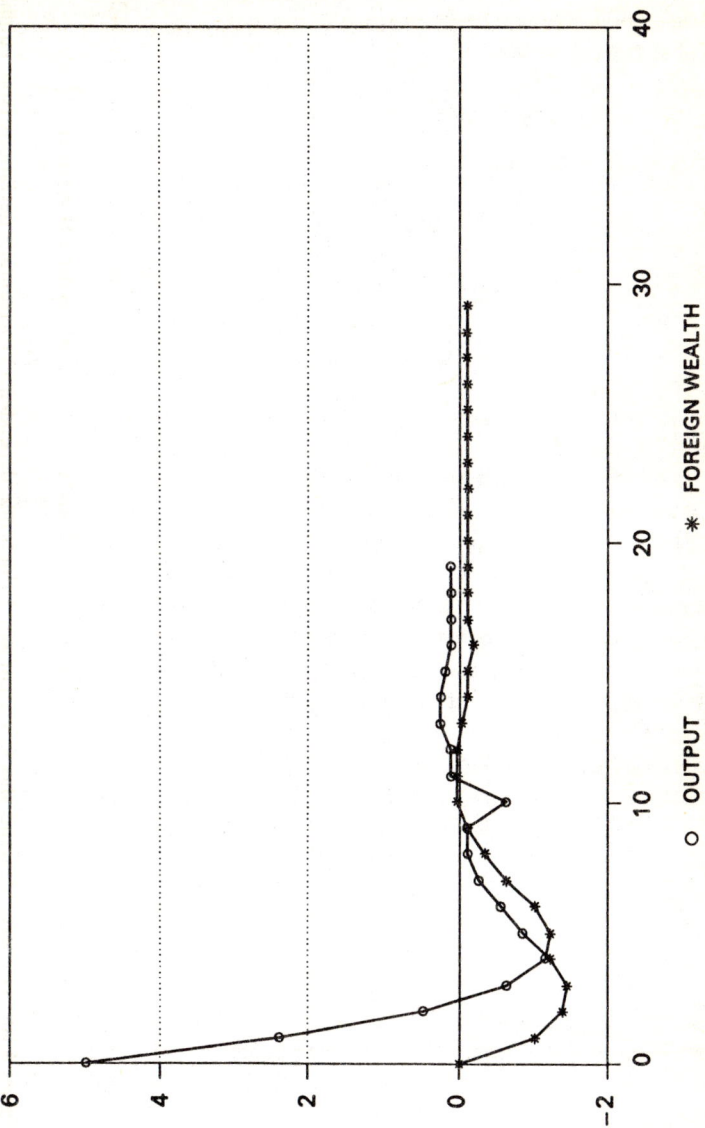

Figure 4.11 Domestic demand shock: assignment 4 (high interdependence) (percentage deviations from equilibrium)

○ OUTPUT   * FOREIGN WEALTH

4.4.3 A fall in foreign demand for domestic goods

We shall consider a permanent reduction of foreign demand for domestic goods, hence $x^* < 0$. In the simulations $x^* = -5$ per cent in terms of domestic output.

4.4.3.1 *New equilibrium values*

Under Assignments 1 and 2:

$$z_\infty = \{-(\mu/\epsilon)(\alpha r^* - \tau - \delta k_2)/[\beta_1(\tau + \delta k_2) - r^*(\beta + \tau F_0)]\}x^*$$

$$F = (-\beta_1\alpha + \beta + \tau F_0)x^*/[\beta_1(\tau + \delta k_2) - r^*(\beta + \tau F_0)]$$

$$a_\infty = (\alpha r^* - \tau - \delta k_2)x^*/[\beta_1(\tau + \delta k_2) - r^*(\beta + \tau F_0)]$$

Current account equilibrium requires permanent changes in both F and a. The exchange rate must depreciate,[37] whereas net domestic holdings of foreign wealth must increase if $F_0 > 0$ and β is big enough. Cumulated output deviations from equilibrium are negative, since the devaluation of the exchange rate necessary to equilibrate supply and demand for exports has a positive effect on core inflation, which must be compensated for by a cumulated output loss. *Once again fiscal policy limits the effect of permanent real shocks on the country's foreign investment.* The numerical simulations confirm that fiscal control of the current account can be quite effective in limiting permanent wealth transfers (Table 4.5).

Under Assignment 3:

$$z_\infty = -x^*\{(\alpha/\delta n_1\phi\epsilon) - [(\beta + F_0\tau - \delta n_1\phi\mu)/\delta n_1\phi\mu\epsilon\beta_1]\}$$

$$F = 0$$

$$a_\infty = x^*/\beta_1$$

F does not change and the exchange rate depreciation offsets the fall in foreign demand for domestic goods. Aggregate demand equilibrium requires that z be positive if the shock has a stronger impact on output than the devaluation. This is more likely if fiscal control is sufficiently strong.

Table 4.5 Simulation results: long-term effects of a fall in foreign demand for domestic exports (percentage values)

		Assignment 1			Assignment 2	
F_0	z	F	a	z	F	a
High interdependence:						
−30	−11.1	9.0	+13.1	−12.5	0.3	+14.8
−10	−12.1	3.0	+14.2	−12.5	0.1	+14.8
+10	−13.2	−3.3	+15.5	−12.5	−0.1	+14.8
+30	−14.4	−11.3	+17.0	−12.5	−0.3	+14.9
Low interdependence:						
−30	−6.2	18.0	+28.0	−8.1	+0.7	+36.0
−10	−7.1	7.1	+33.0	−8.2	+0.2	+36.0
+10	−9.0	−8.9	+41.0	−8.2	−0.2	+37.0
+30	−10.9	−27.8	+49.0	−8.3	−0.7	+37.0

Note: Percentage deviations from initial equilibrium; z and F are 'normalized' with respect to equilibrium output.

Under Assignment 4:

$$a_\infty = x^*[(r^* - \tau)^* v_1/v_2 - n_1\phi\epsilon]/\{n_1\phi\epsilon + (v_1/v_2)[\tau - r^*(\beta + \tau F_0 - n_1\phi\mu)/\beta_1]\}$$

$$F = -x^*(\tau F_0 - n_1\phi\mu)^*(v_1/v_2)/\{n_1\phi\epsilon + (v_1/v_2)[\tau - r^*(\beta + \tau F_0 - n_1\phi\mu)/\beta_1]\}$$

$$z_\infty = x^*(\tau F_0 - n_1\phi\mu)/\{n_1\phi\epsilon + (v_1/v_2)[\tau - r^*(\beta + \tau F_0 - n_1\phi\mu)/\beta_1]\}$$

The exchange rate depreciates. Cumulated deviations of output from the natural rate are negative if the wealth effect of a devaluation is dominated by the fiscal contraction required to control inflation after the devaluation. Net domestic holdings of foreign assets are a negative function of z.

4.4.3.2 Dynamics

The performance of Assignments 1 and 2 (Figures 4.12 and 4.13) is more or less similar. Initially the jump in the exchange rate undershoots its long-term value. After that, its dynamic path is monotonic. Undershooting occurs because the depreciation feeds inflation and triggers the interest rate feedback: a further depreciation is then required. Output exhibits something of a cycle, with limited swings. Persistence is somewhat reduced when fiscal policy controls the current account.

The exchange rate also undershoots under Assignment 3 (Figure 4.14), but for a different reason. The jump in the exchange rate fuels inflation, and the fiscal contraction has a positive effect on the current account, which turns into a surplus. Then the interest rate is raised and a further devaluation is necessary.

Under the target zones rule (Assignment 4, Figure 4.15) the exchange rate immediately jumps onto its equilibrium value. As under the Mundell assignment (Assignment 3) output must initially fall and foreign wealth accumulate, but in this case both effects are stronger because no exchange rate undershooting occurs.

The analysis of deviations from equilibrium of the policy instruments shows that Assignment 2 gives outcomes which are likely to be preferable to the monetarist rule and the target zones rule is preferable to the Mundell assignment. Obviously the choice between rules 2 and 4 should be made according to the government's preference between tax and exchange rate fluctuations.

Table 4.6   A negative shock to foreign domestic demand: cumulated squared deviations from equilibrium of policy instruments (percentage values)

	Assignment			
	1	*2*	*3*	*4*
Low interdependence:				
r	3.4	0.68	0.23	–
s	–	2.52	11.50	10.8
a	128.3	5.35	9.77	–
High interdependence:				
r	3.2	1.50	1.02	–
s	–	2.15	10.47	23.1
a	355.0	40.20	33.72	–

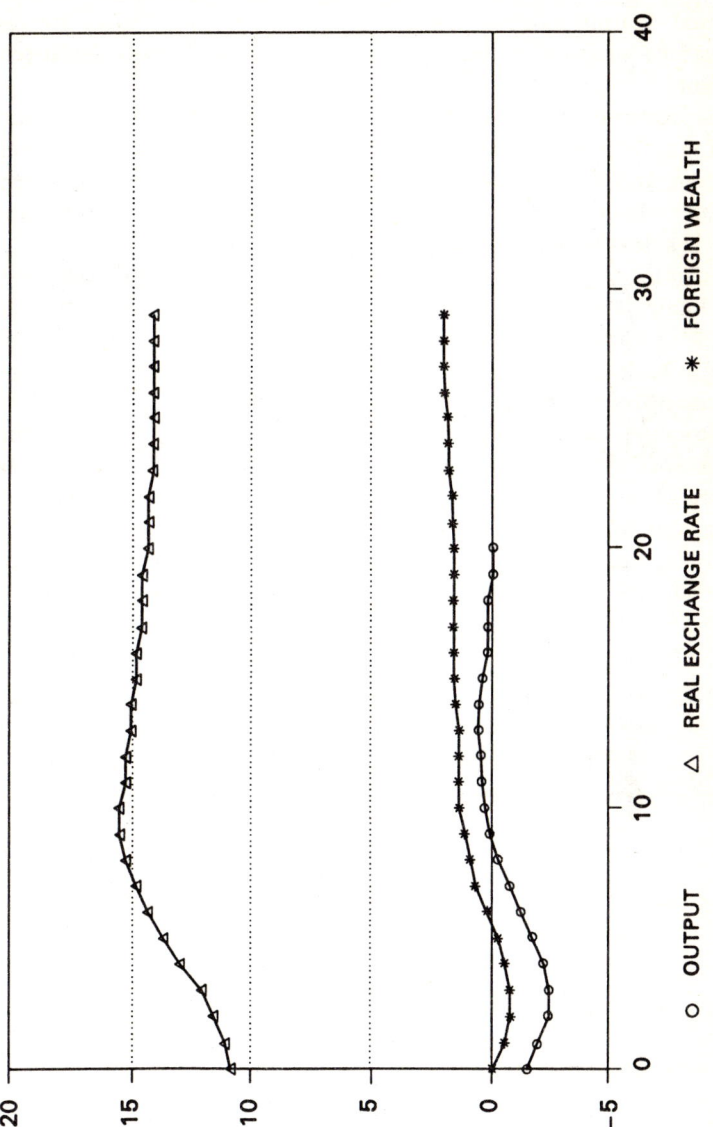

Figure 4.12 Fall in exports: assignment 1 (high interdependence) (percentage deviations from equilibrium)

o OUTPUT   △ REAL EXCHANGE RATE   * FOREIGN WEALTH

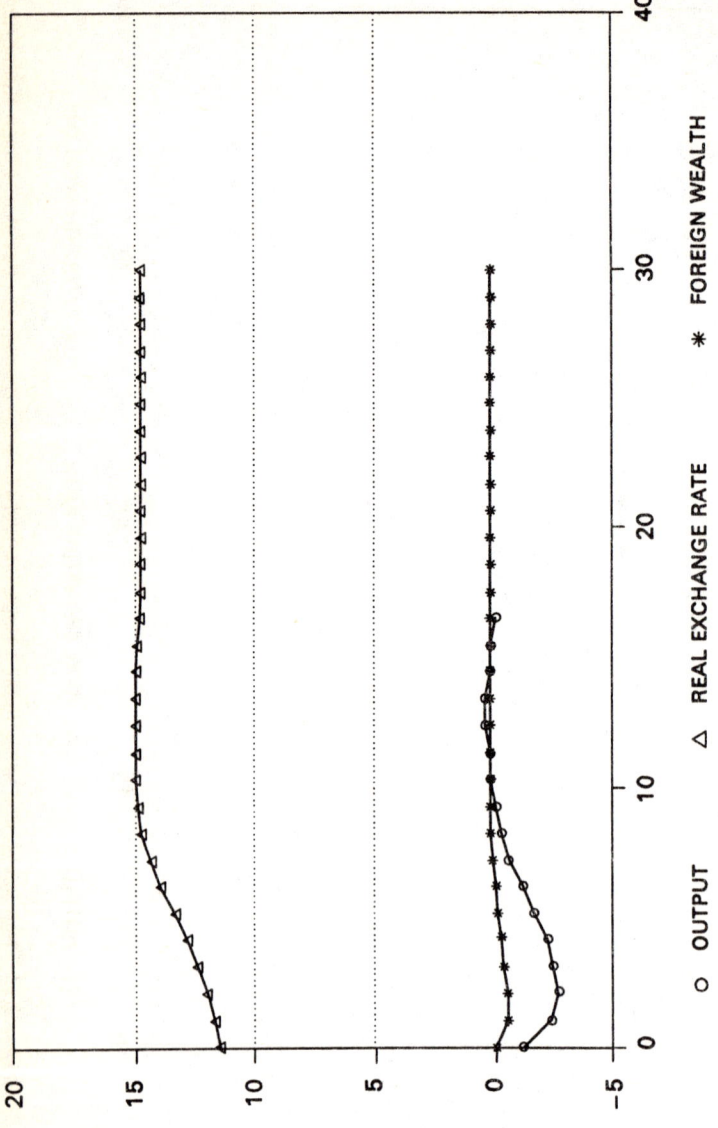

Figure 4.13   Fall in exports: assignment 2 (high interdependence) (percentage deviations from equilibrium)

○ OUTPUT   △ REAL EXCHANGE RATE   * FOREIGN WEALTH

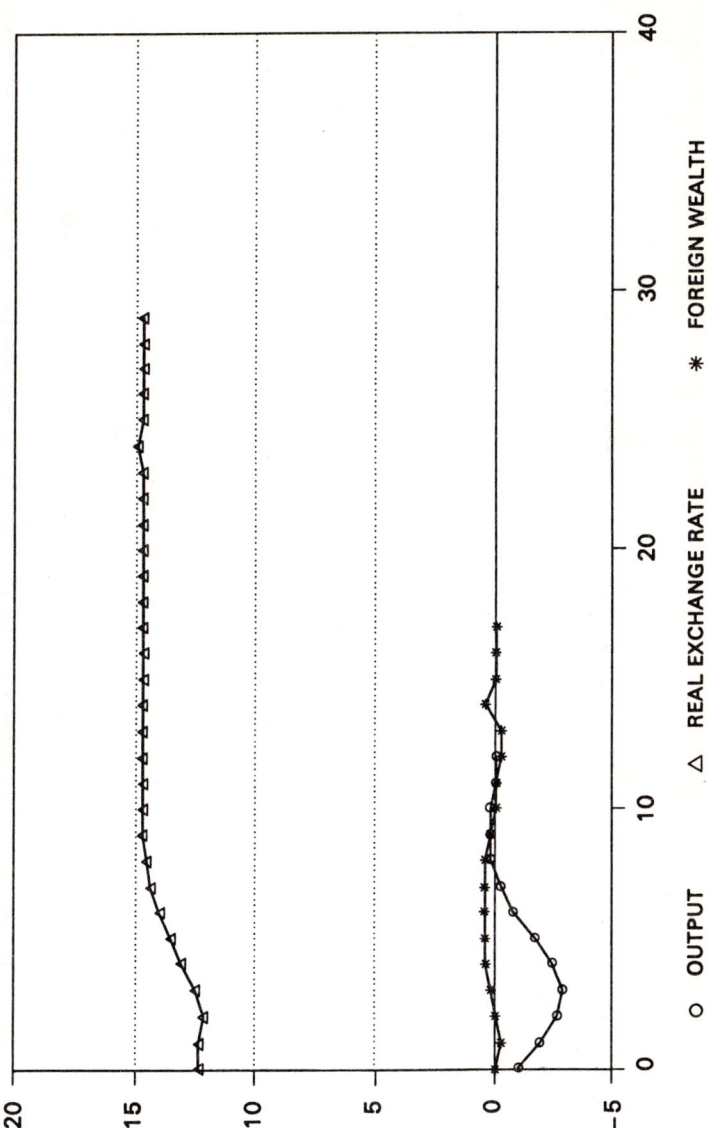

Figure 4.14 Fall in exports: assignment 3 (high interdependence) (percentage deviations from equilibrium)

○ OUTPUT   △ REAL EXCHANGE RATE   * FOREIGN WEALTH

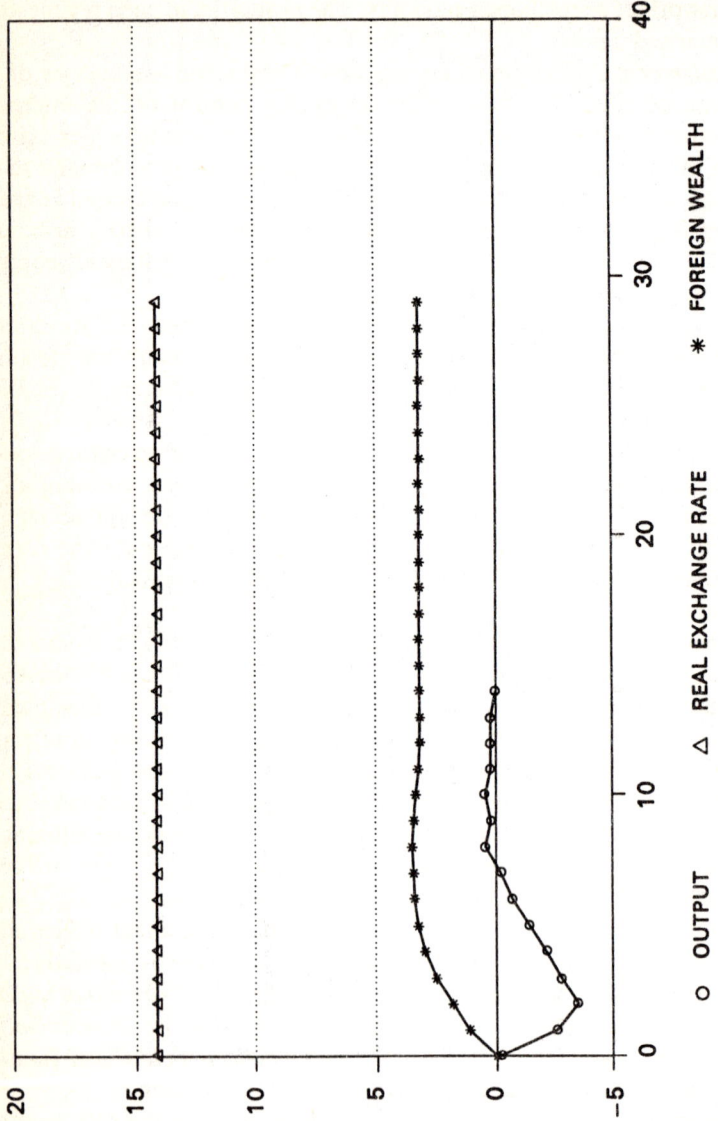

Figure 4.15 Fall in exports: assignment 4 (high interdependence) (percentage deviations from equilibrium)

4.5 CONCLUSIONS

This chapter has analysed alternative policy assignments within the framework of a small open economy. The properties of each regime are summarised below.

Assignment 1. This book stresses two fundamental weaknesses of a monetarist rule. The first is that monetary control of the internal objective does not prevent the risk of dynamic instability, which arises from the interaction between wealth effects on aggregate demand and foreign interest payments on the current account. The second is that under this rule permanent real shocks (especially domestic demand shocks) may cause uncontrolled transfers of foreign wealth and require large adjustments to the real exchange rate.

Assignment 2. By defining a foreign wealth target, the Reversed assignment avoids the risk of instability and limits wealth transfers in the face of real shocks. Furthermore, it significantly improves the overall dynamic performance of the model

Assignments 3 and 4. Under assignment 3 the exchange rate fluctuations necessary to bring down inflation are substantially reduced. If the target zones regime is enforced they do not occur at all. However, the the burden of adjustment is shifted onto the fiscal instrument, requiring a degree of fiscal flexibility which might be difficult to implement.

When real shocks occur, assigning monetary policy to the external objective does not improve on Assignment 4. Fiscal control of the domestic objective coupled with a single exchange rate adjustment seems to be quite effective. To some extent this result confirms Boughton's scepticism about the effectiveness of monetary control of the external objective: one-step changes in the exchange rate seem to be more efficient. Nevertheless the target zones proposal, the ultimate object of Boughton's criticism, still retains validity, being supported by the rather favourable results obtained under rule 4.

Under a target zones regime disinflation has permanent effects on foreign wealth and the exchange rate: this outcome is inevitable if governments wish to avoid exchange rate cycles. *But I stress that under this regime disinflation policy at home might generate international conflict, as it implies a permanent loss of financial wealth and future disposable income for the commercial partners of the country.*[38]

The inclusion of fiscal control in a policy package prevents wealth instability, no matter whether this instrument is assigned to the internal or to the external objective. Not surprisingly, combined use of two weapons substantially improves a purely monetarist rule. But the possible existence of institutional lags in the implementation of the fiscal feedback is not accounted for. This is a widespread criticism of the use of this instrument and some scholars have argued that fiscal control should be assigned to slow-moving variables. Obviously this will be more or less true according to the institutional context of each country, but should fiscal policy be actually considered a not very flexible instrument, then the desirability of proposals like the Reversed Assignment would be further enhanced.

APPENDIX I

In order to render the dynamics more plausible I have removed some simplifications whose only justification was to make the model more analytically tractable. By and large, the modifications introduced to carry out the numerical simulations[39] follow Edison, Miller and Williamson (1987). Exchange rate surprises are assumed to gradually feed on to the consumption price index (Equations 4A.1–2). The policy feedback on inflation involves both proportional and integral control of nominal income (Equations 4A.8, 4A.9, 4A.11, 4A.13) I have 'normalized' the parameters of the government reaction function, so that the anti-inflationary and the current account stabilising policies have the same impact on aggregate demand under each rule. This should facilitate the evaluation of the relative merits of each assignment. The effect of a unit deviation from equilibrium of nominal income is constrained to be:

$$\sigma k_1 = \delta n_1 = \Omega_1 = 0.8$$

Unit deviations from equilibrium of the foreign wealth target have the following impact on output:

$$|\sigma k_2| = |\delta n_2| = |\Omega_2| = 1.34$$

Only the absolute value of the impact on output of wealth control can be normalised, as under Assignment 2 a low level of wealth triggers a tax rise whereas under Assignment 3 the real interest rate is reduced.

Table 4A.1   The model

Block 1. Output and inflation:

$$dp = \epsilon y + \pi + dx \tag{4A.1}$$

$$dx = da - \epsilon 1[x - (\mu/1 - \mu)a] \tag{4A.2}$$

$$y = [\beta a + \tau(a + F) - \sigma r - \delta s + x_d + x^* \tag{4A.3}$$

$$\pi = \phi\epsilon z + \phi x + x_p \tag{4A.4}$$

$$z = \int_0^\infty y \tag{4A.5}$$

Block 2. Wealth accumulation:

$$dF = \beta_1 a - \mu y + x^*/\alpha + r^* F \tag{4A.6}$$

Block 3. Exchange rate dynamics:

$$da = r - r^* \tag{4A.7}$$

Block 4. Policy assignments:

Assignment 1: a monetarist rule

$$dr = k_1(dp + dy) + 0.5k_1(p + y) \tag{4A.8}$$

Assignment 2: reversed assignment

$$dr = k_1(dp + dy) + 0.5k_1(p + y) \tag{4A.9}$$

$$ds = -k_2 dF \tag{4A.10}$$

Assignment 3: Mundell assignment

$$ds = n_1(dp + dy) + 0.5n_1(p + y) \tag{4A.11}$$

$$dr = n_2 dF \tag{4A.12}$$

Assignment 4: target zones rule

$$ds = n_1(dp + dy) + 0.5n_1(p + y) \tag{4A.13}$$

Parameter values:

$\alpha = 1.35$; $\sigma = 1.34$; $\phi = 0.5$; $\epsilon = \epsilon_1 = 0.5$; $\tau = 0.11$; $\delta = 0.80$; $r^* = 0.05$; $k_1 = 0.595$; $k_2 = 0.0168$; $n_1 = 1$; $n_2 = 0.01$,

Low interdependence

$\beta = 0.135$; $\mu = 0.1$; $\beta_1 = 0.1$

High interdependence

$\beta = 0.4$; $\mu = 0.3$; $\beta_1 = 0.3$

APPENDIX II

The state–space form of the model under a target zones regime, when no exchange rate dynamics may occur because real interest rates are equalised across countries, is defined as follows:

$$dz = -\delta n_1 \phi \epsilon z + \tau F + (\beta + \tau F_0 - \delta n_1 \phi \mu)a \qquad (4A.14)$$
$$+ (x_d - x^*) - \delta n_1 \phi \epsilon x_p$$

$$dF = \mu \delta n_1 \phi \epsilon z + (r^* - \mu \tau)F + [\beta_1 - \mu(\beta + \tau F_0 - \delta n_1 \phi \mu)]a \qquad (4A.15)$$
$$- \mu x_d - (1 - \mu/\alpha)x^* + \mu \delta n_1 \epsilon x_p$$

The analysis of stability has shown that under this regime the characteristic equation has one unstable root and equilibrium is a saddlepoint, hence the exchange rate must be regarded as an endogenous variable. In fact, since both F and z are predetermined, dynamics may converge only if the exchange rate is initially set at a level consistent with stability. Intuitively, it should be clear that only a jump in the exchange rate may ensure current account equilibrium when permanent changes of foreign wealth occur. The following discussion will provide a more formal argument.

To find the long-term values of z, F and a it should be taken into account that, as Dixit (1980) and Blanchard and Kahn (1980) have shown,

$$a(0) - a_\infty = v_1(z_0 - z_\infty) + v_2(F_0 - F_\infty)$$

where $[-1, v_1, v_2]$ is the left eigenvector associated with the unstable root and $a(0)$ is the exchange rate level after the initial jump. Therefore overshooting of the exchange rate is a function of initial deviations of predetermined variables from equilibrium. When a target zones regime is enforced in a deterministic setting temporary deviations of the exchange rate from equilibrium cannot occur, as a result $a(0) = a_\infty$ and

$$F_\infty - F_0 = -(v_1/v_2)(z_\infty - z_0) \qquad (4A.17)$$

All dynamic variables are defined as deviations from equilibrium, therefore one may substitute for F in 4A.14 and 4A.15 from the 4A.17. At that stage, having imposed $dz = dF = 0$, finding the long-term values of a, z and F becomes straightforward. It is clear that a_∞, F_∞,

z_∞ are jointly determined. On one hand the real exchange rate must adjust to changes in F to balance the current account. On the other hand, since rational expectations force the exchange rate to jump before the dynamic adjustment begins and this jump affects both wealth accumulation and output, F_∞ and z_∞ cannot be determined independently from a_∞.

Part II

Simple Rules as a Surrogate for Policy Coordination

5 Macroeconomic Policy and Interdependence: The Debate on International Policy Coordination

INTRODUCTION

Part two deals with the issue of policy coordination. This Chapter reviews the literature on the subject and should be regarded as a general introduction to the topics to be discussed in Chapter 6.

Section 1 deals with the issue of interdependence under a flexible exchange rate regime. Section 2 is a brief review of the game–theoretic approach to policy coordination. Section 3 is a background to my own work and is concerned with alternative proposals which involve simple policy rules.

5.1 WHY IS COOPERATION NEEDED. THE RECOGNITION OF INTERDEPENDENCE

In part one it was shown that macroeconomic policies may have substantial spillover effects abroad. Under a monetarist regime changes of the monetary rule, albeit neutral in the long term, may exert prolonged effects on the real exchange rate and on the current account. This happens because, when prices in the goods sector are sticky, expectations in the financial markets cause overshooting of the exchange rate. If the domestic economy is reasonably large, this affects both international trade and the foreign rate of inflation. Secondly, unilateral fiscal policy shifts entail a permanent change in the net external position of each country and alter permanently the real exchange rate and the trade balance. The alternative policy rules we have considered still involve substantial spill-over effects. Foreign wealth targeting may ensure long term stability of the real exchange

111

rate and of trade flows, but it does not prevent swings in the exchange rate. In fact, rules which require the opening of a differential between domestic and foreign interest rates cause exchange rate dynamics and affect inflation abroad. On the other hand, the assignment of fiscal policy to inflation control may require permanent wealth transfers across countries.[1]

If countries are interdependent, decentralized policymaking may cause undesired effects abroad and generate conflict between countries. Typically, uncoordinated policies might result in mutually inconsistent exchange rates and balance of payments targets and eventually determine a generalised reduction of welfare. Advocates of international coordination suggest that governments commit themselves to altering their policies in order to achieve some common goal, for instance the reconciliation of mutually inconsistent targets, or to help each government to achieve its own objectives, on the grounds that this would be beneficial to all coordinating countries.

> The point is that by internalizing the spill-overs of individual policy actions, coordination widens the area of discretion for all participants to approach more closely their objectives.[2]

Assessing the gains from coordination has been the focus of the game–theoretic approach to the analysis of policy coordination. We now turn to a brief review of this literature.

5.2   STRATEGIC INTERDEPENDENCE AND POLICY COORDINATION

Applications of the game–theoretic approach to the issue of policy coordination have grown rapidly in number and relevance over the last few years. Both game theory and the economic theory of externalities and market failures show that decentralised decision-making can generate outcomes which are outside the set of Pareto-optimal outcomes potentially attainable through cooperative solutions. The game–theoretic approach to policy coordination investigates whether and to what extent outcomes generated by decentralised policy actions differ from the outcomes which might prevail under cooperative behaviour. We shall consider static games first.

5.2.1 Static games

In a number of seminal papers Hamada (1976, 1979) investigated the strategic interdependence between national policymakers under different exchange rate regimes. He contrasted non-cooperative outcomes, of the Nash or Stackelberg type, with those which might be achieved through cooperation. In the typical description of policy formation, the behaviour of each government is described by a reaction curve, showing how it will alter one of its policy instruments in response to a change in the policy adopted by the other country. Changes of exogenous variables, such as 'real shocks', determine the shift of the curve. Each government is assumed to maximise a utility function, typically quadratic. The game is a variable sum game, otherwise no benefit from cooperation, as opposed to decentralised policy action, would in principle arise. This is obtained by making the plausible assumption that policymakers have more targets than instruments. Hamada points out that gains from coordination do exist, as cooperation prevents governments from designing mutually inconsistent policies. For instance he shows that under a fixed exchange rate regime, if countries have one instrument, the level of domestic credit, and two targets, domestic output and the level of foreign reserves, a non-cooperative solution leads to over-contractionary policies, as both countries attempt to build up reserves by generating current account surpluses. He shows that the size of the gains from coordination crucially depends on the utility functions of the governments and on the signs of the spillover effects.

Subsequent research has focused on the outcomes occurring under a flexible exchange rate regime. Two complementary studies carried out by Canzoneri and Gray (1983) and Oudiz and Sachs (1985) show that the cooperative outcome outperforms the non-cooperative one. Once more the results depend on the signs of the spillover effects and on the preferences of the government. Canzoneri and Gray argue that if governments assign preeminence to short-term output gains, and the transmission of monetary policy is negative,[3] the Nash equilibrium is associated with over-expansionary monetary policy because each country pursues beggar-thy-neighbour policies by depreciating the exchange rate, and therefore no one can succeed. On the other hand, Oudiz and Sachs show that the Nash equilibrium is over-contractionary if governments are mainly concerned with reducing inflation in the short term and try to export inflation by appreciating the exchange rate. To clarify the issue I discuss the over-contractionary outcome under flexible exchange rates.[4] The model is defined as follows.

$$m - p = k_1 y - k_2 i \tag{5.1}$$

$$y = \beta(e + p^f - p) - \sigma i \tag{5.2}$$

$$p_c = (1 - \mu)p + \mu(e + p^f - p) \tag{5.3}$$

$$i = i^f \tag{5.4}$$

$$m^f - p^f = k_1 y^f - k_2 i^f \tag{5.5}$$

$$y^f = -\beta(e + p^f - p) - \sigma i^f \tag{5.6}$$

$$p_c^f = (1 - \mu)p^f - \mu(e + p^f - p) \tag{5.7}$$

where $m - p =$ log of real money balances; $y =$ log of real output; $e =$ log of the nominal exchange rate; $p_c =$ log of consumer price.

There are two symmetric countries. Foreign variables are denoted by the superscript f. The model is standard so it requires only a brief comment. It is composed of an *IS* curve, Equations 5.2 and 6, and an LM curve, Equations 5.1 and 5. Capital is perfectly mobile, Equation 5.4. In equations 3 and 7 we describe the deflator of domestic consumption for each country, μ being the share of imports in domestic consumption. Output prices are fixed and normalized at

$$p = p^f = p_0 > 0$$

p_0 may also be considered as an initial price shock. Exchange rate expectations are static. The model should be solved in order to determine the signs of the spillover effects.

$$y = \theta_1 m - \theta_2 m^f - (\theta_1 - \theta_2)p_0 \tag{5.8}$$

$$y^f = \theta_1 m^f - \theta_2 m - (\theta_1 - \theta_2)p_0 \tag{5.9}$$

$$e = (m - m^f)/2\beta k_1 \tag{5.10}$$

$$p_c = p_0 + \mu(m - m^f)/2\beta k_2 \tag{5.11}$$

$$p_c^f = p_0 - \mu(m - m^f)/2\beta k_2 \tag{5.12}$$

where:

$$\theta_1 = (2\sigma k_1 + k_2)/2k_1(\sigma k_1 + k_2)$$

$$\theta_2 = k_2/2k_1(\sigma k_1 + k_2)$$

Spillover effects are negative: the appreciation of the domestic real exchange rate raises output abroad. It is easy to see why this happens. The monetary contraction at home raises the domestic interest rate, but this is inconsistent with the uncovered interest parity condition (Equation 5.4). Equilibrium requires that the exchange rate appreciates, depressing output at home and raising it abroad, so that interest rates are equalised across countries.

Given the assumption that p and p^f are fixed, consumer price deflation can only be pursued by appreciating the exchange rate. From Equation 5.10 we see that deflation is achieved only if the monetary stance is more contractionary at home than abroad.

Comparison of coefficients θ_1 and θ_2 highlights another key feature of the model. When the two countries adopt the same policy stance, the negative spillovers originated by domestic policy tend to offset the impact of foreign policy on foreign output and vice versa, but since $\theta_1 > \theta_2$ the domestic impulse will dominate in each country.[5]

To analyse the implications of the game, the familiar loss function must be introduced. This is assumed to be identical for the two policymakers.

$$U = y^2 + \tau(p_c)^2 \tag{5.13}$$

$$U^f = (y^f)^2 + \tau(p_c^f)^2 \tag{5.14}$$

where τ is the importance attached to the consumer deflator relative to output.

Under a Nash equilibrium[6] each policymaker minimises the loss function by taking as given the behaviour of the other government. By differentiating Equation 5.13 the domestic government should set:

$$y(dy/dm) = -\tau p_c(dp_c/dm) \tag{5.15}$$

substituting Equations 5. 8 and 5.11 into Equation 5.15 yields the reaction function of the domestic government:

$$m = \sum_1 m^f + \sum_2 p_0 \qquad (5.16)$$

where:

$$\sum_1 = \theta_1 \theta_2 + (\tau \mu / 2\beta k_2)^2 / (\theta_1)^2 + (\tau \mu / 2\beta k_2)^2$$

$$\sum_2 = \theta_1(\theta_1 - \theta_2) - (\tau \mu / 2\beta k_2)2 / (\theta_1)^2 + (\tau \mu / 2\beta k_2)^2$$

The Nash equilibrium obtains when $m = m^f$. The implications for output and the price level are as follows. If $m = m^f$, then:

$$m = \{\theta_1(\theta_1 - \theta_2) - (\tau \mu / 2\beta k_2)/\theta_1(\theta_1 - \theta_2)\}p_0 < 0$$

$$p^c = p_c^f = p_0$$

$$y = y^f = -(\tau \mu / 2\beta k_2 \theta_1)p_0$$

The non-cooperative outcome implies a loss of output for both countries, and neither country manages to achieve a reduction of consumption prices. In fact, in the symmetric case the two countries pursue the same policy, and neither can succeed in appreciating the exchange rate.

In discussing the cooperative case it is assumed that a 'global planner' undertakes the optimisation, so as to internalise the externalities of the independent policy decisions in the optimisation process. Each country is assigned the same weight.[7] When policy-makers do not cooperate and the Nash equilibrium prevails, each government has the perception that:

$$dy/dm = \theta_1 \text{ and } dp_c/dm = (\tau \mu / 2\beta k_2)$$

whereas the true derivatives are

$$dy/dm = \theta_1 - \theta_2 \text{ and } dp_c/dm = 0$$

A deflationary policy can only be implemented by appreciating the exchange rate, but this outcome is prevented because the two countries have the same target, so p_c cannot be deflated. Thus the optimal policy involves accommodation of the initial price shock, so as to avoid output losses:[8]

$$m = m^f = p_0$$

In principle, the case for coordination might seem straightforward, but this result is open to an obvious criticism. Implementing coordinated policies would require binding rules and appropriate penalties, otherwise each country would be better off cheating on the agreement. The incentive for an individual country to free-ride on the action of others and to renege on cooperative agreements lies at the roots of the so called 'enforcement problem'[9] which has been regarded as one of the major obstacles to policy coordination due to the absence of supranational authorities capable of enforcing cooperative agreements. A way out which is common to game theory, is the design of appropriate threat strategies. Some scholars[10] have taken the view that emphasis on moral hazard problems has perhaps been excessive: in a multi-period context, the early gains from reneging on the cooperative policy must be contrasted with the future welfare losses caused by likely retaliation from partner countries.

On the other hand, Currie and Levine (1987) pointed out that the commonly-used threat of reverting to Nash non-cooperative behaviour (tit-for-tat) is not necessarily a credible deterrent, as it might amount to a threat to fully destabilise the system. As a consequence, a strong incentive might exist for each country to renege first. The results emerging from the literature are somewhat mixed. However the debate on the free-rider problem has stressed the importance of a multi-period setting for a proper assessment of the gains from and the obstacles to policy coordination. Indeed, some conclusions emerging from the literature following the static games approach must be reconsidered when economic actors, both governments and the private sector, take into account the future implications of current behaviour.

5.2.2 Dynamic games

The introduction of dynamics substantially alters the nature of the game being played, bringing two important points of realism into a static game. The first is that the pay-offs of non-cooperative, beggar-thy-neighbour policies may look very different in a multi-period game. For instance, if the initial appreciation of the exchange rate is to be followed by long-term depreciation[11] the early inflation gains will be reversed in the future, as inflation is reimported through a depreciating exchange rate.[12] To the extent that forward-looking governments realise the longer-term implications of their actions, beggar-thy-neighbour policies lose appeal and, by the same token, gains from cooperation are reduced. Second, when the governments undertaking intertemporal optimisation face a forward-looking private sector, the familiar time inconsistency problem arises. Rogoff (1985b) has argued that policy coordination can be counterproductive if it undermines the credibility of governments' commitment to control inflation. He draws on the work of Barro and Gordon (1983), which we have already reviewed in Chapter 1.

The Barro model is built on the assumption that government and wage setters have different objectives. The government is keen to reduce real wages through monetary 'surprises' in order to achieve a relatively higher output target. The wage setters have a relatively higher wage target and are then prepared to accept lower output. If the wage setters realise that the government has an incentive to 'reoptimise' and shift the policy towards a more expansionary stance, then they will try to anticipate future surprises by setting a higher wage rate from the start. Thus, an inflationary bias is regarded as inherent to the interaction between government and wage setters as long as their objectives differ and both adopt forward-looking behaviour. In the open economy, the government incentive to exploit the short-term rigidity of nominal wages is weakened by the inflationary consequences of the depreciation that would follow the monetary shock. Forward-looking wage setters realise this and lower their claims, as they perceive that the government is now less likely to alter its policy. But if countries cooperate, and cooperation takes the form of a fixed exchange rate, the inflationary bias is likely to reemerge, as wage setters perceive that governments might also agree to jointly adopt unexpected expansionary policies. As a result, inflation under cooperation might be higher than inflation under decentralised policymaking.

The logic of the argument is indeed quite simple. If an inflationary bias is inherent to the closed economy because government policies are time-inconsistent, the deflationary bias inherent to the sort of Nash equilibria prevailing in an open economy under flexible exchange rates has the desirable feature of offsetting it by reducing the government incentive to reoptimise its policies. To make this point Rogoff appeals to a standard result from game theory: in a multi-player game, cooperation between a subset of players may make matters worse for those cooperating if the remaining players adopt non-cooperative behaviour. But this result does not survive to extensions of the model: Carraro and Giavazzi (1988) show that under no circumstances will policy coordination decrease welfare in a two-economy model with three sectors for each economy, namely governments, firms and wage setters. The theoretical results on this issue may thus look somewhat inconclusive.

However, this strand of literature has the merit of stressing the importance of reputation. In fact the adoption of cooperative reputational policies may solve the Rogoff conundrum as in this case cooperation is extended from a subset of players, the two governments, to the entire set of players. In fact reputational policies may be thought of as policies where governments and the private sector cooperate, with the government acting as a leader.[13]

Currie and Levine (1987) investigate the gains from coordination with or without precommitment. They set up a two-country model with three players, the two governments and one private sector, assumed to be forward-looking. In this context policies are classified by whether they are designed cooperatively and whether policies are reputational or non-reputational. Reputational policies rely on precommitment, non-reputational policies are designed in such a way that the government has no incentive to reoptimise in the future. The results as to the relative desirability of a non-reputational coordinated policy versus a non-reputational non-coordinated policy were inconclusive, as the ranking of the two policies crucially depended on the nature of the shock. Cooperation without reputation decreased welfare in the case of aggregate supply disturbances, but was more beneficial under demand shocks. The worst performance was achieved under a non-cooperative reputational policy, which also seemed to be prone to instability. This was confirmed in a later paper[14] which assessed the empirical relevance of this issue.

Under reputational policies governments rely heavily on the effect of announcing future policy actions. To the extent that these announcements are believed, policies become effective before the governments actually move their instruments. With discounting this has the advantage of reducing the welfare loss. Under flexible exchange rates, reputational monetary policies typically exploit the exchange rate as the expected interest rate path affects the spot exchange rate. But if governments pursue the same policy without cooperating, the announcement effects tend to offset each other and the final outcome is over-deflationary or over-expansionary. Currie, Levine and Vidalis found that for some discount parameters of the welfare function the system would become unstable.

By contrast, it was discovered that cooperative reputational policies markedly improve welfare on all the alternatives, because they enable governments to exploit the benefits of reputation and to avoid the welfare losses deriving from the setting of mutually inconsistent targets.[15] Their main conclusion therefore is that benefits from coordination and reputation should be considered as mutually interdependent. Governments may exploit the benefits from reputation only if they coordinate. But substantial gains from coordination may only arise when policies are reputational.

5.3   THE CASE FOR SIMPLE COORDINATED POLICY RULES

The criticisms raised in Chapter 1 against optimal policies still apply to fully optimising policies in the domain of policy coordination. Currie, Levine and Gaines (1989) developed a methodology for exploring the issues of reputation and sustainability in the context of simple rules[16] for policy coordination. The issue is important, because we know from the above discussion that reputation is necessary to reap fully the benefits from coordination and simple rules are meant to enhance the policymakers' credibility in the eyes of a sceptical private sector. Their study[17] began by showing that simple coordinated rules,[18] which assign both monetary and fiscal policy to inflation and output targets, may involve a negligible welfare loss relative to the fully optimal policy.[19] The second step was to contrast simple coordinated rules with non-cooperative simple rules.[20] Under some circumstances at least, the simple commitment to follow the same rule turned out to be preferable. This important result strengthens the case for simple rules as a SURROGATE for the far-reaching agreements implied by fully optimal policy coordination because it implies that rules may cause a small relative loss of welfare even when governments retain a certain degree of independence in implementing the policy.

Some theoretical support would therefore seem to exist for simplicity in the design of or even as a surrogate for coordinated policies.

We now turn to a discussion of proposals which involve simple coordinated policy rules. Several simple rules for policy coordination have been put forward over the last few years. In this brief review we shall focus on three proposals:

- The McKinnon proposal for a return to a fixed exchange rate regime.
- The target zones proposal, as it has been put forward by Williamson.
- The simple rules separately advocated by the 'Cambridge Group', working with Meade,[21] by Boughton (1989), and Genberg and Swoboda (1988).

These three proposals are considered part of the same strand of literature because, despite some non-negligible differences, they share a strong emphasis on the need for current account targeting and allow for temporary fluctuations of real exchange rates.

The rules reviewed in this section should be regarded as policy coordination schemes because they are proposed with the obvious aim of internalising, for each country, the externalities of individual policy actions. As will soon become clear, the design of simple coordinated rules requires a two-step strategy. The first is concerned with the definition of targets which are not mutually inconsistent, so as to avoid the excessive global deflation or inflation which may occur under uncoordinated policies. The second step is concerned with the definition of the rules which should enable each country to achieve its own targets. The proposals we are going to consider differ because their proponents do not share the same view about the working of an economic system,[22] or apparently imply a different judgement about what causes negative externalities,[23] or attach a different cost to the use of the same policy instrument.[24]

5.3.1 The McKinnon proposal

McKinnon has long advocated returning to a system of fixed exchange rates, which he regards as the necessary condition for ensuring the survival of a free trade regime. He points to the working of the international monetary system during the late 19th century as an example for a reform of the international monetary system and for international policy coordination.[25] In his view that regime worked reasonably well because countries pursued coordinated policies in defence of international gold parities.[26] Without actually returning to a gold standard, McKinnon advocates the sort of monetary cooperation needed to ensure fixed nominal parities and roughly the same rate of inflation across countries. Following Dornbusch (1988), his view may be summarised in a few key propositions:

- The doctrine which predicts that variations of exchange rates may achieve current account equilibrium is a false one: gains in competitiveness trigger an increase in domestic real expenditure which offsets the initial improvement of the current account. As an alternative, McKinnon recommends sound fiscal policies as a means of ensuring current account equilibrium.
- The purchasing power parity theory is a good guide to equilibrium exchange rates. This approach involves the identification of the level of nominal exchange rates that would equalise the price levels of internationally tradable goods across countries during a period of substantial equilibrium of trade flows.[27]
- Currency substitution shocks are the key determinant of exchange rate instability.

Therefore nominal parities should be fixed according to purchasing power parity and the aggregate monetary base of the three main industrial countries should be managed so as to ensure price stability in the world economy. Each country should thus follow a domestic credit target and stabilise the exchange rate by means of symmetric, unsterilised intervention. The mechanism which would ensure the convergence of national inflation rates would rely on the favourable effect of the fixed exchange rate regime on inflation expectations[28] and on the impact on trade and employment of the temporary appreciation in the terms of trade. In fact, nominal exchange rates being fixed, inflation differentials will change real exchange rates in ways which shift demand away from high inflation countries and eventually ensure the convergence of inflation rates.

5.3.1.1 *Criticisms of the McKinnon proposal*

The first criticism is concerned with McKinnon's belief that variations in the real exchange rate cannot achieve current account equilibrium. Meade's general equilibrium analysis has shown that the correct policy mix for balancing a current account deficit involves a combination of depreciated real exchange rates and a cut in domestic absorption.[29] The analysis in previous chapters has confirmed that devaluation is effective in bringing the net external position of a country into equilibrium, as long as it does not excessively stimulate domestic inflation.

The second criticism is concerned with the reliance on the purchasing power parity. Current account models of the exchange rate that follow the seminal work of Branson, which has already been discussed at some length, show that macroeconomic equilibrium may prevail at different levels of the real exchange rate. According to this approach, the real exchange rate ensures current account equilibrium for given output levels and a given net external position. An increase in net domestic holdings of foreign assets raises domestic demand for goods relative to foreign demand and this causes an appreciation in the terms of trade. Furthermore, exchange rate flexibility may be needed to accommodate the inflation differential which stems from divergent rates of growth in productivity.[30] Another important objection to the McKinnon approach is that if tradables in the industrial economies are imperfect substitutes it makes very little sense to look for exchange rates that ensure purchasing power parity.

Last but not least comes scepticism about the presumption that currency substitution is the main source of interest rate instability. In line with Poole's (1970) celebrated analysis, I would argue that exchange rate pegging might be heavily sub-optimal if real disturbances arise. For example, if an inflationary shock occurs which is not due to an inopportune expansion of the money supply, an accommodative policy allowing for a higher price level without causing permanently higher inflation might be desirable. But this shock would put a strong deflationary pressure on the trade sector under a fixed exchange rate regime.[31] Indeed some degree of managed exchange rate flexibility might be helpful in limiting the negative effects of adverse real shocks on output and inflation.

5.3.2 The target zones proposal

Williamson points out two reasons for dissatisfaction with a regime of unmanaged float. The first is that it allows too much volatility in the exchange rate, due to the inherent instability of the international financial markets. The second is that it does not place enough pressure on countries to coordinate their economic policies. On the other hand Williamson, unlike McKinnon, does not advocate a return to a fixed exchange rate regime. In fact he believes that a flexible, but not unmanaged, exchange rate performs a desirable function in allowing the reconciliation of differential inflation rates. Even more important in his view is the possibility – which a flexible exchange rate does guarantee – of easily adjusting the terms of trade when this is necessary to obtain current account equilibrium. Another reason for advocating flexibility of the exchange rate is that it allows a moderate degree of temporarily anticyclical policies whenever the economic conditions of each individual country should require them. Finally Williamson sees a role for a flexible exchange rate in temporarily accommodating speculative pressures which would be too costly to offset through exchange rate intervention. He believes that announcing the exchange rate target and making known the commitment of governments to cooperate in achieving it would reduce uncertainty about the formation of expectations and about the short-term volatility of exchange rates. In his own words:

> The target zones proposal envisages a limited number of the major countries negotiating a set of mutually consistent targets for their exchange rates . . . . The aim would be to set exchange rate targets at fundamental equilibrium exchange rates, that is, at the real values that on average in the medium term are expected to reconcile the internal and external balance . . . . The participating countries would be expected to conduct their macroeconomic policies with a view to . . . preventing their [real] exchange rates going outside a broad zone of $\pm 10\%$ around the target.[32]

As it is defined above, the target zones proposal leaves many questions unanswered. One of its obvious weaknesses is the absence of a nominal anchor for domestic anti-inflationary policies. This criticism arises because, given the commitment of monetary policy to protecting both the target zone and the flexibility of the nominal exchange rate, some other policy instrument is needed to achieve the domestic target. Williamson accepts such criticism and does not underestimate the importance of policy coordination in guaranteeing the sustainability of a target zones regime. As a guideline for implementing a coordinated policy he has put forward the following three propositions.

- The average level of world interest rates should be assigned to control aggregate nominal income
- Interest rates differentials should aim at limiting currency deviations from their targets.
- National fiscal policies should be designed with the aim of achieving nominal income targets.

This version of the target zones proposal has been modified by Williamson and Miller (1987), who suggest that fiscal policy in each country should be assigned to domestic demand rather than nominal income.

Boughton (1989) has strongly criticised the proposal. He points out that under a flexible exchange rate, fiscal policy has a comparative advantage over the monetary instrument in controlling the current account, because any attempt to improve the current account by depreciating the exchange rate would cause an increase in domestic demand and suck in more imports, whereas the effect of a fiscal contraction would be unambiguously positive. On the other hand monetary policy would seem to be more effective in controlling the domestic target because a fiscal policy shift would push the interest rate in the same direction so that the necessary exchange rate variation might in principle offset the fiscal stimulus.[33] In our view Boughton's criticism might be correct for the conducting of policy in the short term. In fact it should not be necessary to rely on monetary policy to determine the equilibrium target. As we shall see in Chapter 6, Edison, Miller and Williamson (1987) have shown with the aid of a small two-country model that control of domestic targets might be achieved by assigning fiscal policy to the domestic target, leaving monetary policy with the task of equalising interest rates across countries as long as destabilising speculative attacks on the exchange rate do not occur. To the extent that this policy involved only temporary current account fluctuations and no permanent international redistribution of wealth, that is, no revision of the fundamental exchange rate would be necessary, Williamson would not advocate monetary control of the current account.

A [current account] deficit of one year that is offset by a surplus one year or two later has no enduring effects on consumption, investment, inflation or any other variable of welfare significance. On the contrary, short-term variations in the current account provide a valuable shock absorber: it is only when they cumulate over the medium term that one needs to be troubled with the sustainability and optimality of borrowing from or lending to the rest of the world.[34]

The most obvious weakness of Williamson's proposal is a potentially excessive reliance on fiscal policy, a rather inflexible instrument which governments seem to find more difficult to adapt to changes in the economic climate than is the case with monetary policy. As Williamson himself has stressed,[35] coordination of national fiscal policies has so far met with failure. This is not to say that fiscal policy should not play a role in a policy mix aiming at macroeconomic stabilisation. Indeed, this book stresses the importance of fiscal policy in stabilising an open economy, but its use should be geared toward targets which may be regarded as a source of concern in the longer term. It is to these proposals that we now turn.

5.3.3 Alternative proposals involving fiscal control of the current account

In this section we consider the so-called 'IMF view',[36] also known as the reversed assignment, and a proposal outlined by Weale et al. (1989). To some extent these two proposals may look similar, but some important differences will emerge during this review.

The IMF view has been articulated by Genberg and Swoboda (1988) and Boughton (1989). Both share the belief that

> as a general rule, expenditure changing policies have the most direct and quantitatively strong influence on the current account. Expenditure-switching policies, in contrast, affect the exchange rate significantly but have only a limited impact on the current account . . . fiscal policy has a comparative advantage over monetary policy as an instrument for current account adjustment as opposed to domestic aggregate demand stabilisation.[37]

Genberg and Swoboda are mainly concerned with the correction of current account imbalances. Their framework is closely related to the monetary approach under the assumption of rational expectations. They implicitly assume that the correct policy mix may be sufficient to achieve a balance in the current account, and neglect the dangers of real exchange rate misalignments. Within this framework they argue in favour of the assignment of fiscal policy to current account control on the ground of the comparative advantage that this instrument supposedly has over monetary policy. As far as policy coordination is concerned, their main prescription is that governments should implement sound fiscal policies, apparently because they are convinced that unsound ones are the fundamental source of negative externalities. In fact they argue that, if national fiscal policies follow diverging paths and this has undesirable consequences for the global economy as well as for each individual economy, the best remedy is to redress such policies instead of pursuing exchange rate adjustments by means of a monetary policy. One is therefore left to suppose that Genberg and Swoboda regard the attainment of each country's internal target as a matter best tackled under decentralised policy action.

Boughton is concerned with a more general blueprint for macroeconomic stabilisation. In his view the main source of governmental concern for a balanced current account rests on the intergenerational transfer of disposable income that current account imbalances imply. He also emphasises the fact that the impact of monetary policy on the current account balance is ambiguous, and he advocates fiscal control of the external target. As a consequence, he argues that governments should agree about desired current account targets, which should not necessarily be zero, and assign domestic fiscal policies to this objective. Given this assignment, and given that monetary policy has little or no impact on the current account, Boughton argues that each country should independently pursue its own internal target by means of monetary control. This would obviously imply that swings in the exchange rate would become tolerable since in the medium term they would not be associated with excessive external imbalances:

> the international coordination of monetary policy is neither necessary nor sufficient for attaining the targets, fiscal policy coordination, however, is necessary and, if monetary policy is aimed correctly at internal balance, sufficient as well.[38]

One difficulty with this proposal is that, while advocating a reasonable solution to the control of trade imbalances, it would leave room for conflict arising from the international transmission of inflation (or deflation) through the exchange rate. Under this regime nothing would prevent the world economy from being locked into sub-optimal Nash equilibria of the kind discussed in Hamada. A second difficulty is that changes in the real exchange rate level lead to reallocation of resources between tradables and non-tradables, and this has important implications too, as excessive appreciation might fuel calls for protectionism, one of the evils that coordination should particularly avoid. Finally, as Vines (1989) pointed out, there is nothing in Boughton's proposal which is aimed at reducing undesirable volatility in the exchange rate.[39]

The 'Cambridge group'[40] is not directly concerned with the issue of policy coordination as its members focus on macroeconomic policy design in a single country. Nevertheless their approach is of interest here as it is relevant in defining targets. They point at a wealth target as an important element in policy design. This has already been discussed at some length in Chapter 1, but it is interesting to note that they stress the importance of allowing deficits in the current account so as to enable a country to achieve its overall wealth target. For example, it might be acceptable for a country to run a current account deficit as long as this led to a build-up of its productive capital, which would generate income to service the current deficit.[41]

One major caveat is that wealth targets should be coordinated as long as they imply an international redistribution of wealth. In the context of this book, where output is assumed to be constant and no capital accumulation takes place, setting a wealth target is tantamount to setting a foreign wealth target. Also, given that output is constant in the long term, a foreign wealth target would necessarily imply a long-term real exchange rate target.

Thus, the proposal of the 'Cambridge Group' has substantially different implications than the 'IMF view' because neither Genberg and Swoboda nor Boughton are very concerned with this aspect; they stress the importance of avoiding excessive current account imbalances, whatever the level of the exchange rate. Meade and his associates recommend the combined assignment of fiscal and monetary policies to both the domestic and external targets, although they recognise that fiscal policy has a comparative advantage over monetary policy in controlling the current account. This might imply that, for each assignment, the relative strength in using a particular instrument should depend on the comparative advantage of the instrument itself. In Chapter 6 we shall assess the performance of the following simplified version of this proposal using 'decoupled' control rules:

- Coordinated use of monetary policy, so as to enable each country to achieve its domestic target. At the world level monetary policy is assigned to a global nominal income target, as in the Williamson proposal. Real interest rate differentials are assigned to nominal income differentials. This combined strategy ensures that countries do not pursue independent policies which might turn out to be excessively inflationary or deflationary.
- Differentials in the stance of national fiscal policies control an internationally agreed wealth target. Countries whose current net external position is above target are required to expand, whereas countries whose current level of foreign wealth is below target are required to contract.

There could be objections that under this assignment the level of the exchange rate would be left to 'market forces' and that this might leave room for foreign exchange instability. But the announcement of a long-term target for both wealth and the real exchange rate might provide an anchor to prevent the exchange rate from drifting away. Furthermore, coordinated intervention and a limited degree of flexibility of the monetary instrument[42] might significantly reduce the danger from destabilising speculation.

5.3.4 Empirical evidence

Empirical evidence on the relative performance of the alternative proposals is still scant. A recent study by Taylor (1988) stresses the negative consequences of a regime of fixed exchange rates and provides some indirect support for the IMF view. Taylor provides a seven-country model where expectations drive the exchange rate and influence the labour market, as in Taylor's model of sticky wages (1979), long-term output is set at the natural rate and fiscal policy is exogenous. Taylor argues that under a wide set of disturbances, independent interest rate policies which aim at controlling a domestic target, be this a price level or a nominal income target, perform better than a fixed exchange rate regime where monetary policy is aimed at maintaining nominal parities. Under this second rule, interest rates in all countries move simultaneously as average inflation rises above target, and the real exchange rate fluctuations, which are determined by inflation differences, avoid a persistent divergence from the national rates of inflation.

The reason why a decentralised monetary policy performs better can be outlined easily. Suppose that in one country inflation unexpectedly rises. Under a fixed exchange rate regime the domestic interest rate is raised only when and to the same extent that world inflation rises. The policy feedback is therefore slow and weak in the domestic country and unnecessarily affects the foreign economies. The real exchange rate swing caused by the inflation differential has a delayed effect on the individual economies, due to the J-curve effect. As a consequence, deflationary feedback in the domestic economy operates too late. At the same time foreign economies face unnecessary deflation in the initial phase of the cycle. Real exchange rate fluctuations are higher under the flexible exchange rate regime, but fluctuations in the flow of trade are not. This is very much in line with Boughton's argument that monetary policy has negligible effects on the current account, although it does influence profitability in the traded goods sector.

Taylor's study seems open to a significant criticism: it does not account for the wealth redistribution which takes place through current account imbalances.[43] In fact this effect might prove to be quite important. In Chapter 6 we shall simulate a small theoretical model which is analytically very similar to Taylor's, as both are derived from Carlozzi and Taylor (1985). It will be shown that the decentralised monetary policy advocated by Taylor may cause huge swings in the current account and even overall instability.

Frenkel, Masson and Goldstein (1988) provide a model where exchange rate expectations correctly anticipate the policy stance. They first try to assess whether decentralised policy action without sharp shifts would improve the macroeconomic performance. To do this they simply smooth, over time, the paths of policy variables.[44] The outcome is that the smoothness of the targets would actually increase. They argue that this should not come as a surprise, as actual policies were indeed not exogenous during the simulation period but responded to such exogenous shocks as the oil price rise, therefore smoothing was already embedded in the historical data. They find that the target zones proposal is effective in limiting current account imbalances as fiscal policy stabilises domestic targets, but at the cost of large budget deficits. By contrast, the exchange rate paths are smoothed only to a limited extent, and this at the cost of strong swings in the interest rate. But this result might be due to an unconvincing feature of their simulation approach: they assume that future shocks are correctly anticipated, as is the policy feedback. Perhaps their results would have been markedly different if it had been assumed that foreign exchange markets would anticipate the state's contingent policy response but not the shock.

Another criticism comes from Williamson, who has pointed out that, despite the introduction of rational expectations, the model fails to account for the beneficial role of exchange rate targeting on 'bubbles' and 'fads', despite the fact that this is one of the main goals of the target zones proposal. Furthermore, they do not discuss the evolution of the global economy, but there are theoretical reasons to believe that the coordinated world monetary policy advocated by Williamson is likely to improve the actual path of a global economy which is determined by non-cooperative policy decisions. Also it is not entirely clear how the monetary policy rule was applied. They state that uncovered interest parity holds among the industrialised countries, but that a fiscal expansion appreciates the exchange rate.[45] It is only at this stage that monetary policy is activated to keep the exchange rate close to the target. But this is not the kind of policy that advocates of the target zone proposal have suggested. In fact, Edison, Miller and Williamson (1987) provide a small theoretical model where uncovered interest parity holds and real interest rates are equalised across countries in the face of changes in the fiscal policy stance, so that no exchange rate dynamics occur in the absence of fads.[46] One would expect this result to be replicated in the simulations carried out by Frenkel, Masson and Goldstein.

Currie and Wren-Lewis (1989) investigate two alternative rules, the target zones proposal and the Boughton or reversed assignment, by simulating the GEM econometric model for the seven major countries. They define a welfare function which includes output, inflation, fiscal policy and the exchange rate. They then optimise the values of the parameters to be included in the feedback rules. One major criticism of this procedure is that it selects the strength of the policy control under the assumption that shocks are known.[47] This is likely to introduce a bias in favour of simulations under the feedback policies relative to the historical paths, but should not affect the comparison between alternative assignments. The target zones rule turned out to perform better than the Boughton assignment.

One major difficulty with the latter assignment was that the exchange rate changes induced by monetary control of the domestic target affected the current account with considerable delay, due to the J-curve effect. As a result, the delayed response by the fiscal policy to swings in the exchange rate influenced the domestic target in a way that complicated the task of the monetary policy and introduced greater overall variability of the targets. It could be argued that if the lagged fiscal feedback had been calibrated more carefully to account for the J-curve effect, the Boughton assignment might have performed significantly better.[48] Currie and Wren-Lewis point out that the preferable outcome associated with the target zones proposal depends crucially on the arguments of the welfare function, which includes the exchange rate but does not consider the current account. When the current account is part of the welfare function the Boughton assignment performs better, at least for a few countries.

Williamson's counterargument is that in principle there are no strong reasons for assigning a welfare cost to swings in the current account, as long as they are temporary,[49] because they will be easily accommodated by the financial markets. But the trouble with the Currie and

Wren-Lewis experiment is that their econometric model does not account for wealth effects, so it is not possible to find out whether the target zones proposal is able to prevent undesired wealth transfers across countries. If target zones implied this outcome,[50] at least under a certain range of shocks, then favour might shift to the Boughton rule, which is designed to prevent wealth redistribution. This issue will be investigated in Chapter 6.

5.4　CONCLUSIONS

This chapter has discussed several issues which have emerged from the debate on policy coordination. In the context of a growing interdependence it may be advantageous for governments to pursue their goals cooperatively instead of acting independently, as decentralised policy action may yield outcomes which lay outside the set of Pareto-efficient outcomes. The game–theoretic approach stresses the potential gains from coordination, but also emphasises the importance of reputation if cooperation is to actually improve welfare.

Time-inconsistent coordinated optimal policies without precommitment are likely to be counterproductive where the private sector is forward-looking. This conclusion has given support to advocates of simple policy rules which are easily understood and monitored. Several proposals have been put forward over the last few years. To some extent, an empirical evaluation of the performance of these rules has already been carried out, with the aid of large econometric models. This pragmatic approach may be illuminating, but often it falls short of pinpointing the theoretical determinants of the behaviour of the economy and of the reasons why one proposal should be preferred to another.

Furthermore, wealth effects are often neglected, despite their importance in determining long-term equilibria, both in large econometric models and in the simpler models which aim to provide an analytical discussion of the issue. In Chapter 6 we will construct a small theoretical model where wealth is transferred internationally via the balance of payments. Within this framework the performance of alternative simple rules for policy coordination will then be assessed.

6 Simple Rules for Policy Coordination: An Evaluation of Alternative Assignments

INTRODUCTION

In this chapter we evaluate the performance of some simple rules which have emerged from the debate on policy coordination, focusing on two alternatives already considered in Chapter 4: the target zones proposal and the reversed assignment. At this stage we carry out our policy experiments within the framework of a two-country model which explicitly accounts for interdependence between economies.

Edison, Miller and Williamson (1987, henceforth EMW) have examined the target zones proposal by using a small theoretical model of this kind. In their study, monetary policy in each country is assigned to the real exchange rate target, and coordinated fiscal policy is assigned to reducing the inflation differential between countries. However, their work suffers from a serious shortcoming: although they claim that the exchange rate target should be set with the aim of achieving current account equilibrium, no account is in fact given in their model of the way in which the current account would evolve as a consequence of the policies they advocate. In this chapter we shall study that question and show that such current account behaviour may have potentially worrying implications for their scheme. This will be done by analysing an extended version of the EMW model, by explicitly modelling the current account and introducing wealth effects in aggregate demand, as was done in earlier chapters. The results obtained in Chapter 4, Section 4.1, will be broadly confirmed.

Consideration will then be given to another problematic aspect of the target zones proposal which has so far received scant attention. According to EMW, the policies for the control of world and national targets should be regarded as more or less independent. In fact this may no longer be possible when the behaviour of the current account is brought into the picture. Let us consider their proposal once more. They assign *monetary policy* to the control of *average world inflation*, prescribing that average world interest rates should be raised if global inflation rises above target. This rule has implications for the reduction of national imbalances which have probably been underestimated. It is well known that fluctuating interest rates redistribute wealth among debtor and creditor countries and may cause current account disequilibrium. The EMW global anti-inflation policy would do just this and would, I argue, probably make the task of reducing national divergences more complicated, if foreign investment were to be considered a source of active concern for national governments (Louvre agreement,1987).

As an alternative to the target zones proposal we shall consider the reversed assignment, which sets a different rule for the control of national imbalances. In this scheme *interest rate differentials* are assigned to *inflation divergences* and *coordinated fiscal stances* are assigned to control an *agreed international distribution* of *financial wealth*. Within this second framework countries with a *surplus* should carry out a *fiscal expansion* whereas countries running a *deficit* should carry out a *fiscal contraction*.

The rest of the chapter is laid out as follows. Section 1 provides the technical details of the model. Sections 2, 3 and 4 present the results obtained from the alternative assignments.

6.1 THE MODEL

The model's structure and parameter values correspond to those of EMW, who follow Carlozzi and Taylor (1985), except for wealth effects on aggregate demand and the current account. As a matter of fact this is a straightforward extension, in a two-country setting, of the model set out in Chapter 4, Appendix I.

It is assumed that the world economy is composed of two national units, the home and the foreign economy, which are identical in size and structure (Table 6.1). Since the two economies are isomorphic, it becomes possible and analytically convenient to split the model into two blocks (Aoki, 1981), referred to as 'world averages' and 'national differences'.

$$x_a = (x_h + x_f)/2; \quad x_d = x_h - x_f$$

where the subscripts h, f, a, d, relate variable x respectively to the home economy, the foreign economy, the world averages and the national differences. This split highlights the two conceptual tasks of international policy coordination: (a) definition of targets for the world economy; and (b) control of national imbalances, whose transmission across countries occurs through the exchange rate and the current account.

Furthermore, the definition of world averages and national differences may simplify the analysis by making it possible to solve the two blocks independently. However, this can happen only up to a certain stage of the model – not for the full model.

Table 6.1   The model

The home economy:

$$y_h = -\mu r_h - s_h + \pi y_f + \delta c + \theta(cF_0 + F)$$

$$dp_h = \Phi y_h + z_h + dx_h$$

$$z_h = \epsilon(dp_h - z_h)$$

$$dx_h = \sum E(dc) + \beta(\sum c - x_h)$$

The foreign economy:

$$y_f = -\mu r_f - s_f + \pi y_h - \delta c - \theta F$$

$$dp_f = \Phi y_f + z_f + dx_f$$

$$dz_f = \epsilon(dp_f - z_f)$$

$$dx_f = -\sum E(dc) + \beta(-\sum c - x_f)$$

Exchange rate and wealth dynamics:

$$E(dc) = dc$$

$$E(dc) = r_h - r_f$$

$$dF = T + r^*F + F_0 r_f$$

$$T = 2\tau_1 c - \tau_2(y_h - y_f)$$

Table 6.2   The model split into two blocks

World averages:

$$y_a = -\mu r_a - s_a + \pi y_a + 0.5\theta c \tag{6.1a}$$

$$dp_a = \Phi y_a + z_a \tag{6.2a}$$

$$dz_a = \epsilon(dp_a - z_a) \tag{6.3a}$$

World differences:

$$y_d = -\mu r_d - s_d - \pi y_d + 2\delta c + \theta(cF_0 + 2F) \tag{6.1b}$$

$$dp_d = \Phi y_d + z_d + dx_d \tag{6.2b}$$

$$dz_d = \epsilon(dp_d - z_d) \tag{6.3b}$$

$$dx = 2\sum E(dc) + \beta(2\sum c - x) \tag{6.4}$$

$$E(dc) = r_d \tag{6.5}$$

$$E(dc) = (dc) \tag{6.6}$$

$$dF = T + r^*F + F_0 r_f \tag{6.7}$$

$$r_f = r_a - 0.5r_d \tag{6.8}$$

$$T = 2\tau_1 c - \tau_2 y_d \tag{6.9}$$

Dynamic paths for the target variables:

$$dm_a = \sigma_1 z_a - \sigma_2 y_a \tag{6.10a}$$

$$dm_d = \sigma_1 z_d - \sigma_2 y_d \tag{6.10b}$$

In the block relating to world averages output is driven by demand, namely monetary and fiscal policy, plus the wealth effect of the real exchange rate[1] (Equation 6.1a). Consumer price inflation (Equation 6.2a) corresponds to wage inflation, which depends on current output deviations from the natural rate and on core inflation. Core inflation dynamics (Equation 6.3a), driven by a partial adjustment mechanism, are linked to current consumer price inflation.

National divergences differ from world averages because of wealth effects and exchange rates. Uncovered interest parity is assumed to hold, hence the expected rate of change of the real exchange rate is set equal to the difference between the home and the foreign real interest rate (Equation 6.5). Agents in the financial markets are assumed to form expectations rationally and to have full access to the relevant information. Therefore the expected variation of the exchange rate

Table 6.3 Alternative policy assignments

The target zones assignment:

$$dr_a = \alpha_1(dm_a - dp_a - dy_a) + \alpha_2(m_a - p_a - y_a) \tag{6.12}$$

$$ds_d = \Omega_1(dm_d - dp_d - dy_d) + \Omega_2(m_d - p_d - y_d) \tag{6.13}$$

The 'monetarist' assignment

$$dr_a = \alpha_1(dm_a - dp_a - dy_a) + \alpha_2(m_a - p_a - y_a) \tag{6.14}$$

$$dr_d = \Omega_3(dm_d - dp_d - dy_d) + \Omega_4(m_d - p_d - y_d) \tag{6.15}$$

The reversed assignment

$$dr_a = \alpha_1(dm_a - dp_a - dy_a) + \alpha_2(m_a - p_a - y_a) \tag{6.16}$$

$$dr_d = \Omega_3(dm_d - dp_d - dy_d) + \Omega_4(m_d - p_d - y_d) \tag{6.17}$$

$$ds_d = -\Omega_5 dF \tag{6.18}$$

---

1. *Definition of variables (deviations from equilibrium)*
$y =$ real output, measured relative to the 'natural rate' (in logs).
$r =$ short term real interest rate.
$c =$ real exchange rate.
$s =$ index of fiscal stance (scaled to have a unit effect on y).
$p =$ consumer price index (logs).
$z =$ core inflation (a moving average of p).
$x =$ the markup of prices on wages (equivalent to the cost of foreign inputs for a unit of domestic output).
$m =$ nominal income target.
$F =$ net domestic holdings of foreign assets, defined in foreign currency.
$T =$ trade balance.
$d =$ differential operator.

2. *Parameter values*
$\mu = 1.2$; $\sigma = 0.25$; $\epsilon = \beta = 1$; $\Phi = 0.25$; $\theta = 0.08$; $\sigma_1 = -0.25$; $\sigma_2 = 0.5$; $\alpha_1 = -0.83$; $\alpha_2 = -0.42$; $\Omega_1 = 1$; $\Omega_2 = 0.5$; $\Omega_3 = -0.83$; $\Omega_4 = -0.42$; $\Omega_5 = 1$; $\sum = 0.25$; $r^* = 0.05$.

3. *Low interdependence*
$\pi = 0.1$; $\delta = 0.1$; $\tau_1 = 0.06$; $\tau_2 = 0.048$.

4. *High interdependence*
$\pi = 0.3$; $\delta = 0.3$; $\tau_1 = 0.224$; $\tau_2 = 0.188$.

corresponds to its actual rate of change (Equation 6.6). As in EMW, part of national consumer price divergences (Equations 6.2b and 6.4) are accounted for by the gradual adjustment of prices to exchange rate 'surprises'.

Wealth redistribution between the two countries takes place through the current account flow (Equation 6.7). As in previous chapters, alternative forms of wealth are not considered so that we may emphasise the link between wealth effects and current account imbalances. It is assumed that the two countries exchange assets using foreign currency, F, whose rate of return corresponds to the foreign real interest rate. The real instead of the nominal interest rate is included because account is taken of changes in the real value of wealth due to inflation abroad. The term $r_f F$ is linearised, with r^* and F_0 being the initial levels of the foreign real interest rate and of foreign wealth. The initial outstanding stock of wealth is of crucial importance for the results and we shall consider various cases[2] in the range $-0.5 < F_0 < +0.5$. Note that when disequilibrium occurs at the world level and monetary policy is activated the two blocks of the model cannot be solved independently. This is so because, unless $F^* = 0$, world real interest rate changes will redistribute wealth among countries and activate the national differences block.

The trade balance depends on relative deviations of national outputs from the natural rate and on the real exchange rate (Equation 6.9). To be consistent with the formulation of the current account flow, it is assumed that the trade balance is expressed in terms of foreign currency units.

Unlike EMW, the dynamic path of the real exchange rate is connected with both averages and differences by means of its wealth effect on aggregate demand (Equations 6.1a and 6.1b). This is another reason why the two blocks cannot be solved independently. In fact the wealth effect of the real exchange rate operates asymmetrically and affects average aggregate demand. Suppose that, *ceteris paribus*, the domestic price level rises. In this case the real exchange rate appreciates and a negative wealth effect occurs in the home economy whereas nothing similar happens abroad. As a result, average aggregate demand falls.[3]

Domestic holdings of foreign assets are an argument of aggregate demand – when they increase demand rises at home and falls abroad.[4] As a consequence, output differences are enhanced.

Money GDP levels,[5] world averages and national differences, are set as the intermediate target for inflation control (Equations 6.4 and 6.11b). EMW define a path for both targets which is *not* independent from inflation and output dynamics. The reason for doing so is to dampen cyclical fluctuations: 25 per cent of core inflation is 'accommodated' and 50 per cent of the output cycle is resisted

(Equation 6.4a, Equation 6.11d). This choice has been criticised[6] as too 'accommodative' and inconsistent with the spirit of nominal income targets, which should help prevent excessive wage claims by threatening a fall in output and employment. There is another reason for adopting an exogenous nominal income target. EMW obviously select an ad hoc target path in order to improve the dynamic performance of the model under the target zones proposal, but I suspect that such a choice might be less beneficial or even provoke adverse results under the reversed assignment. In this case evaluating the genuine merits of the two rules would be impossible. Therefore, in Section 4 the policy experiments will be replicated under the assumption of exogenous money GDP targets.

In all the experiments which follow, the model is subjected to shock, assuming a 10 per cent surge in world inflation, with national differences also being 10 per cent. This implies that the initial rate of inflation is 15 per cent in the home economy and 5 per cent in the foreign economy. The consequences of the real demand shocks considered in Chapter 4 are not discussed because the original results obtained in the experiments are already clear from the analysis of the disinflation policy.[7]

The model allows for four policy instruments. Two are related to the world averages block; the average real interest rate and the average fiscal policy stance. Two refer to national differences: real interest rates differentials and divergences of national fiscal policy stances. It is assumed that policy tools gradually adjust to deviations of the targets from their desired values: the policy experiments differ in the nature of these gradual adjustments.

In Sections 2 and 3 we will investigate the performance of the two assignments under the endogenous target path selected by EMW. In Section 4 we consider the case of exogenous money GDP targets.

6.2 THE EMW ASSIGNMENT

EMW make use of *two* instruments only. They assign 'average' monetary policy to the control of world money GDP (Equation 6.12), dispensing with 'average' fiscal policy altogether. The asymmetric stance of national fiscal policies is targeted at the reduction of differences between national rates of inflation: the country whose rate of inflation is above average *contracts*, whereas the country whose inflation rate is below average *expands*. Monetary policy is used to hold down the exchange rate at its target zones level. In this model, perfect capital mobility constrains real interest rates to be always equal across countries, since anything else would cause fluctuations in the exchange rate (Equation 6.6). Neither real interest rate differentials nor real exchange rate dynamics ever occur. Implicitly, monetary policy is left to act as a short-term reserve weapon against exchange rate bubbles not accounted for in the model. In the EMW experiment the real exchange rate target stays constant throughout the adjustment period and is set with reference to external equilibrium. The current account does not appear in the model so there is no way of assessing the current account implications of their proposal. The aim of this section is to do exactly that.

To facilitate a better understanding the analysis will be undertaken in stages. At first the wealth effect of the real exchange rate[8] and the debt service in the current account will be ignored.[9] Then a model will be constructed where the foreign debt service appears in the current account. This substantially complicates the picture, but it will be assumed, as a preliminary step, that no shock occurs at the world level so that world interest rates stay constant.[10] Finally, by implementing the full model,[11] we will assess the implications that the assignment of world monetary policy to average inflation has in terms of wealth redistribution and current account disequilibrium as part of the overall adjustment process.

6.2.1 A model where the trade balance is the only source of wealth transfer

The current account equation becomes $dF = T$.

Real interest rate differences being constrained at zero, curbing inflation differentials requires a fiscal contraction in the home economy and a symmetric expansion abroad.[12] Obviously, each country's demand for foreign goods depends, *ceteris paribus*, on its own rate of growth. As a consequence of the asymmetric fiscal policy the home economy runs current account surpluses throughout the adjustment period. This leads to a permanent redistribution of wealth from the foreign economy to the home economy. The change in domestic holdings of foreign assets is related to the accumulated divergence of national outputs:

$$F_\infty - F_0 = -\tau_2 \int_0^\infty y_d$$

$$\int_0^\infty y_d = (z_{d\infty} - z_{d0})/\epsilon\Phi = -40\%$$

where F_∞ is the new equilibrium level of domestic holdings of foreign assets.

If the two economies exhibit a low degree of interdependence, the increase of F is about 2 per cent of real GDP. If the degree of interdependence is higher, international wealth redistribution amounts to about 8 per cent of GDP. Long-term equilibrium requires that the permanent deviation of F from its initial value be compensated by a permanent bias of fiscal policy. Wealth effects do not seem to significantly alter the dynamic path of output and inflation with respect to the original EMW results.

6.2.2 Reduction of national imbalances when the debt service is taken into account

At this stage the simulation exercise still only involves world differences. It is clear that, once national differences have died out, permanent changes in domestic holdings of foreign assets will have to be offset by real exchange rate variations in the opposite direction if the current account is to be in equilibrium. This point has been made repeatedly in the literature on exchange rate determination (Branson, 1979; Dornbusch, 1987), but it is worth recalling because under this assignment the exchange rate cannot be regarded as exogenous and set independently from the policy exercise being carried out. Given that divergences of national real interest rates are ruled out, no real exchange rate dynamics can take place, and the adjustment must occur once and for all, right from the beginning. As shown in Chapter 4, the new equilibrium is a saddlepoint: stability requires an immediate jump by c into its new equilibrium value. Note that the inclusion of foreign investment service introduces an unstable root as a consequence of the chosen policy mix and is quite independent from the values of the structural parameters.

When monetary policy controls domestic inflation the danger of wealth instability arises[13] if $r^* > \tau_2\theta$: an increase in F will increase foreign interest payments more than it will depress imports through a fall in domestic expenditure, therefore leading to the destabilising outcome of cumulative current account surpluses. In this case potential instability arises irrespective of whether r^* is greater or less than $\tau_2\theta$. If the inflationary gap between the two economies is to be driven down, a negative differential must arise in the rates of real GDP growth. As a consequence, the home economy must run current account surpluses and accumulate foreign assets. The expansionary stimulus to domestic expenditure which originates from wealth accumulation will have to be matched by a permanent fiscal contraction. Eventually, when $y_d = 0$, the increased stock of foreign investment will still exert positive pressure on the current account, to be compensated for by a real exchange rate appreciation (Table 6.4). $F_\infty - F_0$ turns out to be lower when foreign investment service is included in the current account equation. This is so for two reasons. First, the initial appreciation worsens competitiveness in the home economy, and weakens the positive impact of lower domestic growth on the current account. Second, the permanent appreciation of the terms of trade dampens the amplitude of the required output divergence between the two economies (see Equation 6.3d).

$$\epsilon\Phi \int_0^\infty y_d = z_{d\infty} - z_{d0} - 2\epsilon \sum (c_\infty - c_0)$$

Table 6.4 Permanent real exchange rate and foreign wealth changes and relative output loss necessary when foreign investment service is included in the current account but monetary policy does not influence national differences

Interdependence	Dc	DF	$\int_0^\infty y_d$
Low	−0.8%	+1.5%	−38.4
High	−0.8	+6.0%	−38.4

Figures 6.1 and 6.2 show the dynamic paths of core inflation, foreign wealth and the real exchange rate.

6.2.3 Simulating the full model

Permanent changes in F and c are significantly affected by the *sign and value of F_0* (Table 6.5). To a lesser extent inflation divergences are altered as well (Figures 6.3–5. When the home economy is a net creditor, higher world interest rates enhance the accumulation of foreign assets. This addition can be quite substantial when foreign

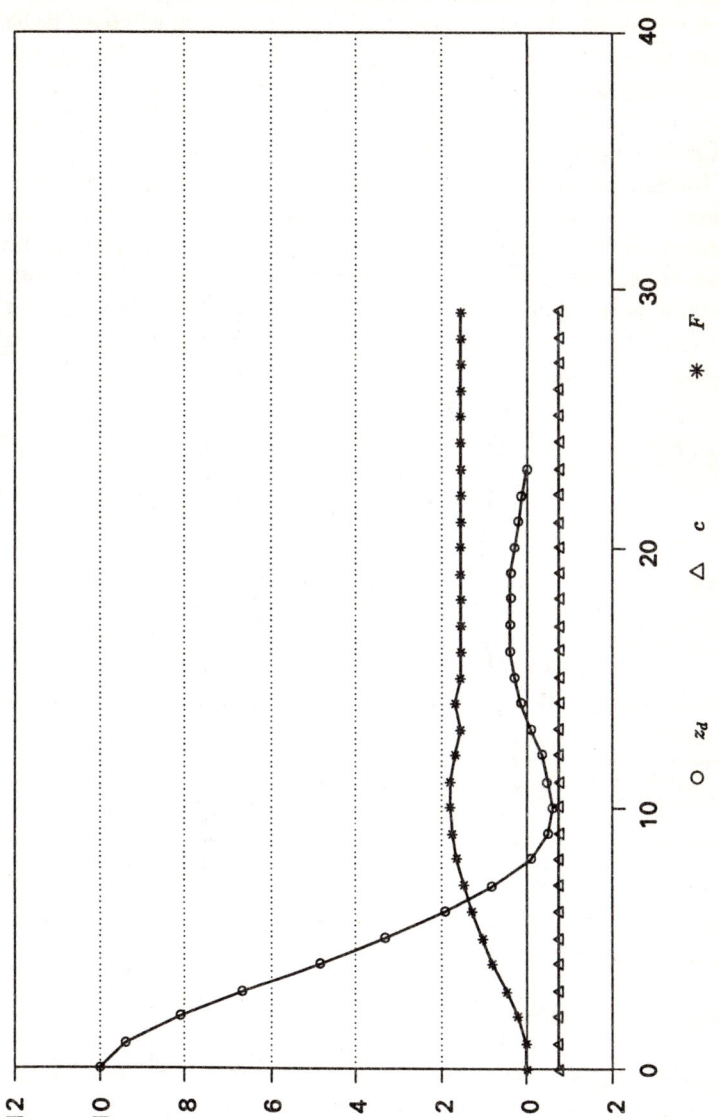

Figure 6.1   EMW policy assignment: $F_0 = 0$ (low interdependence)

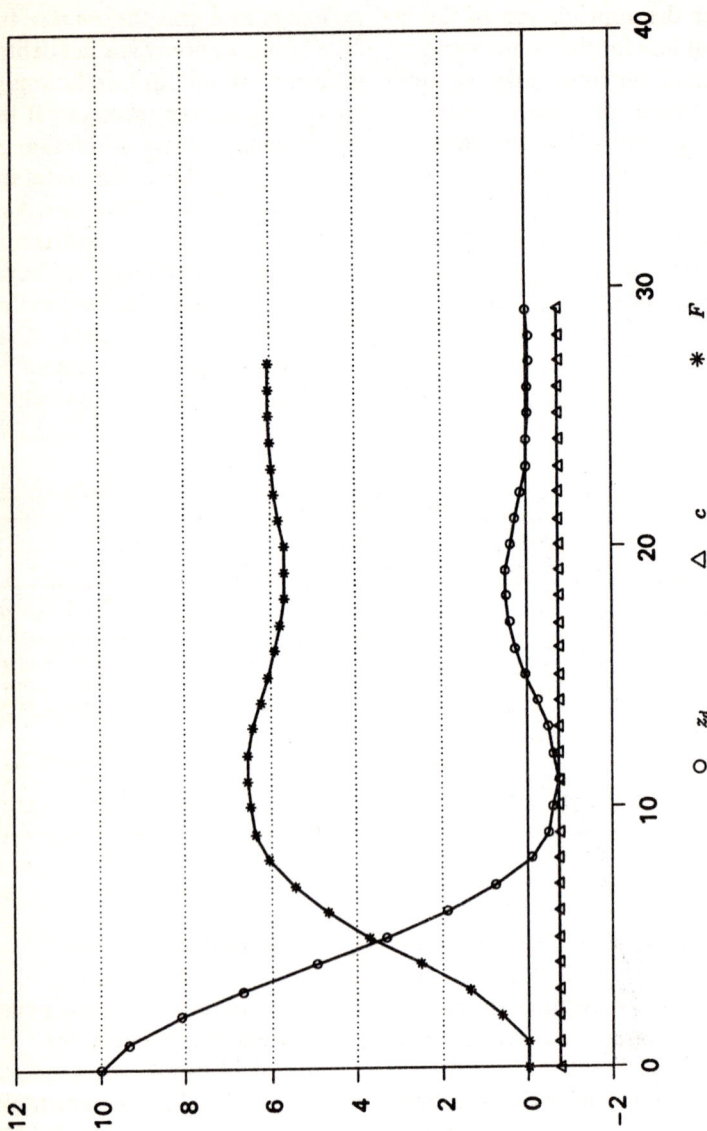

Figure 6.2 EMW policy assignment: $F_0 = 0$ (high interdependence)

investment is a significant proportion of real GDP. At the same time, the *higher* the income elasticity of the trade balance the *stronger* the increase of F_∞; the *lower* the price elasticity of the trade balance the bigger the appreciation of the real exchange rate and the *smaller* the output loss for the home economy. If the home economy is a net debtor the final outcome may be quite different. World anti-inflationary policy raises real interest rates and worsens the current account. If the starting level of foreign debt is sufficiently high the loss of foreign assets, determined by restrictive world monetary policy, dominates the accumulation of F caused by the reduction of national differences. As a consequence, current account equilibrium requires a permanent depreciation of the real exchange rate. This spurs inflation at home and curbs it abroad. Correspondingly, the total output loss associated with the reduction of national imbalances must be higher. Also, depreciation in the terms of trade initially exerts a positive impact on inflation differentials, but this perverse effect dies out quite quickly.

Table 6.5 Permanent wealth, exchange rate changes and output loss required when world monetary policy affects the current account (percentage changes)

Interdependence		$F_0 = -0.5$	$F_0 = -0.3$	$F_0 = -0.1$	$F_0 = 0.1$	$F_0 = 0.3$	$F_0 = 0.5$
Low	$DF =$	−10.3	−5.6	−0.8	+3.9	+8.7	+13.4
	$Dc =$	+5.3	+2.8	+0.4	−2.0	−4.4	−6.9
	$\int_0^\infty y_d =$	−50.6	−45.6	−40.8	−36.0	−31.2	−26.2
High	$DF =$	−3.3	+0.4	+4.1	+7.8	+11.5	+15.2
	$Dc =$	+0.4	−0.1	−0.5	−1	−1.5	−2.4
	$\int_0^\infty y_d =$	−40.8	−39.8	−39.0	−38.0	−37.0	−35.2

6.2.4 Concluding remarks on the target zones proposal

The previous sections have shown that an anti-inflationary policy under a target zones regime might have undesirable implications.

– Correction of national differences implies a permanent redistribution of wealth and a permanent change in the terms of trade. The size of the wealth transfer grows when the income elasticity of the trade balance is higher.

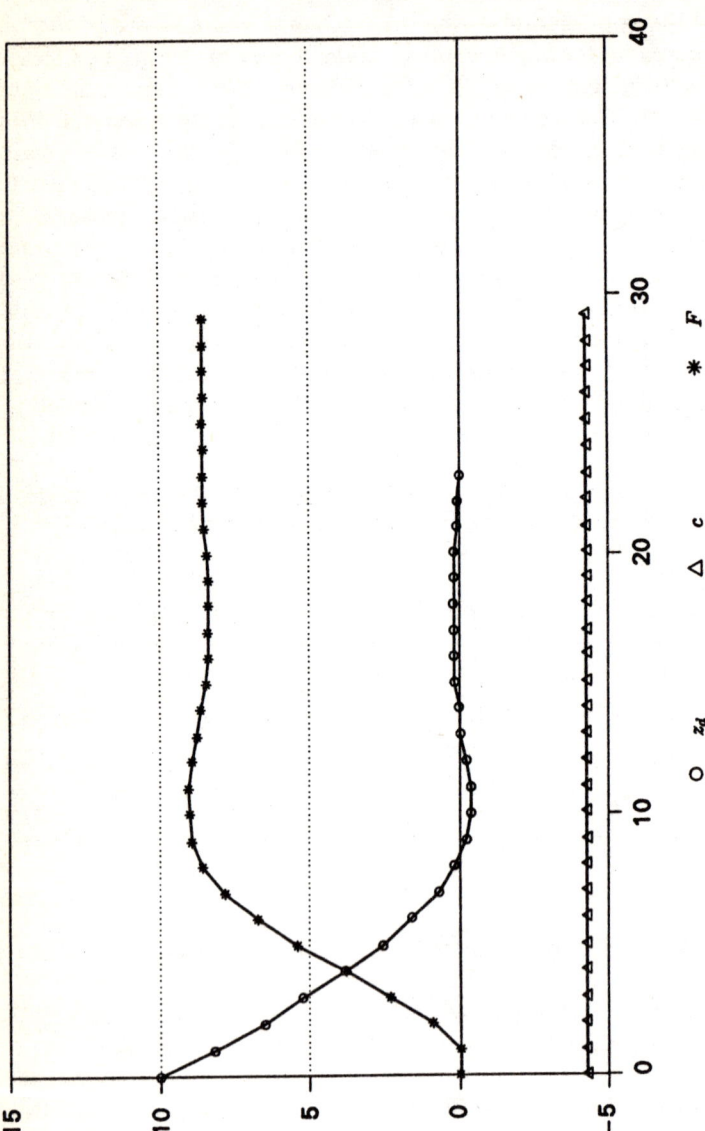

Figure 6.3 EMW policy assignment: $F_0 = 0.3$ (low interdependence)

○ z_d △ c * F

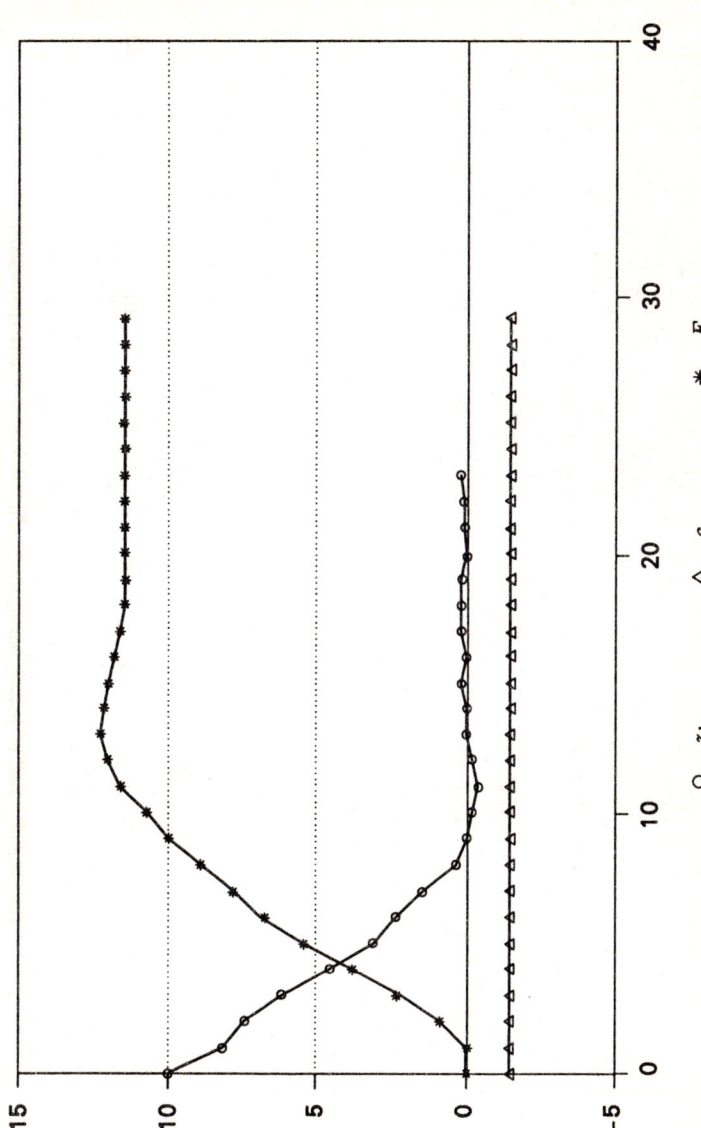

Figure 6.4 EMW policy assignment: $F_0 = 0.3$ (high interdependence)

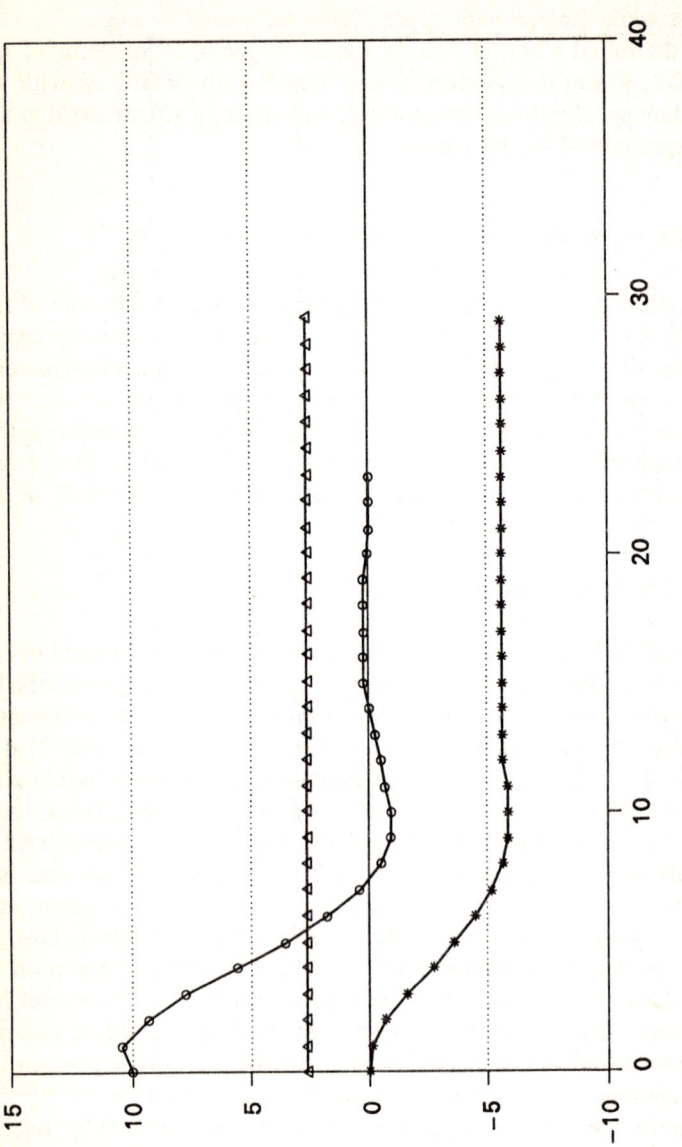

Figure 6.5   EMW policy assignment: $F_0 = -0.3$ (low interdependence)

- For each country the total output cost of reducing inflation is affected by the sign and amplitude of the change in the terms of trade. A permanent depreciation will add to the required output loss while a permanent appreciation will lower it.
- If the initial stock of foreign wealth is not small in terms of real GDP, a world monetary policy significantly interferes with the reduction of national imbalances, and strongly affects the sign and magnitude of wealth transfers.

6.3   EXPLORING ALTERNATIVE POLICY RULES

Rules alternative to the target zones proposal involve active use of real interest rate differentials and activation of real exchange rate dynamics. Obviously this might reproduce those real exchange rate misalignments that the proposal aims to avoid. However, having shown that real exchange rate stability cannot be achieved without cost and that this cost might be substantial, in this section we investigate to what extent misalignments are inevitable if countries coordinate and yet allow real interest rates to diverge.

6.3.1   The 'monetarist' alternative

The standard alternative to a target zones rule is the assignment of real interest rate differentials to differences in money GDP. I have labelled this 'monetarist' (although it departs from the standard monetarist orthodoxy by establishing a closed-loop rule) because it is restricted to the use of monetary policy only and completely disregards fiscal policy as a viable instrument for stabilisation purposes. It has already been shown in Chapter 4 why the reversed assignment should be preferred to this rule. We briefly reconsider the issue at this stage. EMW take into account the 'monetarist' rule and show that real exchange rate misalignments occur. Also, early gains in inflation control, brought about by the initial appreciation of the exchange rate, are reversed when the terms of trade move back into equilibrium. My model has replicated their experiment and the results show that when the two countries exhibit a low degree of interdependence, fluctuations in the world interest rates actually cause the global system to become completely unstable. If interdependence is high the model regains stability but exhibits prolonged persistence. In this case, due to the stronger effect of the terms of trade on aggregate demand, fluctuations in the exchange rate are greatly dampened but huge swings occur in the stock of foreign wealth, fluctuating in a range of ± 15 per cent when F_0 is different from 0. After 60 periods, wealth is still significantly removed from equilibrium. It is well known (Kouri, 1976; Dornbusch and Fischer, 1980) that wealth effects provide an endogenous correction mechanism for disequilibrium in the international distribution of foreign wealth; unfortunately they seem to be too weak to effectively dampen fluctuations. This raises the issue of the need for an active fiscal policy as part of a system which ensures external equilibrium.

6.3.2 Policies for internal and external equilibrium: the reversed assignment

Under this set of rules monetary policy controls money GDP differences, while national fiscal policy stances control international wealth distribution, Equations 6.16–6.18. The fiscal policy gradually adjusts over time according to current account deviations from equilibrium. This implies that at any point in time s is targeted on F.

Although integral control of foreign wealth is not imposed, no permanent change of F can occur. In equilibrium, $y_d = 0$, $dc = 0$ and $dF = 0$. For exchange rate dynamics to be nil, $r_d = 0$. Since s_d is a linear function of F, $c = F = 0$ is the only combination of wealth and the exchange rate which ensures current account equilibrium when output is at the 'natural rate' in both countries.

The working of this policy assignment can be described as follows. Reducing differences in inflation requires a positive differential between domestic and foreign real interest rates. This in turn triggers an immediate appreciation of the real exchange rate. Thus inflation differentials are affected in two ways: appreciation of the terms of trade brings in early gains, to be reversed later when the exchange rate depreciates moving back towards equilibrium; higher interest rates and the loss of competitiveness depress demand for domestic goods and slow down the pace of wage inflation. Apart from the effect that fluctuations in world interest rates have on wealth accumulation, the current account turns into a deficit if the loss of competitiveness reduces net exports to a greater degree than the higher real interest rates reduce imports.[14] The external deficit triggers a contractionary fiscal policy stance, thereby causing further downward pressure on wage inflation.

6.3.3 Control of the national differences

We begin with an analysis similar to that in Section 3.2 so as to explore the results in stages. It is first assumed that a shock affects inflation only, so that world monetary policy is not activated. The current account equation becomes:

$$dF = 2\tau_1 c - \tau_2 y_d - F_0 0.5 r_d + r^* F$$

$-0.5 r_d$ represents the change in the foreign real interest rate required to control money GDP targets. With low interdependence and $-0.5 \leq F^* \leq 0$ the jump in the real exchange rate is about -7 per cent so it can be absorbed quite quickly. After seven periods its deviation from equilibrium is below 1 per cent, since then c fluctuates in a band of approximately ± 2 per cent. The initial appreciation in the terms of trade has a favourable impact on inflation, but at the cost of slightly higher persistence later on. The output cycle is dampened if compared with the corresponding results obtained in Section 2.3. Domestic holdings of foreign assets fluctuate in a band with a maximum range is ± 1.5 per cent. When $0 < F_0 \leq +0.5$ the initial exchange rate path keeps a lower profile at the cost of wider positive deviations from equilibrium later on. The fall in the foreign interest rate[15] worsens the current account and requires a stronger fiscal contraction, which will be more prolonged the weaker the income elasticity of the trade balance. At the later stage of the cycle, the stronger fiscal control will exert an excessively contractionary effect on money GDP growth, to be compensated for by a negative interest rate differential, which triggers a depreciation of the real exchange rate. Obviously, the less effective fiscal policy is on the current account, the more prolonged and complex the output cycle becomes. In fact simulations show that if τ_2 is strong enough the effect of r_f on the current account makes very little difference to the overall dynamic performance of the model. In this case the initial appreciation of the exchange rate is substantially reduced and fluctuations in the terms of trade occur in a much narrower band.[16] Also, the pattern of the exchange rate cycle does not seem to be significantly affected by the sign and magnitude of F_0. Figures 6.6–6.9 provide some examples of dynamics.

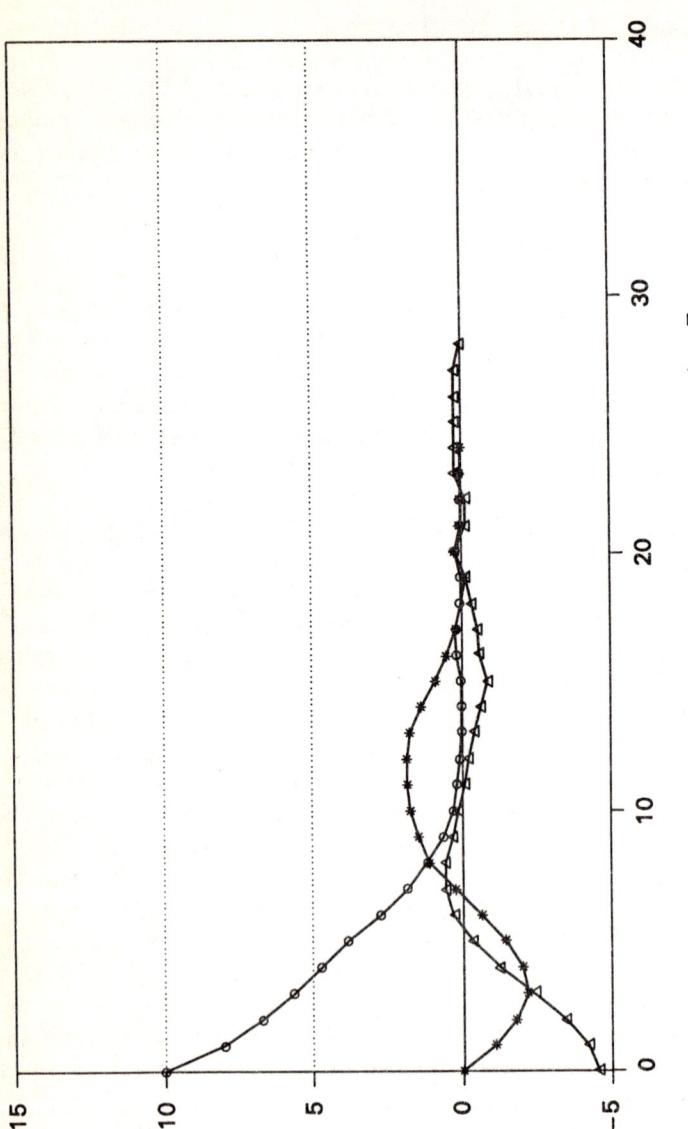

Figure 6.6 Reversed policy assignment: $F_0 = 0.3$ (high interdependence, differences only)

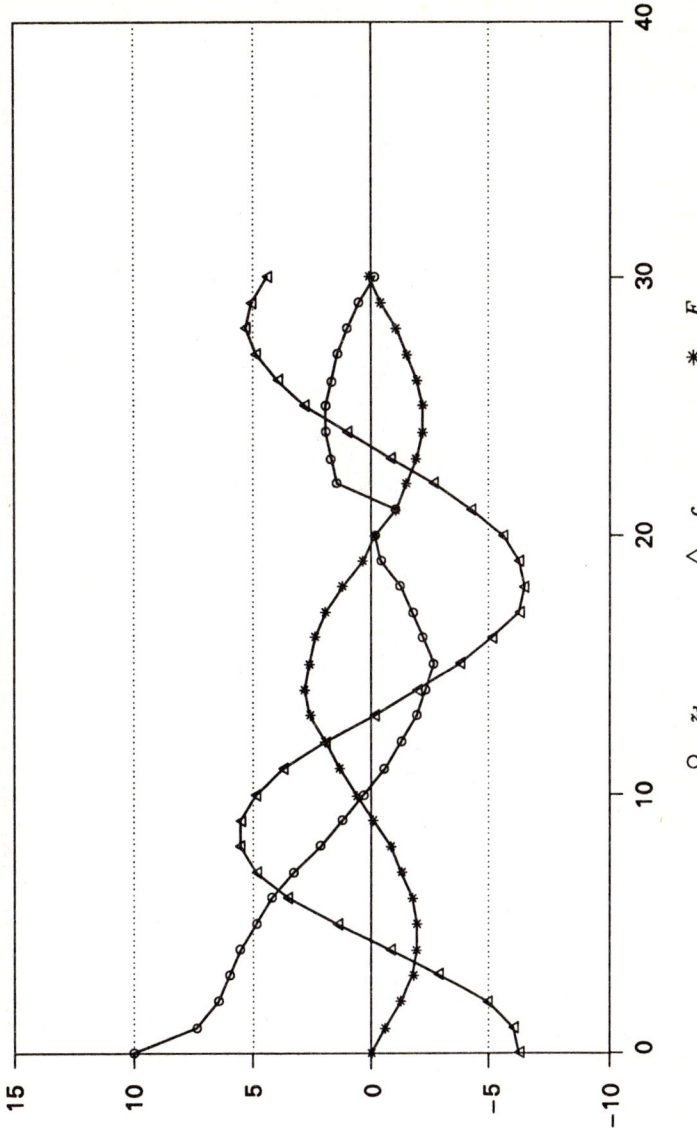

Figure 6.7 Reversed policy assignment: $F_0 = 0.3$ (low interdependence, differences only)

○ z_d △ c * F

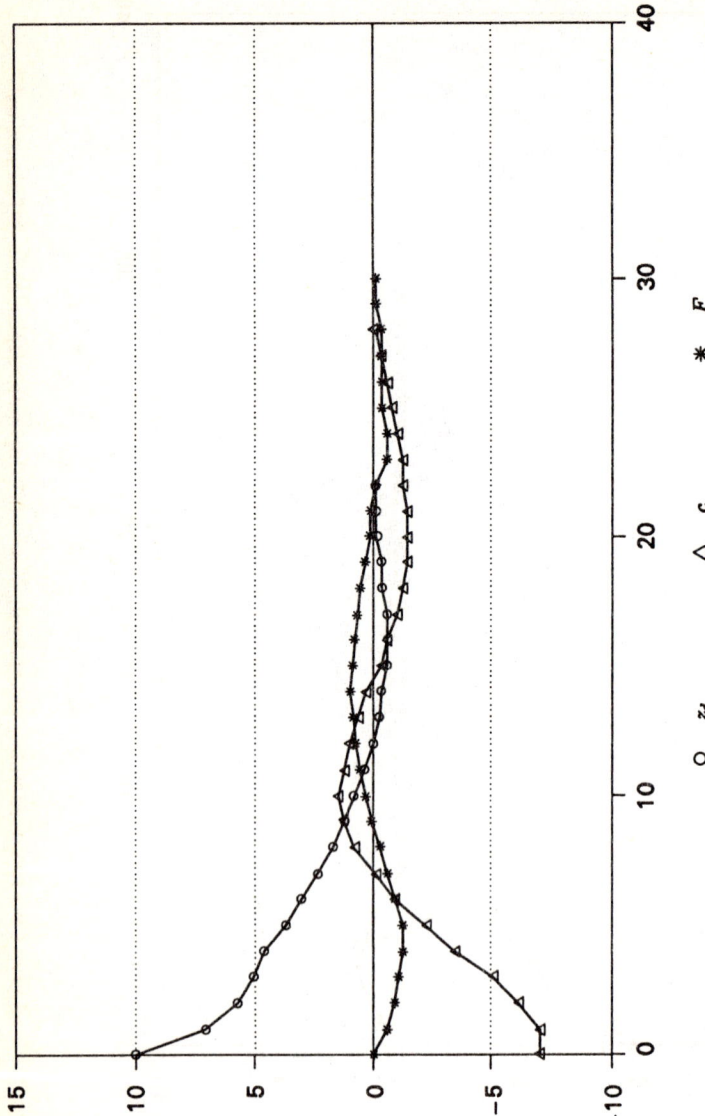

Figure 6.8 Reversed policy assignment: $F_0 = -0.3$ (low interdependence, differences only)

O z_d Δ c * F

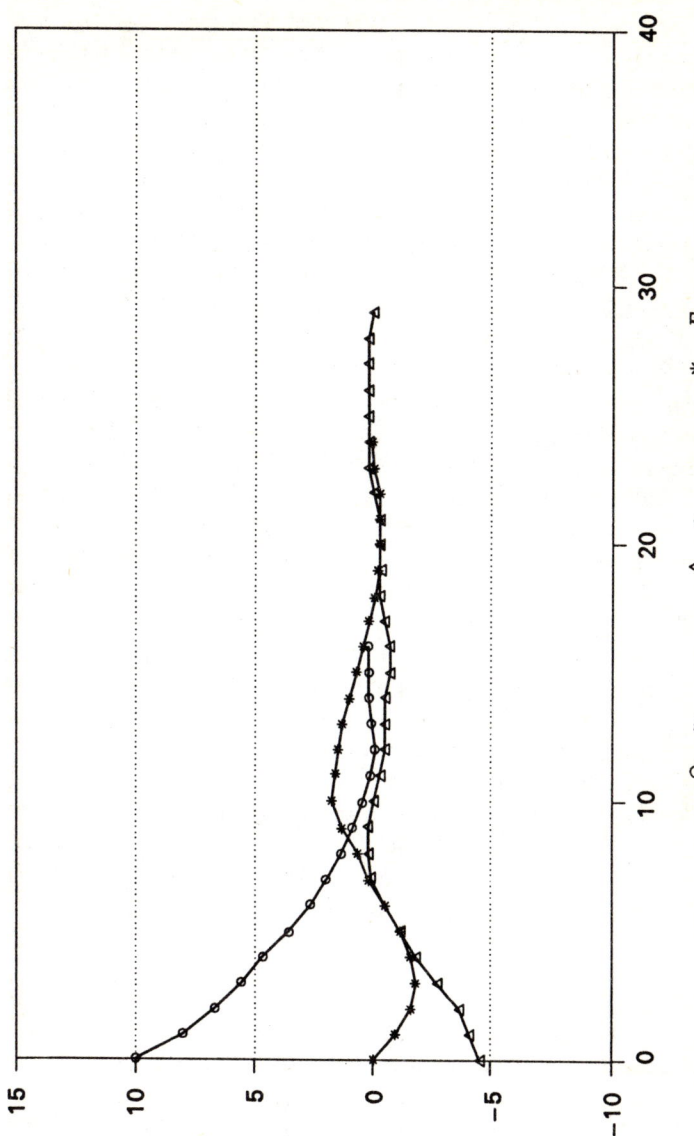

Figure 6.9 Reversed policy assignment: $F_0 = -0.3$ (high interdependence, differences only)

6.3.4 The full model

I shall now investigate the implications of monetary control of average inflation. As in Section 2.4 it is assumed that both average and differential inflation are set initially at 10 per cent. When interdependence between countries is low fluctuations become much wider than those analysed in Section 3.3 (Figures 6.11 and 6.12). Fiscal policy avoids the danger of instability[17] but is not very effective in limiting fluctuations. Both the exchange rate and foreign wealth exhibit huge swings. When $-0.5 < F_0 \leq -0.1$ higher world interest rates during the first eight years cause a redistribution of wealth from the home economy to the foreign one in a range of between 2 per cent and 9 per cent. The loss of foreign wealth requires a prolonged fiscal contraction that will affect the current account only gradually over time, complicating the task of monetary policy.

In order to keep money GDP close to its target, the restrictive fiscal policy must be compensated for by negative interest rates differentials. This in turn causes a depreciation of the exchange rate. By and large, dynamics follow the pattern discussed above, when the effects of world monetary policy were not taken into account, but fluctuations at the later stage of the cycle are much wider. When $0.1 < F_0 \leq 0.5$ the surge of world real interest rates has a strong positive effect on the home economy's current account. In spite of the strong initial loss of competitiveness, the current account is driven into a surplus, forcing the fiscal stance to become expansionary. Terms of trade must depreciate further before regaining equilibrium.

For a higher degree of interdependence (Figures 6.10 and 6.13), exchange rate fluctuations are far narrower. Although similar in pattern, the terms of trade cycle is substantially dampened. This is so because relative prices exert a more powerful influence on the balance of trade, and because the fiscal policy is more effective in controlling financial wealth. Therefore world real interest rates exert a smaller impact on the current account and the dynamic adjustment becomes far more satisfactory.

The policy assignment presented in this section exhibits a dynamic pattern for output and inflation which only marginally differs from the results obtained under the target zones regime. And yet permanent wealth transfers between the two economies and permanent real exchange rate adjustments are *completely avoided*. However, the model exhibits something of an exchange rate cycle, and although a permanent redistribution of wealth is avoided, something of a cycle

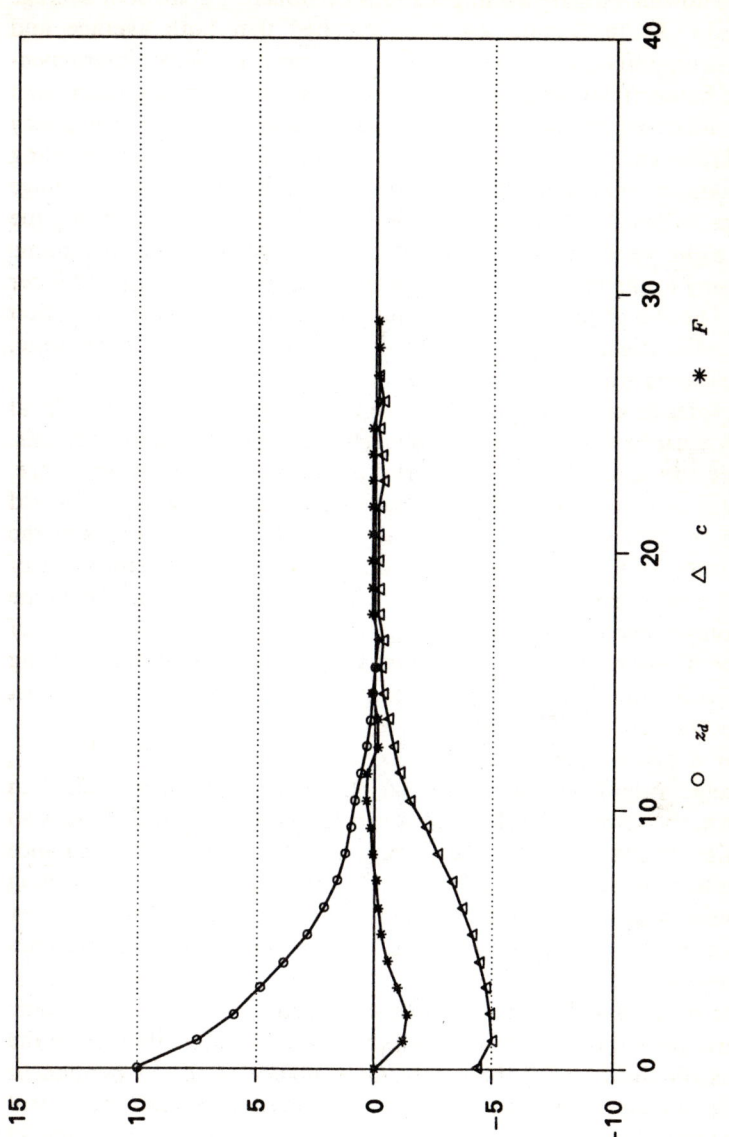

Figure 6.10 **Reversed policy assignment: $F_0 = 0.3$ (high interdependence, full model)**

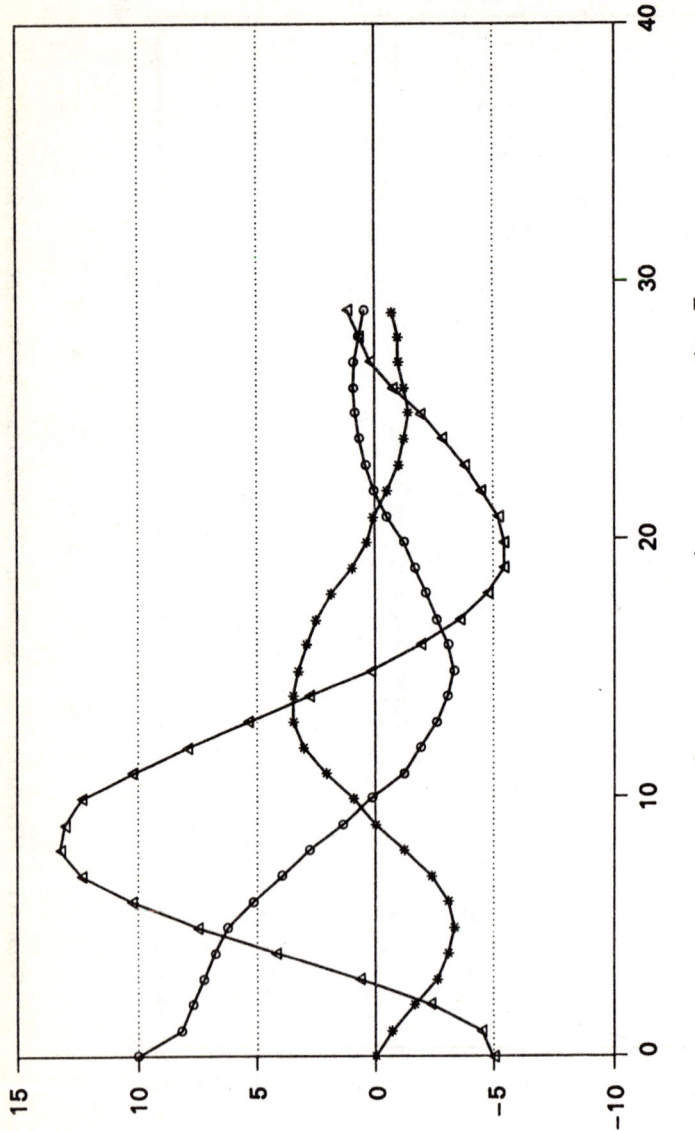

Figure 6.11 Reversed policy assignment: $F_0 = 0.3$ (low interdependence, full model)

O z_d $\triangle$ c * F

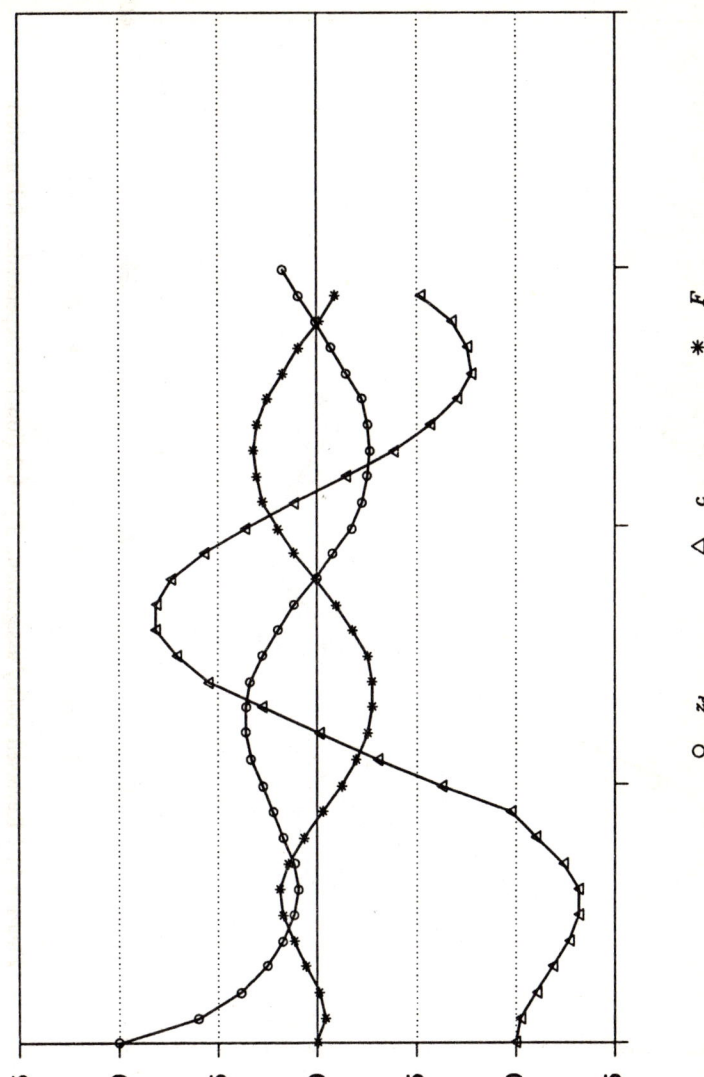

O z_d $\triangle$ c $*$ F

Figure 6.12   **Reversed policy assignment:** $F_0 = -0.3$ (low interdependence, full model)

ancient bacterial parents, both of which may have played, and still may be playing, a major evolutionary role in this unfortunately large group.

In eu...

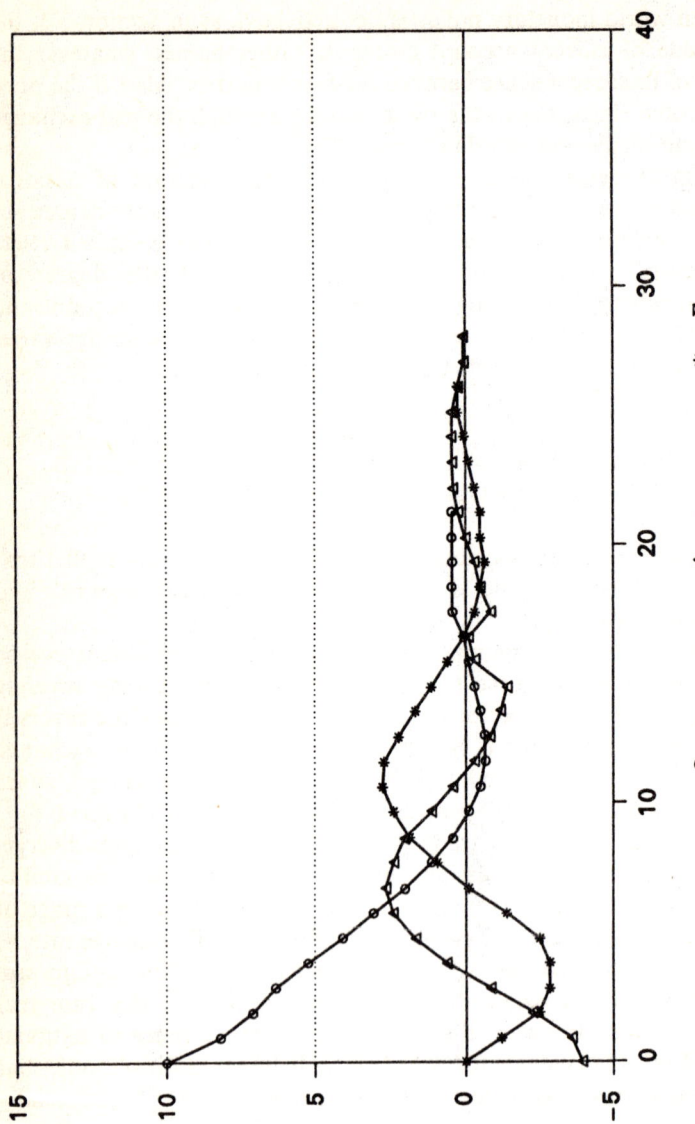

Figure 6.13   Reversed policy assignment: $F_0 = -0.3$ (high interdependence, full model)

appears necessary in wealth, too, as the model converges towards long-term equilibrium. It is now possible to say whether these cycles are likely to be large or small.

When world monetary policy is not activated, as in Section 3.3, the amplitude of current account swings is rather limited whatever the degree of interdependence between the two countries. Also, if the price and income elasticities of the trade balance are high the real exchange rate cycle is substantially dampened.

World monetary policy interferes with the reduction of national imbalances by redistributing financial wealth. If the degree of interdependence is high, world monetary policy has a limited effect on wealth and terms of trade. By contrast, if the degree of interdependence is low, huge fluctuations in the current account and real exchange rate can occur. Also, the pattern of these swings varies according to the initial distribution of foreign wealth.

6.4 THE PERFORMANCE OF THE TWO ASSIGNMENTS UNDER EXOGENOUS MONEY GDP TARGETS

In this section exogenous money GDP targets are set. This implies that $\sigma_1 = \sigma_2 = 0$. The full model is simulated under the target zones rule and the reversed assignment.

Under the EMW assignment the model exhibits persistent cycles: setting an exogenous time path for nominal income targets severely worsens the dynamic performance of the model. Under the reversed assignment convergence is faster: the relative variability of exchange rate, output, inflation and the fiscal stance under the target zones proposal is higher over 30 periods than over the first 10 (Table 6.6).[18]

Stabilising the terms of trade when national inflation rates diverge, as required by the EMW assignment, causes a great deal of variability in the nominal exchange rate (Table 6.7) which fluctuates in a range of ± 20 per cent. By contrast, swings in the the nominal exchange rate, e, are significantly reduced when real exchange rate fluctuations are allowed and fiscal policy controls foreign wealth. In this case real 'misalignments' do occur; they ensure faster convergence of national inflation rates but cause a distortion of trade flows. However, note that under the reversed assignment output variability is smaller, especially when the appreciation of the initial terms of trade is stronger. Furthermore, avoiding misalignments requires a great deal of fiscal intervention (Table 6.8),[19] whereas under the reversed assignment the use of the fiscal instrument is more limited, especially when income elasticities are high. This is not surprising because the fiscal instrument, which controls foreign wealth by altering domestic expenditure on imports, is more effective when income elasticities are stronger. As a result, the degree of fiscal intervention is smaller.

For low trade elasticities F fluctuates in a range of about ± 2 per cent when fiscal policy controls financial wealth. The EMW rule halves these swings. For high trade elasticities this outcome is reversed, precisely because in this case the impact of the fiscal policy on the trade balance is enhanced.

Table 6.6   The relative variability of some key variables under the two assignments*

	y_d	F	z_d	s_d	e
Low income elasticities:					
a**	1.02	0.5	1.3	1.19	1.33
b	1.09	0.5	1.4	1.26	1.48
High income elasticities:					
a	1.44	3.6	1.52	2.6	2.4
b	2.46	5.8	2.2	3.1	4.4

*   Relative variability is measured as follows: $V = (v_1)^{-1/2}/(v_2)^{-1/2}$; where v is the sum of cumulated squared deviations from equilibrium and subscripts 1 and 2 refer to the target zones proposal and to the alternative assignment respectively.
** a = relative to the first 10 periods; b = relative to the first 30 periods.

6.5   CONCLUSIONS

This chapter stresses the consequences that the policy assignment generally associated with the target zones proposal has in terms of international wealth redistribution. It has been shown that the equilibrium exchange rate cannot be regarded as exogenous to the disinflationary process. If policy is concerned with a reduction in the underlying rate of core inflation, then a permanent redistribution of wealth between countries must occur. As a consequence, if the current account is to end up in equilibrium, the real exchange rate must adjust in the opposite direction. The *higher* the income elasticity of the trade balance the *larger* the necessary wealth redistribution between the two

Table 6.7 Time path for nominal and real exchange rates under the two assignments (percentage deviations)

	Low income elasticities			High income elasticities		
	Target zones	Reversed assignment		Target zones	Reversed assignment	
Time elapsed	e	e	c	e	e	c
0	0.4	−6.6	−6.6	−1.8	−10.4	−10.4
1	9.6	1.6	−6.0	7.0	−3.2	−10.1
2	16.2	7.7	−4.3	13.4	1.0	−9.3
3	19.5	12.0	−1.9	16.8	3.6	−8.0
4	19.0	14.3	0.9	16.9	5.0	−6.3
9	−13.8	−1.3	6.6	−13.4	0.1	0.2
10	−17.6	−6.1	5.1	−18.2	−1.5	0.6
11	−18.3	−9.9	3.0	−20.3	−2.5	0.7
12	−15.7	−12.0	0.7	−19.2	−3.1	0.5
19	18.6	8.5	−1.6	18.1	1.9	0.2
26	−14.3	−5.6	1.6	−18.9	−1.5	−0.2

Table 6.8 Time path for the fiscal stance in the home economy under the two assignments (percentage deviations)

	Low income elasticities		High income elasticities	
	Target zones	Reversed assignment	Target zones	Reversed assignment
Time elapsed				
1	−2.6	−1.5	−2.6	−1.1
2	−4.9	−3.2	−5.1	−2.1
3	−6.5	−4.6	−7.0	−2.7
4	−7.1	−5.5	−8.0	−3.0
9	2.7	−0.1	1.9	−0.1
10	4.7	1.9	4.6	0.7
11	5.8	4.6	6.5	1.3
12	5.9	4.9	7.4	1.6
19	−5.3	−3.2	−6.9	−1.0
26	4.7	2.0	5.4	−0.8

economies. Flucuations in world interest rates may substantially affect the amplitude and the direction of wealth redistribution.

As shown in Section 3, it is possible for disinflation to be achieved without consequential redistribution of wealth. It does however appear difficult to avoid exchange rate and wealth cycles. By considering alternative sets of structural parameters we were able to assess what factors might influence the likely size of these cycles. The analysis suggests that the performance of the reversed assignment is enhanced if countries are highly interdependent, especially if income elasticities are high. This is important because in the corresponding case the EMW policy assignment imposes a particularly large redistribution of wealth.

In Section 4 we evaluated the performance of the two rules when the nominal income targets are exogenous. The balance unambiguously shifts in favour of the reversed assignment. The only relative strength of the target zones proposal is the stabilisation of the terms of trade. In fact, avoiding misalignments requires greater inflation and output variability. Furthermore, we found that variability in the nominal exchange rate is strongly increased under the target zones proposal. This seems a rather undesirable feature at a time when many governments seem to favour policies which stabilise nominal rates even at the cost of misalignment of the terms of trade[20] as it is widely recognised that stabilising nominal rates may help to curb inflationary expectations. Another weakness of the target zones proposal is the relatively high degree of fiscal intervention, which might simply be not feasible. By and large, greater variability in the fiscal instrument, the nominal exchange rate, the inflation rate and output seems a rather high price to pay for the stabilisation of the terms of trade.

Under both assignments global monetary policy complicates the task of reducing national differences. Under the target zones rule the total wealth transfer increases, whereas under the reversed assignment swings in the terms of trade and wealth become wider when $F*$ is significantly different from zero.[21] This brings up the issue of adopting a global fiscal policy as a useful complement to the monetary instrument in controlling average money GDP targets. This point has not been raised in the debate on rules for policy coordination. Advocates of the proposals considered here agree with the view that monetary policy alone should control global inflation, but overlook the current account implications of such assignment. The results in this book point out that these undesirable consequences might be somewhat reduced by using fiscal intervention to control global targets, and I can see no reason why fiscal activism should be restricted to the correction of national differences. Besides, using fiscal policy at the global level would clearly be beneficial for the correction of national imbalances,[22] therefore it is possible that using the fiscal instrument at both levels would not raise the overall degree of fiscal intervention. This would probably be more likely under the reversed assignment, when national fiscal policies are directly linked to foreign wealth transfers.

7 Concluding Remarks

This final chapter reviews briefly the main results of the book and outlines directions for future research.

The original conclusions are discussed in Chapters 3, 4 and 6. Chapter 3 presented a model for exchange rate determination which allows for sticky prices, wealth effects and imperfect capital mobility. The analysis has stressed the danger of instability inherent in an open economy under a monetarist rule. This risk of instability is shown to exist because the process of wealth accumulation, operating through the current account, is deliberately not controlled under a monetarist regime.

Chapter 4 assessed the relative performance of four alternative policy assignments which involve simple feedback rules. This was done by means of algebraic analysis and numerical simulations in a small theoretical model. The rules considered can be described as follows.

Rule 1, a monetarist rule, assigns a real interest rate feedback to a nominal income target. Rule 2, the reversed assignment, adds fiscal control of a foreign wealth target to the monetary control of the internal objective. Rule 3, the Mundell assignment, establishes fiscal control of domestic nominal income and monetary control of the foreign wealth target. Finally, Rule 4 applies to a small country the kind of assignment advocated by Williamson in the target zones proposal: the government dispenses with monetary policy altogether and assigns fiscal policy to the domestic target. Briefly, the main results were as follows.

Rule 1 appears to be prone to the same risk of instability highlighted in Chapter 3. In a recent study, Currie and Levine (1990) investigated the issue of current account stability and argued that in a growing economy even a small wealth effect in aggregate demand would stabilise the foreign debt to income ratio. Nevertheless I believe that, even if the risk of instability were remote (although this cannot be taken for granted), the issue remains important because our simulations show that if wealth effects are small the amplitude of swings increases and 'real' demand shocks involve larger transfers of foreign wealth. Indeed, as discussed in Chapter 1, policymakers should be concerned both with the sustainability of current account imbalances and with the level of the foreign-debt to income ratio.

166

Rule 4 is effective in controlling the domestic objective and obviously achieves stability of the exchange rate. On the other hand it requires a high degree of fiscal intervention, which governments might find hard to adhere to. Furthermore, we discovered that the reduction of inflation is necessarily associated with a permanent change in the (equilibrium) real exchange rate and to a permanent transfer of foreign wealth from abroad. This appears to be a key difference between the target zones assignment and the other rules.

Rule 3 does not seem to perform much better than Assignment 4 in controlling the domestic and foreign targets, and it still involves a significant degree of volatility in the exchange rate. This might seem paradoxical, as it involves one additional instrument – monetary policy. The explanation probably is the limited influence of monetary policy on the external position of a country.

Finally, Rule 2 avoids the risk of dynamic instability inherent in a monetarist assignment and is very effective in controlling the foreign wealth target. It requires a relatively limited degree of fiscal intervention when compared to the target zone rule. On the other hand it cannot eliminate swings in the exchange rate.

Rules 2 and 4 emerge as the most suitable candidates for a macroeconomic stabilisation policy, and the choice between the two should obviously depend on the relative costs associated with the deviations from equilibrium of the exchange rate and of use of the fiscal instrument.

In part two of the book, Chapter 6 represents the original contribution of this work to the debate on simple rules and policy coordination. In a two-country setting we have considered a disinflation experiment, and we have assessed the relative performance of three alternative proposals, which assign the same instrument to the control of global, or average, inflation, but differ in their strategies for reducing international inflation differentials. The first rule is the well known target zones proposal. The second is a standard monetarist rule. The third is a two-country version of the reversed assignment.

The monetarist rule appears to be prone to instability, or at least to wide swings in foreign wealth and the exchange rate. Under the target zones regime the interesting result obtained in Chapter 4 is confirmed. The reduction of inflation differentials requires a permanent wealth transfer in favour of the high inflation country. This wealth transfer may be increased or partially offset according to the external position of the home economy prevailing at the beginning of the policy experiment. This result is the obvious consequence of the monetary contraction necessary to curb global inflation: as world real interest rates are increased wealth is transferred from the debtor to the creditor country.

Under the reversed assignment, disinflation requires less fiscal intervention than under the former rule. Also, no permanent change in foreign wealth and in the real exchange rate is necessary. But exchange rate fluctuations do occur. Indeed, the performance of the rule is highly sensitive to the strength of trade balance elasticities: it definitely improves when interdependence is higher. The policy performance is unambiguously complicated by the wealth redistribution caused by the fluctuation in world interest rates.

We also found that the setting of exogenous nominal income targets renders the target zone rule less appealing, as it implies greater relative variability of fiscal intervention, the nominal exchange rate, the inflation rate and output. This seems a rather high price to pay in exchange for stabilisation of the terms of trade.

Future research should extend in two directions the work done so far. The first should be an assessment of the performance of the simple rules considered here in the context of a model where a broader definition of wealth is taken into account. This would involve the inclusion in the model of both the government budget constraint and the accumulation of 'real' capital. An illuminating example of how such a research programme might be carried out has beeen provided by Weale *et al.* (1989).

The second line of research which could prove rather promising is the analysis of simple fiscal rules in the context of a monetary union, as the ongoing process of European economic integration has brought this issue to the centre-stage of the debate on stabilisation policies for open economies.

Notes and References

1 The Design of Simple Rules for the Modern Economy

1. See Vines, Maceijowski and Meade (1983) and Weale, Blake, Vines and Meade (1989).
2. Tobin (1983).
3. Sargent and Wallace (1975).
4. We shall deal with this subject in sections 2.2 and 2.3 of this chapter.
5. Friedman (1968).
6. Okun (1981).
7. Layard and Nickell (1985).
8. See McKinnon (1988).
9. See the illuminating discussion in Koromzay et al. (1987) about the 'misalignment' of the dollar in the 1980s.
10. See Taylor (1979).
11. More attention will be devoted to this subject in Part II.
12. For instance, the government may raise output and employment through a monetary expansion only by tricking the private sector into believing that the inflation rate will be below its actual level.
13. Fischer (1977).
14. See Currie (1985).
15. For a general review of the subject see Blackburn (1988).
16. For simplicity we refer to the deterministic case.
17. Bellman (1957).
18. This might be due to existing distortions which make the 'natural' level of output too low.
19. Kydland and Prescott (1977), quoted in Christodoulakis et al. (1989).
20. See Barro and Gordon (1983) and, for a more general treatment, Levine (1988).
21. Currie and Levine (1985b).
22. See Currie and Levine (1985b).
23. See Currie and Levine (1985b).
24. This has been clearly shown by Christodoulakis and Levine (1987).
25. See Weale et al. (1989).
26. See Weale et al. (1989).
27. See Doyle and Stein (1981).
28. See Rustem et al. (1979).
29. See Currie, Holtham and Hughes Hallett (1988).
30. This definition is drawn from Vines et al. (1983).
31. In the sense of Phillips (1957).
32. This was discussed in Weale et al. (1989), Chapter 2.
33. Needless to say, the two targets are closely related, as setting a price level target implies integral control of inflation.

34. McKinnon (1988) has advocated the return to a fixed exchange rate regime. A detailed account of his proposal is given in Chapter 5.
35. Tobin (1983), Vines *et al.* (1983), McCallum (1990).
36. Weale *et al.* (1989).
37. See Corden (1991) .
38. Corden (1991).
39. For instance, Muellbauer and Murphy (1990) argue that domestic financial liberalisation coupled with distortions in the housing markets might generate outcomes which resemble an adverse shock.
40. This happened in Chile, see Mellor (1990).
41. Evans (1990).
42. According to the 'new view', governments should perhaps announce a complete neglect of the current account, but the policy would probably lack credibility in the face of unsustainable deficits (think of the unsound spending boom example).
43. Boughton (1989), Weale *et al.* (1989), Williamson (1987), Vinals (1986).
44. We shall investigate the working of this proposal in Chapters 4 and 6.
45. This definition is drawn from the seminal works of Branson (1979) and Kouri (1976).
46. And the corresponding national wealth target.
47. This implies that the government is only concerned with deviations of the current account balance from the socially optimal path.
48. See Currie and Levine (1985b), Edison, Miller and Williamson (1987) Weale *et al.* (1989), Currie and Wren-Lewis (1989).
49. See Meade (1983), Williamson (1987), Boughton (1989), Weale *et al.* (1989).
50. See Barro (1974).
51. The reason we do so in Chapter 6 is that since we wish to provide a further evaluation of the target zones proposal, we want to keep the model as close as possible to the original version formulated by Edison, Miller and Williamson (1987).
52. For an illuminating description of why this must happen see Weale *et al.* (1989) pp. 168–74.
53. Hall and Mishkin (1982), Hayashi (1985), Deaton (1987), Jappelli and Pagano (1989), Guiso and Jappelli (1991), Zeldes (1989).
54. See Vines *et al.* (1983), Chapter 2.

2 Open Economy Models: The Macroeconomic Approach

1. See Dornbusch (1990).
2. Mussa 1977.
3. Stockman (1983).
4. Calvo (1983, 1985).
5. Quoting Dornbusch (1990): '. . . one suspects that we will all use the new classical approach having learned to assume rigourously everything that the macroeconomic approach already assumed as critical features of the operation of the economy. I use the term to "assume rigourously" to

denote the current fashion of introducing ad hocery at a lower level, and then deriving its implications rigorously.'

6. Dornbusch (1976). For an extension, including the role of unanticipated disturbances, see Wilson (1979).
7. The model is loglinear.
8. In the original Dornbusch model fiscal policy was not explicitly taken into account. Nonetheless this assumption is made here as it has commonly been done in the literature originating from Dornbusch's seminal work. For sake of simplicity we shall maintain the original Dornbusch assumption that the nominal instead of the real interest rate appears in aggregate demand.
9. In the next chapter a more general model will be presented, where fiscal policy does affect the price level.
10. Assuming that foreign prices are stable.
11. Blanchard and Kahn (1980).
12. On the rationale for imposing the transversality condition see Sargent and Wallace (1975).
13. The general solution for this class of dynamic systems is:

$$p_t - p_\infty = AU_u\exp(\theta_u t) + CU_s\exp(\theta_s t)$$

$$e_t - e_\infty = A\exp(\theta_u t) + C\exp(\theta_s t)$$

where $[U_u, 1]$ and $[U_s, 1]$ are the eigenvector associated with the unstable and the stable root, respectively θ_u and θ_s. C and A are arbitrary constants. Imposing the transversality condition we set $A = 0$ and choose to analyse the only stable dynamic path.
14. For formal proof of this assertion see Gandolfo (1972).
15. According to this simple version of the Dornbusch model fiscal shocks are instantaneously offset by exchange rate jumps and do not involve any dynamics at all, but less restrictive assumptions about the degree of capital mobility and the inclusion of financial wealth in demand for money would yield different results.
16. The original Dornbusch and Fischer model is set out in implicit form. To simplify the exposition we log-linearise it, at the cost of making some restrictive assumptions. Variables are expressed as deviations from equilibrium.
17. Following Driskill (1980) and Eaton and Turnovsky (1983) we have linearised W around equilibrium, w_1 being the initial share of foreign wealth on W. I have chosen to approximate wealth around equilibrium by a Cobb–Douglas function: $W = H[M^{1-\alpha}(eF)^\alpha]_0$, where H is an arbitrary constant. Taking logs and remembering that if W is to be a good approximation to actual wealth we must set $\alpha/(1 - \alpha) = (eF/M)_0$ it is easily shown that $\alpha = (eF/W)_0$.
18. Variables are defined as deviations from equilibrium, therefore national savings become negative when $W > 0$.
19. See Blanchard (1985).
20. As this Chapter only aims to review well-known results.

21. This issue has been raised by Branson in a study to be reviewed in the next section.
22. The sign of $\pi_{2,3}$ cannot be defined a priori because unlike Dornbusch and Fischer we introduce interest rate effects in aggregate demand.
23. See discussion above.
24. Dornbusch and Fischer consider this case only.
25. Note that when $[(w_1 - 1)\tau + w_1\beta + w_1\sigma/k] < 0$ (Figure 2.3), the reduction of the price level necessary to equilibriate aggregate demand would raise real wealth and generate a cumulative current account deficit. In this case the exchange rate devaluation is necessary to stimulate demand and to reduce the price fall, so that real wealth decreases and the current account turns into a surplus.
26. Eaton and Turnovsky (1983).
27. I have loglinearised the original Branson model.
28. Note that wealth effects in the money market offset each other in the foreign assets market.
29. This must be so because, holding de constant, the interest rate increase necessary to equilibrate the foreign assets market would be too weak for equilibrium to obtain in the money market. As a result, de must rise.
30. Equilibrium in the the financial markets requires a constant level of wealth.
31. Note that while in the short term de ensures portfolio equilibrium, in the long term $de = 0$ so that F must adjust.
32. Dornbusch (1990).
33. Smith (1989) and Engle and Flood (1985) made attempts to explore the subject but their results are not entirely satisfactory.

3 Monetarist Macroeconomic Policy Rules in a Small Open Economy Model

1. See Smith (1989).
2. But he assumes that output and the exchange rate are fixed.
3. Here and in the rest of the book, all the variables are in logs except for interest rates and foreign wealth, F. I linearise real wealth around the initial values of the real exchange rate, 1, and of foreign assets F_0, which is assumed to be larger than 0. For a detailed exposition of the procedure followed here see Smith (1989).
4. i^* is defined as the real foreign interest rate because it is assumed that the foreign price level is stable.
5. Note that s might also describe the effect of any other domestic demand shock.
6. For a closed economy model where core inflation is a weighted average of backward- and forward-looking behaviour see Taylor (1979).
7. Engle and Frankel (1984).
8. This assumption bears no influence on the stability analysis, which is the main issue to be discussed in this Chapter.
9. i_0^* and F_0 are the initial levels of the interest rate and of foreign wealth.
10. Note that $\beta_1 < \beta$ and $\alpha > 1$ because it is assumed that individual sources of foreign demand affect aggregate demand more than the trade balance.

11. This issue has been investigated in the seminal work of Cagan (1956).
12. I refer to the impact of the money supply on inflation because the stronger this effect, the bigger the reduction of the real interest rate and of the output expansion.
13. Hence it is assumed that $\beta_1 - \mu\pi(\beta + \tau F_0) > 0$.
14. Modigliani (1966).
15. Currie *et al.* (1986).
16. In fact it seems to be generally accepted that wealth effects take a long time to significantly influence the economy. See, for instance, Engle and Flood (1985).
17. Note that in this case nominal and real exchange rate dynamics must coincide because p is fixed.
18. Points to the right of aa.
19. Points to the left of aa.
20. Therefore if agents in the financial markets choose the appropriate initial exchange rate level the economy converges to equilibrium.
21. Blanchard and Kahn (1980).
22. Note that if $\beta_1 - F_0 i^* < 0$ condition 3.20 does not hold either: the model cannot be saddlepath stable.
23. Smith (1989).
24. For a similar result see Driskill (1981).
25. s might also describe a real domestic demand shock.
26. As in Smith (1989).

4 Simple Policy Rules for the Open Economy: Evaluating Alternative Proposals

1. Frenkel and Johnson (1976).
2. Boughton (1989), Evans (1990).
3. Dolado and Vignals (1991).
4. These are open-loop equations in which the tax rate and the real interest rate are treated as exogenous policy instruments, whose closed loop behaviour is specified below. As regards using the real rather than the nominal interest rate as the monetary policy instrument see Edison, Miller and Williamson (1987).
5. Equation 4.2 implies that $p = (1 - \mu)w + \mu e$, where w and e represent the prices of domestic and foreign goods respectively, and μ is the import content of expenditure. Thus it is straightforward to show that $p = w + \mu a$. For a similar definition of inflation see Miller (1985).
6. A shock to the level of core inflation will be added below.
7. We assume zero inflation abroad, therefore nominal and real foreign interest rates must coincide.
8. The real interest rate is treated as a policy instrument (as in Miller, 1985, and Edison, Miller and Williamson, 1987). This implies that the nominal rate of interest is adjusted according to the feedback policy rule plus contemporaneous changes in the rate of inflation.
9. The determinant $|A|$ equals the product of the roots. Condition 4.13 below is necessary but not sufficient for stability to obtain because $|A|$

might be positive as a result of all three roots being positive. But the plausible numerical values chosen for the simulations performed in Section 5 would suggest that this is unlikely to occur in practice.

10. Note that this assumption has been made only in order to render the model simple enough to be analytically manageable.
11. Under the assumption of perfect capital mobility.
12. This implies that $\beta_1 - \mu(\beta + F_0\tau) > 0$.
13. Holding z constant.
14. Under the assumption that $r^* > \mu\tau$.
15. When $r^* < \mu(\tau + \delta k_2) tr A^* < 0$, $|A^*| > 0$, thus two roots are negative and one is positive.
16. This is necessary for the financial markets to be in equilibrium.
17. $r = k_1\pi = k_1(\phi\epsilon z + \mu a)$; so $dr = \phi\epsilon y$ when $da = 0$.
18. At this point $a < 0$, which of its own would make $y < 0$, and $r = 0$, thus F must be positive.
19. Both of which will tend to increase the current account balance.
20. The trace of the transition matrix is equal to the sum of the roots. If it is negative at least one negative root must exist, ruling out the possibility of three positive roots when $|A| > 0$.
21. It might appear that condition 4.17 imposes an unduly strong constraint on the policy as it puts a ceiling on the strength of the wealth control. However, note that 4.17 is a sufficient but not a necessary condition for stability to obtain. The control parameters selected for the numerical simulations did not satisfy condition 4.17, but this did not impair stability.
22. This will become apparent from the analysis of simulations.
23. The rationale for this assignment relies on the presumption that a devaluation improves the current account.
24. Which is zero, since the model is set in deviations from equilibrium.
25. In this case uncovered interest parity holds.
26. This assumption is by no means necessary to show that stability obtains. It is made here as this case is more akin to Boughton's example.
27. This is a standard result from the overshooting literature discussed in Chapter 2.
28. This issue will be investigated in greater detail in Chapter 6.
29. This result adds to the straightforward case of a foreign demand shock.
30. In order to obtain a more realistic description of dynamics I have simulated a model where some of the simplifications necessary to carry out the algebraic analysis have been removed.
31. See Chapter 2, Section 4.
32. Explained in Appendix II.
33. This is a standard result in the literature since the work of Buiter and Miller (1982).
34. But the country carrying forward the disinflation ends up with an appreciated currency anyway.
35. This may be easily derived from condition 4.13.
36. It might be expected that by including the government budget constraint in the model, the prolonged fiscal contraction would reduce domestic

holdings of government debt, so that eventually this negative wealth effect would keep aggregate demand in equilibrium.
37. This seems obvious when the fiscal feedback is activated, and assuming that $\tau > \alpha r^*$ this must also be true under Assignment 1.
38. This issue will be explored in greater detail in Chapter 6.
39. A two-country version of this model is presented in Chapter 6.

5 Macroeconomic Policy and Interdependence: The Debate on International Policy Coordination

1. This issue will be discussed at greater length in the next Chapter.
2. See Artis and Ostry (1986).
3. This means that a monetary expansion in the home country depreciates the exchange rate, raises domestic output and has a contractionary effect abroad.
4. This model has been set out in McKibbin (1988).
5. This point is important in determining what happens when countries choose to adopt an identical policy, as discussed below. In principle, negative spillovers might more than offset the influence of domestic policy in each country.
6. The Nash equilibrium is the only form of non-cooperative outcome that is discussed here. A more general treatment of the subject would involve at least the analysis of the Stackelberg equilibrium, where one country acts as a leader and is assumed to take into account the reactions of the other country when setting its own policy.
7. Therefore we ignore the bargaining process which might eventually yield a cooperative outcome giving different weights to each country.
8. Note that the cooperative outcome generated by the model implies that a fixed exchange rate regime is Pareto-efficient, but different, more general models would imply alternative conclusions.
9. Frankel (1989).
10. See Frankel (1988 and 1989).
11. Indeed this is the final outcome one would predict from the models laid out in Chapters 2 and 3.
12. See Buiter and Miller (1982) for a formal demonstration of the long-term ineffectiveness of exchange rate appreciations on the total output cost necessary to permanently curb inflation.
13. Currie and Levine (1987a).
14. Currie, Levine and Vidalis (1987).
15. It has already been shown that in the closed economy reputational policies generally outperform non-reputational time consistent policies. The trouble with non-cooperative reputational policies is that the mutual inconsistency of policies reduces the 'gains from reputation'.
16. In the sense that it involves proportional and integral control of some specific target.
17. They run simulations of a reduced version of the OECD model, Interlink.

18. This term means that the functional form of the rules is identical in the two countries and that control parameters are the result of a joint optimisation exercise.
19. Assuming that the covariance matrix of disturbances is known.
20. This term means that countries were committed to the same policy rule but were free to choose the strength of the control parameters.
21. Weale *et al.* (1989).
22. Contrast for example the purchasing power parity approach followed by McKinnon with the fundamental real exchange rate approach of Miller-Williamson.
23. Boughton overlooks the trade distortions potentially caused by real exchange rate fluctuations, whereas this is a primary source of concern for both Williamson and McKinnon. Instead, he argues that governments should set mutually consistent foreign wealth targets.
24. Meade and his associates criticise Williamson's assignment of fiscal policy to the domestic objective for two reasons. First, they point out that in many countries fiscal policy is not sufficiently flexible to be used for inflation control. Secondly, they argue that this assignment might cause adverse cost-push effects in the labour market.
25. McKinnon (1988).
26. By contrast, Eichengreen (1985) argues that central banks sterilised gold flows more often than intervening to reinforce their impact on the domestic market. Furthermore, interest rates tended to move together, whereas the 'rules of the game' would have implied the widening of differentials.
27. For a more detailed explanation see McKinnon and Ohno (1987).
28. See Giavazzi and Pagano (1986).
29. Meade (1951).
30. See Dornbusch (1988) for a clear example of how differences in productivity growth may substantially complicate the task of equalising inflation rates across countries.
31. Williamson (1988b) raises this criticism.
32. Williamson (1987).
33. Indeed Boughton's criticism is a combination of the well-known Fleming–Mundell conclusion about the effectiveness of fiscal policy under perfect capital mobility and of the equally well-known Laursen–Metzler effect.
34. Williamson (1989).
35. Williamson (1988b).
36. I have mutuated this definition from Currie, Levine and Gaines 1989.
37. Genberg and Swoboda (1988).
38. Boughton (1989).
39. This criticism would also apply to the paper by Genberg and Swoboda.
40. Weale *et al.*(1989).
41. This argument has been used very recently, in the face of the external deficits incurred by the US and the UK.
42. The target zones proposal also shares these features.
43. But the majority of large-scale econometric models share this short-coming.

44. They simply consider five-year moving averages for each policy instrument.
45. Frenkel, Masson and Goldstein (1988), p. 33.
46. In the next chapter we will discuss the Edison, Miller and Williamson paper at great length.
47. See Williamson (1988b).
48. I do not believe that accounting for the J-curve effect would decisively affect the simplicity and appeal of this rule.
49. This might not be true when these swings are large and their correction becomes very difficult, so that the incentive to renege on previous commitments increases.
50. As has been shown in Chapter 4.

6 Simple Rules for Policy Coordination: An Evaluation of Alternative Assignments

1. The reason why the real exchange rate affects average output will be explained later.
2. I remind the reader that F is normalised as a fraction of equilibrium output.
3. The same result would obtain as a consequence of a (*ceteris paribus*) nominal exchange rate appreciation.
4. Following Modigliani, the numerical value of the wealth effect is slightly bigger than the equilibrium real interest rate. I have also considered larger values, but my results were not altered substantially.
5. Miller and Williamson (1987) point at domestic demand as the intermediate target for inflation control. We do not explore that possible alternative here for the sake of simplicity.
6. Weale *et al.* (1989).
7. However, the results are available from the author on request.
8. This is not infrequent in the literature. For instance, Smith (1989) and Currie *et al.* (1986) excluded the revaluation effects on financial wealth caused by real exchange rates, by assuming that it is held in foreign currency by domestic residents.
9. As in Bandhari *et al.* (1988).
10. Alternatively, we might have assumed that fiscal policy is assigned to control average inflation.
11. At this final stage we shall also consider the influence of the real exchange rate on average aggregate demand.
12. Basically, Sections 2.2 and 2.3 should be regarded as an informative complement to Section 4.1 in Chapter 4, the different results in terms of the total wealth transfer being explained by the slightly different parameter values adopted in this chapter.
13. See the discussion in Chapters 3 and 4.
14. The plausible parameter values that we use imply this outcome.
15. r_d is positive.

16. With high interdependence the performance of the monetarist rule substantially improved too, but the results could not match those obtained under the reversed assignment.
17. Except for a very large value of F_0.
18. This result is robust to changes in the strength of the trade elasticities.
19. The fiscal stance in both countries exhibits wide swings, being initially strongly negative and then positive, but the average s_d must be contractionary in order to achieve a bigger cumulated output loss in the home economy.
20. Consider, for instance the success of the European Monetary System.
21. It is well known that contractive monetary policy contributed to the serious difficulties of the highly indebted third world countries. If current trade imbalances continue, the scenario depicted in this chapter might become plausible for developed countries too.
22. Because it would limit the size of the wealth transfers generated by the global monetary policy.

Bibliography

Adams, C., and D. Gros (1986) 'The Consequences of Real Exchange Rate Rules for Inflation: Some Illustrative Examples', *IMF Staff Papers*, vol. 33, Sept, pp. 439–76.

Alogoskoufis, G. (1989) 'Stabilization policy, fixed exchange rates and target zones', in M. Miller, B. Eichengreen and R. Portes, *Blueprints for Exchange Rate Management* (Academic Press).

Alogoskoufis, G. (1989) 'Monetary, Nominal Income and Exchange Rate Targets in a Small Open Economy', *European Economic Review*.

Aoki, M. (1981) 'Dynamic Analysis of Open Economies', New York, Academic Press 1981.

Artis, M. and T. Bayoumi (1990) *Savings, Investment, Financial Integration, and the Balance of Payments*, IMF, Staff Studies for the World Economic Outlook (Washington, Sept.).

Artis, M. and D. Currie (1981) 'Monetary and Exchange Rate Rules: A Case for Conditional Targets', *Oxford Economic Papers*.

Artis, M. and O. Ostry (1986) 'International Economic Policy Coordination', Royal Institute for Economic Affairs, 1986.

Bakus, D. and J. Driffill (1985) 'Inflation and Reputation', *American Economic Review*.

Barro, R. (1974) 'Are Government Bonds Net Wealth?', *Journal of Political Economy*, 82, p. 1095–118.

Barro, R. (1985) 'Recent Developments in the Theory of Rules versus Discretion', *Economic Journal*, Supplement, pp. 23–37.

Barro, R. and G. Gordon (1983) 'Rules, Discretion and Reputation in a Model of Monetary Policy', *Journal of Monetary Economics*, vol. 12, pp. 101–21.

Bean, C. (1983) 'Targeting Nominal Income: An Appraisal', *Economic Journal*.

Begg, D. (1982) *The Rational Expectation Revolution in Macroeconomics* (Oxford University Press).

Bellmann J. M. (1957) *Dynamic Programming* (Princeton).

Bandhari, J. *et al.* (1988) 'Capital Mobility and Exchange Rate Overshooting', *European Economic Review*.

Bilson, J. (1978) 'Rational Expectations and the Exchange Rate', in J. Frenkel and H. Johnson, *The Economics of Exchange Rates*.

Blackburn, K. (1988) *Credibility and Reputation in International Macroeconomic Policy Games*, University of Southampton discussion papers.

Blanchard, O. (1985) 'Debt, Deficits and Finite Horizons', *Journal of Political Economy*, vol. 93, pp. 223–47.

Blanchard, O. and M. Kahn (1980) 'The Solution of Linear Difference Models under Rational Expectations', *Econometrica*, vol. 48, pp. 1305–11.

Boughton, J. (1989) 'Policy Assignment Strategies with Somewhat Flexible Exchange Rates', in M. Miller, B. Eichengreen and R. Portes, *Blueprint for Exchange Rate Management* (Academic Press).

Branson, W. H. (1979) 'Exchange Rate Dynamics and Monetary Policy', in A. Lindbeck (ed.), *Inflation and Unemployment in Open Economies*, pp. 189–224.

Branson, W. H. (1983) 'Macroeconomic Determinants of Real Exchange Rate Risk, in R. Herring, *Managing foreign exchange rate risk* (Cambridge University Press).

Bryant, R. *et al.* (eds) (1989) *Empirical Macroeconomics for Interdependent Economies* (Washington: Brookings Institution).

Bryant, R. and R. Portes (eds) (1987) *Global Macroeeconomics: Policy Conflict and Cooperation*, London: Macmillan).

Buiter, W. (1981) 'The Superiority of Contingent Rules over Fixed Rules in Models with National Expectations', *Economic Journal*, vol. 91, September, pp. 647–70.

Buiter, W. and R. Marston (1985) *International Economic Policy Coordination* (Cambridge, Mass: Cambridge University Press).

Buiter, W. and M. Miller (1982) 'Real Exchange Rate Overshooting and the Output Cost of Bringing Down Inflation', *European Economic Review*, vol. 18, pp. 85–124.

Cagan, P. (1956) 'The Monetary Dynamics of Hyperinflation', in M. Friedman (ed.) *Studies in the Quantity Theory of Money* (Chicago).

Calvo, G. (1983) 'Staggered Contracts and Exchange Rate Policy', in J. Frenkel, *Exchange Rates and International Macroeconomics* (University of Chicago Press and NBER).

Calvo, G. (1985) 'Currency Substitution and the Real Exchange Rate: the Utility Maximizing Approach', *Journal of International Money and Finance*.

Campbell, J. and G. Mankiw, (1989) 'Consumption, Income and Interest Rates: Reinterpreting Time Series Evidence', in O. Blanchard and S. Fischer (eds), *NBER Macroeconomics Annual* (MIT Press).

Campbell, J. and G. Mankiw (1991) 'The Response of Consumption to Income', *European Economic Review*, vol. 35, pp. 723–56.

Canzoneri, M. B. and J. Gray (1983) 'Monetary Policy Games and the Consequences of Non-Cooperative Behaviour', *International Economic Review*.

Carlozzi, N. and J. Taylor (1985) 'International Capital Mobility and the Coordination of Monetary Rules', in Bandhari (ed.), *Exchange Rate Management under Uncertainty* (MIT Press) pp. 186–211.

Carraro, C. and F. Giavazzi (1988) *Can International Policy Coordination really be Counterproductive?*, NBER working paper 2669.

Christodoulakis, N. and P. Levine (1987) 'Linear Rational Expectations Models: A Frequency-Domain versus Optimal Control Approach to Policy Design, mimeo.

Christodoulakis, N. *et al.* (1989) 'Macroconomic Policy using Large Econometric Models: Methodology and Application', *Oxford Economic Papers*, vol. 43, pp. 25–58.

Claessens, S. (1991) 'Balances of Payments Crises in an Optimal Portfolio Model', *European Economic Review*, vol. 35, pp. 81–102.

Cooper, R. (1986) 'Economic Interdependence and Coordination of Economic Policies', in R. Cooper, *Economic Policy in an Interdependent World* (Cambridge, Mass: Cambridge University Press).

Cooper, R. and J. Sachs (1985) 'Borrowing Abroad: The Debtor's Perspective', in G. Smith and J. Cuddington (eds), *International Debt and the Developing Countries* (Washington, The World Bank).

Corden, M. (1985) 'On Transmission and Coordination under Flexible Exchange Rates', in Buiter and Marston (1985).

Corden, M. (1986) 'Fiscal Policies, Current Accounts and Real Exchange Rates: In Search of a Logic for International Policy Coordination' (Tubingen) *Weltwirtschaftliches Archiv*.

Corden, M. (1991) 'Does the Current Account Matter? The Old View and the New View', paper for conference in honour of J. Polak (Washington: IMF, January).

Currie, D. (1985) 'Macroeconomic Policy Design and Control Theory: a Failed Partnership?', *Economic Journal*, vol. 5, pp. 285–306.

Currie, D., G Holtham and A. Hughes Hallett (1988) 'The Theory and Practice of International Policy Coordination: Does Coordination Pay?', paper presented at the conference 'Macroeconomic Policies in an Interdependent World' (Washington, Dec.).

Currie, D. and P. Levine (1985a) 'Macroeconomic Policy Design in an Interdependent World', in Buiter and Marston, pp. 228–71.

Currie, D. and P. Levine (1985b) 'Simple Macropolicy Rules for the Open Economy', *Economic Journal*, Supplement, vol. 95 pp. 60–70.

Currie, D. and P. Levine (1985c) 'Optimal Feedback Rules in an Open Economy Model with Rational Expectations', *European Economic Review*, vol. 27, pp. 141–63.

Currie, D. and P. Levine (1987a) 'Credibility and Time Consistency in a Stochastic World', *Journal of Economics*.

Currie, D. and P. Levine (1987b) 'Does International Economic Policy Coordination Pay and is Sustainable? A Two Country Analysis', *Oxford Economic Papers*.

Currie, D. and P. Levine (1987c) 'The Design of Feedback Rules in Linear Stochastic Expectations Models', *Journal of Economics Dynamics and Control*, vol. 11, pp. 1–28.

Currie, D. and P. Levine (1987d) 'Assessing the Benefits, Costs and Feasibility of International Macroeconomic Policy Coordination', LBS discussion papers, p. 7.

Currie, D. and P. Levine (1990) 'The Solvency Constraint and Fiscal Policy in an Open Economy', in Alogoskoufis *et al.*, *External Constraints on Macroeconomic Policy: The European Experience* (Cambridge, Mass: University Press).

Currie, D. *et al.* (1986) 'Alternative Financial Policy Rules in an Open Economy under Rational and Adaptive Expectations', *Economic Journal*, vol. 96 (Sept.) pp. 680–95.

Currie, D., P. Levine and J. Gaines (1989) 'The Use of Simple Rules for International Policy Agreements', in M. Miller, B. Eichengreen and R. Portes (eds), *Blueprint for Exchange Rate Management* (Academic Press).

Currie, D., P. Levine and N. Vidalis (1987) 'Cooperative and Noncooperative Rules for Monetary and Fiscal Policy in an Empirical Two Block Model', in Bryant and Portes.

Currie, D. and S. Wren-Lewis (1989) 'A Comparison of Alternative Regimes for International Policy Coordination', in M. Miller, B. Eichengreen and R. Portes, *Blueprint for Exchange Rate Management* (Academic Press).

Deaton, A. (1987) 'Life-cycle Models of Consumption: is the Evidence consistent with Theory?', in T. F. Bewley, *Advances in Econometrics*, vol. 2 (Cambridge, Mass: Cambridge University Press).

Dini, L. (1988) 'Cooperation and Conflict in Monetary and Trade Policies IMDI, US–European round table (Milan, Feb.).

Dixit, A. (1980) 'A Solution Technique for Rational Expectations Models with Applications to Exchange Rate and Interest Rate Determination', University of Warwick mimeo.

Dolado, J. and J. Vignals (1991) 'Macroeconomic Policy, External Targets and Constraints: The Case of Spain', in Alogoskoufis *et al.*, *External Constraints on Macroeconomic Policy: The European Experience* (Cambridge, Mass: Cambridge University Press) pp. 304–41.

Dornbusch, R. (1976) 'Expectations and Exchange Rate Dynamics', *Journal of Political Economy*, vol. 84, pp. 1161–76.

Dornbusch, R. (1982) 'Exchange Rate Risk and the Macroeconomics of Exchange Rate Determination', in Howkins *et al.*, *The Internationalization of Financial Markets and National Economic Policy* (MIT).

Dornbusch, R. (1983) *Flexible Exchange Rates and Interdependence*, Staff Papers, March.

Dornbusch, R. (1987) 'Exchange Rates Economics, 1986', *Economic Journal*, vol. 97 (March), pp. 1–18.

Dornbusch, R. (1988) 'Doubts about the McKinnon Standard', *Journal of Economic Perspectives*, Winter, vol. 2, pp. 104–15.

Dornbusch, R. (1990) 'Real Exchange Rates and Macroeconomics', in S. Honkapohja, *The State of Macroeconomics*, (Oxford: Basil Blackwell) pp. 185–216.

Dornbusch, R. and S. Fischer (1980) 'Exchange Rates and the Current Account', *American Economic Review*, vol. 70, pp. 960–71.

Dornbusch, R. and Y. C. Park (1987) 'Korean Growth Policy', *Brookings Papers on Economic Activity*, vol. 2, pp. 389–454.

Doyle, J. and G. Stein (1981) *Multivariate Feedback Design: Concepts for a Classical/Modern Synthesis* (Institute of Electrical and Electronic Engineers, Trans AC) vol. AC-26, no. 1, pp. 4–16.

Driskill, R. (1980) 'Exchange Rate Dynamics, Portfolio Balance and Relative Prices', *American Economic Review*, vol. 70 pp. 776–83.

Driskill, R. (1981) 'Exchange Rate Overshooting, The Trade Balance and Rational Expectations', *Journal of International Economics*.

Eaton, J. and S. Turnovsky (1983) 'Covered Interest Parity, Uncovered Interest Parity and Exchange Rate Dynamics', *Economic Journal*, vol. 93, pp. 555–75.

Eaton, J. and S. Turnovsky (1985) 'Exchange Risk, Political Risk and Microeconomic Equilibrium', *American Economic Review*, pp. 1068–75.

Edison, H. J., M. Miller and J. Williamson (1987) 'On Evaluating and Extending the Target Zones Proposal', *Journal of Policy Modelling*, vol. 9, no. 1, pp. 199–224.

Eichengreen, B. (1985) 'International Policy Coordination in Historical Perspective: A View from the Interwar Years', in Buiter and Marston.

Engle, R. and R. Flood (1985) 'Exchange Rate Dynamics, Sticky Prices and the Current Account', *Journal of Money, Credit and Banking*.

Engle, R. and J. Frankel (1984) 'The Secular Term in Open Economy Phillips Curves', *European Economic Review*.

Evans, O. (1990) *National Savings and Targets for the Federal Budget Balance in the United States*, IMF Staff Studies for the World Economic Outlook (Washington, Sept.).

Feldstein, M. (1988) 'Thinking about International Economic Coordination', *Journal of Economic Perspectives* (Spring).

Fischer, S. (1977) 'Longer Contracts, Rational Expectations and the Optimal Money Supply Rule', *Journal of Political Economy*, vol. 85, pp. 191–206.

Fischer, S. (1988a) *Rules versus Discretion in Monetary Policy*, NBER working paper 2518.

Fischer, S. (1988b) 'Comment on Miller–Williamson', *European Economic Review*, vol. 32, no. 5, pp. 1048–51.

Frankel, J. (1988) *Obstacles to International Policy Coordination*, NBER working paper 2505.

Frankel, J. (1989) *A Modest Proposal for International Nominal Income Targeting*, NBER working paper 2849.

Frankel, J. and C. Rockett (1986) *International Macroeconomic Policy When Policymakers Disagree on the Model*, NBER working paper 2059, Oct.

Frankel, J. and Froot (1987) 'Using Survey Data to Test Standard Propositions Regarding Exchange Rate Expectations', *American Economic Review*.

Frenkel, J. (1987) 'The International Monetary System: Should it be Reformed?', *American Economic Review*, supp.

Frenkel, J. and Johnson (1976) *The Monetary Approach to the Balance of Payments* (Allen and Unwin).

Frenkel, J. and M. Goldstein (1986) *A Guide to Target Zones*, IMF staff papers, Dec..

Frenkel, J., P. Masson and M. Goldstein (1988) 'International Coordination of Economic Policies: Scope, Methods and Effects', NBER working paper no. 2670, July.

Frenkel, J., M. Goldstein and P. Masson (1989) 'Simulating the Effects of Some Simple Coordinated versus Uncoordinated Policy Rules', in R. Bryant *et al.* (eds), *Macroeconomic Policies in an Interdependent World*, IMF, CEPR, Brookings Institution.

Frenkel, J. and M. Mussa (1984) 'Assets Markets, Exchange Rates and the Balance of Payments', in R. Jones and P. Kenen, *Handbook of International Economics*, vol. II (Amsterdam: North-Holland).

Friedman, M. (1953) 'The Case for Flexible Exchange Rates', *Essays in Positive Economics* (Chicago).

Friedman, M. (1968) 'The Role of Monetary Policy', *American Economic Review*.

Gandolfo, G. (1972) *Mathematical Methods and Models in Economic Dynamics* (Amsterdam: North-Holland).

Genberg, H. and A. Swoboda (1988) 'The Current Account and the Policy Mix under Flexible Exchange Rates', *IMF Staff Papers*, June.

Ghosh, A. and P. Masson (1988) 'International Policy Coordination in a World with Model Uncertainty', *IMF Staff Papers*, June.

Giavazzi, F. and M. Pagano (1986) 'The Advantage of Tying One's Hands', *European Economic Review*, vol. 32, pp. 1055–82.

Guiso, L. and T. Jappelli (1991) 'Intergenerational Transfers and Capital Market Imperfections: Evidence from a Cross-Section of Italian Households', *European Economic Review*, vol. 35, pp. 103–20.

Hall, R. (1986) 'Stochastic Implications of the Life-cycle Permanent Income Hypothesis: Theory and Evidence', *Journal of Political Economy*, pp. 971–86.

Hall, R. and F. Mishkin (1982) 'The Sensitivity of Consumption to Transitory Income: Estimates from Panel Data on Households', *Econometrica*, pp. 461–81.

Hamada, K. (1976) 'A Strategic Analysis of Monetary Interdependence', *Journal of Political Economy*.

Hamada, K. (1979) 'Macroeconomic Strategy and Coordination Under Alternative Exchange Rates', in R. Dornbusch and Frenkel (eds), *International Economic Policy: Theory and Evidence* (Johns Hopkins University Press).

Hayashi, F. (1985) 'The Effect of Liquidity Constraints on Consumption: A Cross-Sectional Analysis', *Quarterly Journal of Economics*, C, pp. 133–206.

Horne, J. and P. Masson (1988) *Scope and Limits of International Economic Cooperation and Policy Coordination*, IMF staff papers, June.

Ishii, N., W. McKibbin and J. Sachs (1987) 'The Economic Policy Mix, Policy Cooperation and Protectionism: Some Aspects of Macroeconomic Interdependence among the U.S., Japan and Other OECD countries', *Journal of Policy Modelling*.

Kenen, P. (1987) *Exchange Rates and Policy Coordination*, Brookings Discussion Papers No. 61, Oct.

Koromzay, V. *et al.* (1987) 'The Rise and Fall of the Dollar: Some Explanations, Consequences and Lessons', *Economic Journal*, vol. 97 (March) pp. 23–43.

Kouri, P. (1976) 'The Exchange Rate and the Balance of Payments in the Short Run and the Long Run: A Monetary Approach', *Scandinavian Journal of Economics*, vol. 78, pp. 255–75.

Kydland, F. and E. Prescott (1977) 'Rules Rather than Discretion: the Inconsistency of Optimal Plans', *Journal of Political Economy*, vol. 85 (June) pp. 473–92.

Jappelli, T. and M. Pagano, M. (1989) 'Consumption and Capital Market Imperfections: An International Comparison', *American Economic Review*, vol. 79, pp. 1088–105.

Layard. P. and S. Nickell (1985) 'Unemployment, Real Wages and Aggregate Demand in Europe', *Carnegie Series on Public Policy*, vol. 23, pp. 143–202.

Levine, P. (1987) *Three Themes from Game Theory and International Macroeconomic Policy Formation*, LBS discussion paper, 16.

Levine, P. (1988) *Does Time Inconsistency Matter?*, CEPR discussion paper', p. 227.

McCallum, B. (1990) 'New Classical Macroeconomics: a Sympathetic Account', in Honkapohja, S. (ed.), *The State of Macroeconomics* (Oxford: Basil Blackwell) pp. 3–32.

McKibbin, W. (1988) 'The Economics of International Policy Coordination', *The Economic Record*, vol. 64, pp. 241–53.

McKibbin, W. and J. Sachs (1988) 'Coordination of Monetary and Fiscal Policies in the Industrial Countries', in J. Frenkel (ed.), *International Aspects of Fiscal Policy* (Chicago).

McKinnon, R. (1982) 'Currency Substitution and Instability in the World Dollar Standard', *American Economic Review*, vol. 77 (June) pp. 320–33.

McKinnon, R. (1988) 'Monetary and Exchange Rate Policies for International Financial Stability: a Proposal', *Journal of Economic Perspectives* (Winter).

McKinnon, R. and K. Ohno (1987) *Purchasing Power Parity as a Monetary Standard*, Stanford University mimeo.

Meade, J. (1951) *The Balance of Payments* (Oxford University Press).

Meade, J. (1982) *Stagflation: Volume 1. Wage Fixing* (Allen and Unwin).

Meade, J. (1983) 'A New Keynesian Approach to Full Employment', *Lloyds Bank Review*, Oct., pp. 1–32.

Meade, J. (1984) 'New Keynesian Bretton Woods', *Three Banks Review*, June.

Mellor, P. (1990) 'Chile', in J. Williamson (ed.), *Latin American Adjustment: How Much Has happened?*, Washington: Institute for International Economics.

Miller, M. (1985) 'Monetary Stabilization Policy in an Open Economy', *Scottish Journal of Political Economy*, pp. 127–40.

Miller, M., B. Eichengreen and R. Portes (1989) *Blueprint for Exchange Rate Management* (Academic Press).

Miller, M. and M. Salmon (1985) 'Policy Coordination and Dynamic Games', in Buiter and Marston.

Miller, M. and M. Salmon (1985) 'Dynamic Games and the Time Inconsistency of Optimal Policies in Open Economies', *Economic Journal*, vol. 95, pp. 124–37.

Miller, M. and P. Weller (1989) 'Exchange Rate Bands and Realignments in a Stationary Stochastic Setting', in M. Miller, B. Eichengreen and R. Portes, *Blueprint for Exchange Rate Management* (Academic Press, 1989).

Miller, M. and J. Williamson (1987) *Targets and Indicators: A Blueprint for the International Coordination of Economic Policy* (Washington, DC: Institute for Economic Affairs).

Modigliani, F. (1966) 'The Life-cycle Hypothesis of Saving, the Demand for Wealth and the Supply of Capital', *Social Research*, vol. 32, no. 2.

Muellbauer, J. and A. Murphy (1990) 'Is the UK Balance of Payments Sustainable?', *Economic Policy*, vol. 11, (Oct.) pp. 347–96.

Mussa, M. (1977) 'Empirical Regularities in the Behaviour of Exchange Rates and Theories of the Foreign Exchange Rate Market', in Brunner and Meltzer, 'Policies for Employment, Prices and Exchange Rates', *Journal of Monetary Economics*, Supplement.

Obstfeld, M. (1985) 'Floating Exchange Rates: Experience and Prospects', *Brookings Papers on Economic Activity*.

Okun, A. (1981) *Prices and Quantities* (Washington: The Brookings Institution).

Oudiz, J. and J. Sachs (1984) *Macroeconomic Policy Coordination among the Industrial Economies*, Brookings Papers on Economic Activity, No.1.

Oudiz, J. and J. Sachs (1985) 'International Policy Coordination in Dynamic Macroeconomic Models', in Buiter and Marston (eds), pp. 274–318.

Phillips, A. W. (1957) 'Stabilization Policies and the Time Form of Lagged Responses', *Economic Journal*, vol. 67, pp. 265–77.

Ploeg, F. van der (1988) 'International Policy Coordination in Interdependent Monetary Economies', *Journal of International Economics*.

Poole, W. (1970) 'Optimal Choice of Monetary Policy Instruments in a Simple Stochastic Macro Model', *Quarterly Journal of Economics*, vol. 84 (May) pp. 197–216.

Rogoff, K. (1985a) 'The Optimal Degree of Commitment to an Intermediate Monetary Target', *Quarterly Journal of Economics*.

Rogoff, K. 91985b) 'Can International Monetary Policy Cooperation be Counterproductive?', *Journal of International Economics* (May).

Rustem, B. *et al.* (1979) 'Iterative Re-specification of the Quadratic Objective Function', in S. Holly, B. Rustem and M. Zarrop, *Optimal control for Econometric Models* (Macmillan) pp. 106–33.

Sargent, T. J. and Wallace, N. (1975) 'Rational Expectations, the Optimal Monetary Instrument and the Optimal Money Supply Rule', *Journal of Political Economy*, vol. 83, pp. 241–53.

Smith, P. (1989) 'Current Account Movements, Wealth Effects and the Determination of the Real Exchange Rate', *The Manchester School*, pp. 353–77.

Stiglitz, J. and A. Weiss (1981) 'Credit Rationing in Markets with Imperfect Information', *American Economic Review*, vol. 71, pp. 393–411.

Stockman, A. (1983) 'Real Exchange Rates under Alternative Nominal Exchange Rate Regimes', *Journal of International Money and Finance*, vol. 2.

Taylor, J. B. (1979) 'Staggered Wage Setting in a Macromodel', *American Economic Review*, vol. 69, pp. 108–13.

Taylor, J. B. (1985) 'International Coordination in the Design of Macro-economic Policy Rules', *European Economic Review*.

Taylor, J. B. (1988) *Policy Analysis with a Multicountry Model*, paper presented at the conference: Macroeconomic Policies in an Interdependent World, Washington, Dec.

Tobin, J. (1983) 'Monetary Policy, Rules, Targets and Shocks', *Journal of Money, Credit and Banking*, vol. 15, pp. 506–17.

Vaubel, R. (1985) *International Collusion or Competition for Macroeconomic Policy Coordination? A Restatement* (Recherches Economiques de Louvain, Dec.).

Vinals, J. (1986) 'Fiscal Policy and the Current Account', *Economic Policy*, vol. 1, pp. 711–44.

Vines, J. (1989) 'Comment on Boughton', in M. Miller, B. Eichengreen and R. Portes, *Blueprint for Exchange Rate* (Management Academic Press).

Vines, D., J. Maciejowski and J. Meade (1983) *Stagflation: volume 2, Demand Management* (Allen and Unwin).

Vines, D. *et al.* (1983) *Wealth Targets, Exchange Rate Targets and Macroeconomic Policy*, CEPR discussion paper no 247.

Weale, M., A. Blake, D. Vines and J. Meade (1989) *Inflation, Wealth and the Exchange Rate: Macroeconomic Policy for an Open Economy* (Unwin Hyman).

Williamson, J. (1985) *The Exchange Rate System* (Institute for International Economics).

Williamson, J. (1977) 'The International Monetary Non-System', in M. Artis and A. Nobay, *Studies in Modern Economic Analysis* (Blackwell).

Williamson, J. (1987) *Exchange Rate Management: the Role of Target Zones*, *American Economic Review*, Papers and Proceedings.

Williamson, J. (1988a) *Whither Macroeconomic Policy Coordination?*, paper presented to the R. Triffin Jubilee, Brussels, 8–9 Dec.

Williamson, J. (1988b) 'Comment on McKinnon', *Journal of Economic Perspectives*, vol. 2 (Winter).

Williamson, J. (1989) 'Comment on Currie and Wren Lewis', in M. Miller, B. Eichengreen and R. Portes, *Blueprint for Exchange Rate* (Management Academic Press).

Williamson, J. and M. Miller (1987) 'A Blueprint for the International Coordination of Economic Policy', *Targets and Indicators*, no. 22 (Washington, Institute for International Economics).

Wilson, C. A. (1979) 'Anticipated Shocks and Exchange Rate Dynamics', *Journal of Political Economy*, vol. 87, pp. 639–47.

Zeldes, S. (1989) 'Consumption and Liquidity Constraints: an Empirical Investigation', *Journal of Political Economy*, vol. 97, pp. 305–46.

Index